LECILE

THIS AIN'T MY FIRST RODEO

LECILE HARRIS

with
Rex Allan Jones

LECILE: THIS AIN'T MY FIRST RODEO

Copyright © 2015 by Lecile Harris and Rex Allan Jones

Grateful acknowledgement is made to those who contributed material for this book:

Hadley Barrett; Baxter Black; Clay Collins; Randy Corley; Mark W. Duncan; Ken Knopp; Mike Mathis; Les McIntyre; Dr. Lynn Phillips; Boyd Polhamus; Donny Sparks; Ronny Sparks; Andy Stewart; Bob Tallman.

Front cover photo: Dan Hubbell

Rear cover photo: Dudley Barker

Published by

CLOWNING AROUND ENTERPRISES, LLC

ISBN: 9780692476963

ACKNOWLEDGMENTS

This book is dedicated to ALL the people who have helped me along the way in my life. It's impossible to name you all individually, because that would be a book in itself of just names; you know who you are.

I do want to thank my mom, Rubye Gray Harris, for helping me to be the person I am today; my dad, Marvin Harris, who taught me my work ethic; and my sister, Mary Jo Harris Wilson, for playing pasture football when we didn't have enough guys.

I haven't devoted a chapter especially to my family, but without them, I couldn't do what I do. Thanks to my wife, Ethel; our children: Matt, Chuck, and Christi; our grandchildren: Justin Harris and Indie Harris Rhoda and Dylan Lalonde and Bailey Gray Lalonde; and our great-grandchildren: J.J. Harris and Cole Harris and Coy Rhoda, who are the icing on the cake. There are in-laws and outlaws too.

Ethel has been the architect of my career and has hung in there for over fifty-eight years. Her support as an early publicist, money manager, and in many other roles has been invaluable. I wouldn't be where I am today without Ethel.

Matt has given me much happiness watching him play sports beginning in the third grade and on through high school. After college, he became our printer at the printing company and also worked for Harper & Morgan Rodeo as the lighting and sound coordinator. He would work the other end of my acts at other rodeos and also work the barrel. Eventually he became invaluable in my acts; we made an unbeatable team. His type of comedy and mine weren't the same but they meshed perfectly. He got so good in my acts that he could play anything from an opera singer to a gorilla. Matt is also one of the best barrel men I've ever worked with.

Chuck played the drums from the age of three. He was good at basketball and baseball, which he loved to play, but music took over his time. He has had countless jobs ever since, all the while playing music. Now he keeps everything running smoothly while I'm on the road. I don't have to worry about security on the thirty acres in Collierville because he keeps things locked up tighter than the penitentiary. We have several different properties and he also checks on all them. Chuck is also one of the best drummers I've ever heard.

Christi has always excelled at everything she ever tried. She was highly motivated because she was the youngest. She took gymnastics and dance and was a cheerleader from the third grade on. When she was in high school, she began modeling for Elite Modeling Agency. She got a scholarship to Memphis State on their championship pom squad, graduated with honors, and then danced with the Beach Boys for a few years. After that she got married and became a wonderful mother to two great kids. She is a fabulous cook, a skilled promoter, and a shrewd business woman. Christi is also a person who everyone loves to be around because of her vivacious, fun, loving personality.

Finally, I want to thank all my fans – especially if you're reading this book. Even after more than sixty years in rodeo, it's still a privilege to entertain you.

CONTENTS

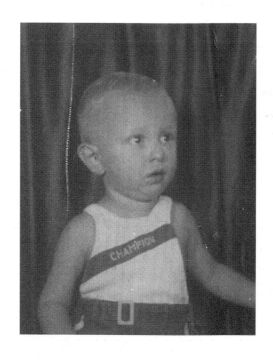

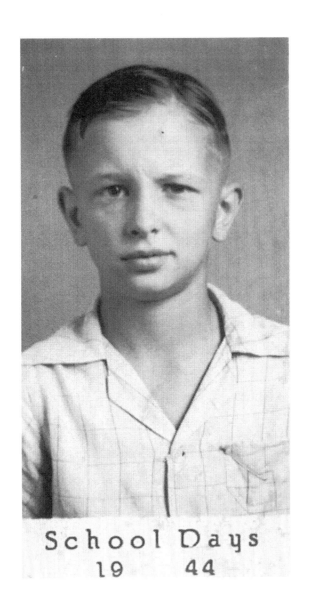

School Days
19 44

DISCLAIMER

There is some language in my book that I don't use in the arena. I'm talking about real life in this book and the way most men talk when they're together, so you parents may want to read it yourselves before you give it to your kids to read. Having said that, whatever's in here that might be objectionable to you, they've probably already heard it on TV or at the movies.

FRIENDLY TRIO—Every rodeo has its clown and this one is Lecile Harris of Collierville, football end for University of Tennessee, Martin Branch. Cuddling up to "Gigani," the colt, is 2-year-old Amy Stuart, daughter of Mr. and Mrs. J. O. Stuart Jr. of 4434 Charleswood, the association's youngest rider.

My first published newspaper interview - 1956. Photo taken at Davis Brockwell's Rodeo in Arlington, Tennessee, where I got my start.

Photo: The Commercial Appeal.

CO-AUTHOR'S NOTE BY REX ALLAN JONES

We've all heard the saying "this ain't my first rodeo," but we rarely hear anyone tell us what their first rodeo actually was. I'm fortunate enough to say that mine was at Ralph Morgan's in Lauderdale, Mississippi as a guest of Lecile Harris.

In my "day job" as a documentary filmmaker making movies about Mississippi and the South, I'm always looking for potential story ideas. One day back in 2012 I was reading the Memphis newspaper and came across a story about a seventy-something-year-old rodeo clown. By the end of the article, I knew I had found the subject of my next film.

One morning soon thereafter, I met Lecile for our interview. He was gracious, maybe a little reserved at first, but grew more loquacious and animated as our conversation went on. I pride myself on being able to make a pretty quick connection with people in these situations, but in this particular case it was especially clear that Lecile and I had hit it off.

We went to the arena that night for the performance, where I shot lots of footage of Lecile's acts and his walking and talking. I was amazed at how beloved he was by the crowd and how that feeling was genuinely returned by him. Everywhere he went, people greeted him like an old friend they hadn't seen since the last rodeo. Lecile, for his part, always went out of his way to visit with them – especially children. How any kid could be scared of clowns after a few minutes with Lecile, I'll never know.

The rodeo ended and it was time to head our separate ways. When I shook hands with Lecile, he said, "You know, I've done a lot of these interview things, and they usually send out some asshole, but you have been a breath of fresh air." Dear reader, I count that statement amongst the highest praise I have ever received.

I went back to the office that next week and told everyone that Lecile was quite simply one of the most impressive personages I had ever met. As I put the movie together, I knew it would be impossible to tell his whole story in a half hour. I asked him if he'd ever considered writing his autobiography, to which he replied, "Yes, people have been on my ass to do that for years, but I've never found anyone I could stand to be around long enough to get it done."

I didn't think much more of it until I saw Lecile again at a rodeo in Jonesboro, Arkansas. I had gone up there to get some more performance footage of him, and as we wrapped things up, he said, "When you get through with this project, I've got something else I want to talk to you about."

You hold in your hands the culmination of that discussion. I'm proud to say that Lecile was able to stand being around me long enough for us to get it done.

FOREWORD BY MARK W. DUNCAN

Anyone can tell a story, but in this life there are very few storytellers. Yes, folks, we live in a world where everyone seems to have a story that they are dying to tell and seeking an avenue in which to deliver it. I have generally found that most folks are wide-ranging in their opinions and narrow-minded in their knowledge, and that although their stories are usually long in duration, they are mostly short on content and substance. That is why, when on those rare occasions that I do find myself in the presence of a real storyteller, I seem to lose myself in the moment and become an active participant in the story rather than a mere casual observer. That is because the best storytellers know three things with absolute certainty: no storyteller is greater than the story; stories must be lived before they can be told; and people must be inspired to listen to a story and not just hear it. Lecile Harris is a storyteller who has known and practiced these truths for over sixty years.

From the moment I first met Lecile, I knew I had met a lifelong friend. At that time, he had never worked a performance for me and I had never seen him in makeup or even watched him perform in the arena. I later learned that I had seen him on "Hee Haw" and in other cameo appearances when I was younger, but those sightings seemed to pale in comparison to the man who had my two young daughters totally enthralled in conversation just a few feet away from me. I believe that children are the best judges of character, and it was evident to everyone present that my girls knew Lecile was a character. To this day I do not know what the story was, but I do know that my daughters were in the presence of a genuine storyteller.

Lecile Harris is a talented entertainer, a dedicated student of his craft, a voice for those who cannot be heard, a creative genius, and a comedic icon – all wrapped up in red and white squares and denim. Yes, Lecile is all of these things and more, but most importantly he is always the consummate professional. He is one of the most influential persons in our sport and he will forever be remembered for putting the "Professional" in the Professional Rodeo Cowboys Association.

So as you find yourself throughout this book in the presence of one of our generation's greatest storytellers, remember that these stories are not intended to be merely read: rather, they were written to be experienced. The book is not an autobiography, a novel, or a fictional work. It is a culmination of the life experiences that have made Lecile Harris a master storyteller and ultimate entertainer. Although he has performed in front of tens of millions of fans during his lifetime, his greatest accomplishment is that we each felt as if he were performing individually just for us. So do not try to read the entire book in one sitting, and for goodness' sake do not hurry through it looking for the ending. Do not set it on the coffee table or display it on a bookshelf. Read it where Lecile intended it to be enjoyed: the toilet.

The stories are designed to last about as long as an ideal BM, so if your legs are asleep when you finish, you need to take a speed-reading course or buy the audio version of the book. If you finish the book in a week, you need more fiber in your diet and an emergency colonoscopy. If you are offended by the stories or content of the book, you should probably write a book of your own and call it "My Pitiful Life." On the other hand, if you find yourself laughing so hard that you mess your britches, then you probably know Lecile as well as I do.

PROLOGUE

A lot of people ask, "Why would you choose to do this for a living?" Especially when I was fighting bulls – why? Why would I want to deal with an animal that weighs fifteen hundred pounds, is as agile as a cat, and wants to stomp me into the dirt?

Let's say there's a cowboy in trouble. He's hung up and can't get his hand out, so obviously it's going to be a wreck. To be able to get yourself in there in a position to untie his hand; to drop him out and allow him to escape unharmed by maneuvering the bull to you; to be able to work yourself out of that position; and to then top that off with a little piece of comedy – there's no greater feeling I can think of.

"Toby the Town Pump" act. That's me on the right without my hat on. I had a bald front wig. Boy, do I look old. The other clown is Dub Pratt.

Photographer unknown.

LECILE

THIS AIN'T MY FIRST RODEO

These ropes came out "TIDE" at the Dixie Nationals Rodeo in Jackson, Mississippi.

Photo: Robbie Freeman.

A BOY NAMED LECILE

I was born on November 6th, 1936 in Lake Cormorant, Mississippi. My mom and dad had moved there from Alabama, and this being the Delta around about the end of the Depression, there weren't but six or eight houses in the whole town. My uncle owned the only mercantile store, and there was nothing else but a cotton gin, a train station, a post office, and a little school. None of those few houses were open, so my uncle allowed my mother and daddy to clean out a storage room in the back of the store there to live until a house became available. And that's where I was born – in the back room of a mercantile store in Lake Cormorant, Mississippi.

Apparently the doctor who delivered me couldn't type very well, because he got my name mixed up on the birth certificate. When the paperwork came back, my dad looked at it and said, "What is this kid's name?" My mother's sister read it and said, "It looks like Lecile to me." Evidently he had misspelled my name – it was supposed to have been Cecil. By the time I got to the first or second grade, that's when I realized that the name Lecile was going to be a problem, because I was being called Lucille, Lisa, Leslie, and every other kind of thing you could think of but Lecile. So I learned to fight real early, and most of it was over my name.

TRIXIE AND THE DOGS

I was four years old the first time I had anything really traumatic happen to me. A house had finally come available in town, so we moved into it. It had a fence around it, and my little dog Trixie and I weren't supposed to go outside that fence. One day he slipped out of the fence, got out on the railroad track, and a train cut him right in two.

That messed me up for a couple of days, and about the time I got straightened up from that, I just had to break out of the little fence I was in and go across the dirt road to the schoolyard to play on this little old swing they had. We lived really close to the Mississippi River levee, and it was full of wild dogs. While I was swinging, a pack of those dogs came out, jumped on me, and dragged me toward the levee. I guess I was going to be their lunch. Fortunately Mr. Riggins, the principal of the school, heard me screaming and the dogs barking and all that commotion, so he came out with a broom and ran them off and saved me. I had just gotten over my dog being cut in two by the train, and then a couple of days later these dogs tried to tote me off, so I didn't care too much for dogs for a while.

We had this table in our living room that had a little lower shelf on it, and every time I got to thinking about those dogs, I'd go lay up under that little table until I felt better. My mother kept that table until she passed away, and I have it now out in my shop. Even today, occasionally I feel like going out there and getting up under that table. It was like my security blanket!

COLLIERVILLE

My daddy eventually got a job working as a mechanic and crew chief at the airport where the "Memphis Belle" and other war planes came for repair, so we moved to Collierville when I was about five years old. The house we lived in was divided into four separate apartments. There was my family, another family, a single lady, and my buddy Stanley White's family. Stanley and I both got into a lot of trouble at school. Whenever our principal retired, he wanted to give his paddle to the one who got the most whippings. He couldn't decide if that was me or Stanley, so we flipped a coin, and Stanley won it. Then he lost the damn paddle. That's just the kind of guy he is.

I ran around with a couple of boys in the neighborhood there named Taylor Stamps and James Richard Treadwell. I first learned to ride bulls by climbing up on a honeysuckle-covered fence and letting them jerk the vines to rock the fence back and forth and try to buck me off just like a bull would do. Another thing we did was go around and pick up little Bull Durham tobacco sacks. They had a drawstring at the top, and they looked like the little sacks that miners would use to carry around their gold. We must have had hundreds of them.

Our house we shared with the other people sat on the tops of brick piers about four feet off the ground. The mortar in the bricks was made from creek sand, not white sand, so it had kind of a gold tint to it. Taylor, James Richard, and I decided this sand in between the bricks looked a whole lot like gold, so we'd take a nail or something and scrape the sand out from between the bricks. Then we'd take it and put it in our little tobacco sacks, just like the gold miners. We scraped on the front side of the house for a few days before somebody saw us and made us stop. Well, all we did was crawl on deeper under the house to the back side where they couldn't see what we were doing.

This house had one bathroom that everybody used, and you got to it by walking down a porch that ran along the back. One morning the single lady went out to go to the bathroom, and when she hit the middle of that porch where we had mined so much sand out of the pier, the whole thing fell in with her. There was an old cistern in the ground there that collected rain water, and she ended up with one leg over in that and one still on the collapsed porch. Our folks got under there and figured out what had happened, because there wasn't any sand in between the bricks, so we got our butts wore out.

We all got BB guns when we turned ten years old, and we shot each other with them all the time. Mine and James Richard's were Roy Rogers models, but Taylor had one you could pump up to give it a lot more power. We were in a gunfight one time and he shot me right in the earlobe. It swelled up a little bit but I figured it would get better, which it eventually did, except I always had a little knot in my ear where he shot me. When I was about sixty years old, that little place on my ear festered up. I took my finger and scratched the top off, and out popped that BB that had been in my ear for fifty-something years.

On the railroad back then they had battery-operated switches that controlled the signals and tracks and that sort of thing. When the batteries ran out of juice, or close to it, the workers would put in new ones and throw the old ones on the side of the tracks. We'd go up and down the tracks picking up these batteries, keeping the ones that still had a little juice in them.

Taylor and I used these batteries to build my first robot. First we shot a blue jay and took his brain out. Next we got my sister's doll, cut its head open, and put the brain in it. Then we hooked a railroad battery up to the brain in this doll, but we couldn't ever get it to do anything. My sister was looking for her doll, so we gave up and I took the doll back to her. A week or so later something got to stinking in Mary Jo's room, and it took most of the night before my mother figured out what it was.

BOOB BRASFIELD

There was a theatrical group called the Bisbee Comedians that brought their show to Collierville. We lived just a few blocks from their campsite. There was a lot behind the fire station big enough for their outfit, and every year they'd make that their last stop. It was a tent show, so they had a big old circus tent with folding chairs and a stage under it.

Us local boys would get jobs with the show. The older ones would do the heavy work like setting up the tents, while the ones who were ten or eleven would work the concessions. Before the show started and between acts, we sold popcorn, snow cones, and saltwater taffy. When the acts started, we'd take our chairs in the front row and enjoy our pay, which was a snow cone and a little sack of popcorn. There were three or four acts a night, so we thought that was a pretty good deal.

The star of the show was a comedian named Boob Brasfield, who was the brother of Rod Brasfield of the Grand Ole Opry. I got to know Boob pretty well. My mother had a restaurant just a few blocks away, and she was an outstanding cook, so I used to bring him fried chicken, cornbread, and turnip greens. He had been on the road eating out the whole season, so he loved all this home cooking. I also got to run his errands, and that just blew me away to do things for him. He'd even invite me into his little camper trailer that he pulled behind his car and used as a dressing room, where we'd visit before his shows.

Boob was my first introduction to comedy. There were little things I saw Boob do that I still do. His fingers were real long and limber, so when he pointed, he could make the end of one turn up right at the tip. Boob's timing was what made him so good. Even at ten years old, I recognized the importance of timing and it never left me. Just like in music, timing is everything in comedy. I think that's why I always worked best with announcers who were also musicians. When you tell a comedic story, it has a timing or a rhythm just like a song. It has beats, and you have to time those beats properly in order to keep the people interested enough so that when it's time to nail the punch line, you know they're ready for it.

Some people say you can't teach timing, but I don't think that's true. If someone has no timing whatsoever, then there's no use in trying, but if someone has some timing, they can improve it over the years – which is now about sixty for me. I still work on my timing and it gets better every year. I used to be in too big of a hurry to let the timing work, but now I can give it that extra beat that makes all the difference in a delivery. Whether you're telling a story or buying a mule or chasing a girl, timing is everything. If your timing is off, you're going to miss something.

MY FIRST FIGHT

My first really knock-down, drag-out fight was in the fourth grade. One day at lunch, this bully named Milton told me he was going to beat me up as soon as school was over. We lived down the railroad track from the school, so I walked it every day. When I got out on the track that afternoon and started home,

Milton saw me and got after me. I was hauling butt down the railroad track and Milton was right behind me. My daddy happened to be driving by at the time, and he saw me running from Milton, but he didn't stop.

When I got home, Daddy was waiting for me with his belt off, and he said, "Do you think that boy can whip you?"

"I don't know. I think so."

"Do you think he can give you a better whipping than I can?"

"No sir."

"Well, you better go back up that railroad track and catch that boy then."

So I put my books down and went back up the track knowing Daddy was sitting there in the yard watching me. As soon as Milton saw me, he came barreling down the track to whip me. I didn't want to get whipped by either one of them, but I figured I'd just get my butt whipped by Milton since I knew that wouldn't hurt as bad as if Daddy did it. But as scared as I was, I just beat the crap out of Milton. And every day after school for the rest of the semester, I chased his butt back up the railroad trying to catch him and whip him again! I had found me somebody I could whip, so I thought I'd just keep it up, although I don't think I ever caught him. But from then on, it seemed like fights just followed me.

MR. OSTEEN

I was always clowning in school when I wasn't fighting. I did things like reach around the back of my head and scratch my right ear with my left hand. A teacher asked me one time why I couldn't scratch my right ear with my right hand – why I had to scratch it like that. She said, "You're just doing that to make people laugh. If you scratch your right ear, scratch it with your right hand, not with your left hand wrapped all the way over your head." So, shortly after that, I scratched my left ear with my right hand, the other way around, and I got sent to the principal's office. Mr. Osteen asked me why I was there, and I told him the teacher had told me not to scratch my right ear with my left hand, and I hadn't. I had scratched my left ear with my right hand. Mr. Osteen just shook his head and tried not to laugh, because he liked me even though I was a frequent visitor to his office.

As I was coming up, I had a friend named Bobby Ballard. He and I ran together all the time and were always getting into trouble. One day I hit him in the head with an eraser and he chased me up the stairs and into the boys' bathroom. It had a long trough in there where you washed your hands, and it stayed stopped up with towels, so it had water in it all the time. I knew Bobby was right behind me, so I picked up this wastebasket and scooped it down through there and filled it with water. Then I went into the first stall, which was right by the door of the bathroom. I got up on top of the commode seat and held the bucket up, and when the door opened, I just dumped it right on over the wall.

Unfortunately I drenched Mr. Osteen. When Bobby had come running up the stairs behind me, he met Mr. Osteen, who was headed for the bathroom too, so Bobby just threw on the brakes and acted like nothing was happening. After I emptied the bucket on Bobby, or so I thought, I laughed so hard I lost my balance. One foot slipped off in the commode, which left me standing there with just one foot on the floor. That's when Mr. Osteen came around the end of the stall with his long gray hair hanging down all wet as a rag, and I mean he was red hot. He looked at me and said, "Lecile, get out of the toilet and go down to the office and wait on me until I get down there, because I'm too mad to come down there right now."

So I went down the hall to the office, every other step going *squish – squish – squish*. When Mr. Osteen got down there, he called me into this little room and shut the door. He was standing there with a paddle curved like your butt, about three inches wide, and it was made out of some kind of thin whippy stuff that just warped your behind. He told me to grab my knees and said, "I have never given anybody over ten licks, but I don't know whether I'm going to be able stop at ten with you, so you better keep count. When I get to ten, you better get out." Well, when he got to ten, I started reaching for the door, but by the time I found the handle and got out, I had taken fifteen or sixteen licks. As I was scrambling out, he hollered at me to go back to class and not come back down there. He started to close the door, but then he told me to come back in. He pulled out a dollar bill and said, "Son, you're never going to make a living clowning around. Why don't you study and be something? I'll bet you this dollar that you don't even graduate."

Years later, on the night of my graduation, he gave me my diploma with that dollar folded up in there. I still have it. Shortly after that, he quit teaching, but he was doing a lot of speaking around town and he always led his talk off with a story. He'd say, "You know, I'm going to tell you folks, you really need to watch what you say," and he would tell them the story about me and that bet. "Lecile Harris has made a living all his life being a clown, so you have to really watch what you say!"

When Mr. Osteen died, his wife told me, Bobby Ballard, Stanley White, and Tom Keough – the group that was always in some kind of mischief – that she wanted us to be his pallbearers. She said, "You all got him this far. You just need to take him home to his grave."

Mr. Osteen was to be buried in a little cemetery about fifty miles from Collierville. Stanley had become a deputy sheriff and, since he knew where the cemetery was, he said we could all ride with him and lead the funeral procession. Come to find out, Stanley really didn't know where the cemetery was at all. We drove and drove and drove, with all the other people following us, until finally the hearse figured it out and everybody else went on to the cemetery. We didn't notice that, so we kept driving around by ourselves until we got to the right place more or less by accident.

When we finally got there, the hearse was backed up to the grave with the door open, and everybody was just sitting there waiting because there was nobody to get Mr. Osteen out. Mrs. Osteen just shook her head and said, "Boys, you messed up at school the whole time he was alive and you messed up his funeral after he died. I don't know why I could have expected any more, and it just wouldn't have been the same if you all had gotten it right." So it got all over town that we, his pallbearers, were late for Mr. Osteen's funeral.

HALLOWEEN PRANKS

My school days were full of mischief. Around Halloween, down on the square in Collierville, the hardware store used to put different things out there to sell. One year they had a regular two-horse wagon for sale. This wagon was probably ten feet long and six feet wide, with three-foot wheels, so it was pretty big. On the night before Halloween, we went downtown, took the wagon apart, and took it up to the school.

Our school building was two stories, with classrooms downstairs and a study hall in a small auditorium upstairs. Of course everything was locked, so to get upstairs, we had to climb up on the gym and onto another building and then crawl through the window of the study hall. After we did all that, we got a rope, pulled the wagon up there one piece at a time, and assembled it on the stage. Then we shut everything up and went home.

The next day, we went to class as usual. Bobby, Tom, and I – the three of us that did the wagon deal – got to study hall first that day and just waited for everyone to come in. When they did, and saw that wagon, nobody could believe their eyes! There was no way you could get it in there, up the stairs, and through the door. The teacher threw a fit when she came in and saw it, so she went to get Mr. Osteen, who told the three of us to come down to his office when the bell rang. When we went down there, he said, "Boys, I don't have any idea how y'all did that, but I know you did. Before the day's over with, I want it off that stage."

I said, "Mr. Osteen, we don't know how in the world they got that up there."

"Well, boys, I don't want to hear any of that mess. I just want that thing off the stage."

So we went back up to the study hall and sat around and figured and drew plans and measured windows and doors and just made a big production of it. After school was over with, we took it apart and carried it out down the stairs, but we never admitted that we put the thing up there.

The study hall teacher had told on us, so we just had to get her back on Halloween night. Bobby and I went to a dairy farm by the house and got us a paper sack full of fresh cow pies, took it to her house, set it up on the front porch right outside her door, lit it, and rang the doorbell. We were in the bushes watching when she came out in a housecoat and slippers, stomped the fire out, and got cow crap all over her feet. I did love that!

GORILLA CRAP

My mother, bless her soul, she was so good to me. We didn't have much money, so she worked all the time selling eggs and doing things like that so she could do a little extra for me and my sister. One of the things she did for me was to let me join the Cub Scouts.

The Cub Scout uniform was blue pants, blue shirt, yellow handkerchief around the neck, and a blue cap. I didn't have all that, but Mother did sell enough eggs to buy me a shirt. I was so proud to have that.

Our troop leader took us on a field trip to the zoo. Back then they didn't have glass in front of the monkeys like they do now; there were just bars. We were standing in front of the gorilla house looking at the gorilla. He would stick his hand out and people would hand him peanuts and popcorn and things like that. He'd eat them and we thought that was funny.

Some smartass in front of us thought it would be hilarious to put a hot cigarette butt in the gorilla's hand. It burned him, so he put his hand in his mouth and licked it, and then he sat on it. What he was doing was crapping in his hand. He pulled it out from under his butt and reared back and slung that crap at the guy who put the cigarette in his hand. He missed him but strung gorilla crap all down the front of my new shirt, from my neck to my waist. I mean it stunk, and that was our first stop at the zoo.

The scoutmaster took my shirt off and washed it off in the goldfish pond, but it still stunk the whole day long. I remember coming home and telling my mother that my shirt smelled like gorilla crap, and she never was really able to get that smell out of it.

COTTON CARNIVAL

Memphis had a cotton carnival back in the late '40s and early '50s, and it was a big deal, with parades and everything. Each school around the county and city would have a prince and princess to represent them. The carnival was at Crump Stadium, which was the big stadium in Memphis back then. Dick Hawley, a TV and radio personality who was the voice of Memphis back then, was the announcer. I must have been a freshman the year this girl named Jo Coats was the princess for our school, and I was the prince.

My mother had bought me some new pants for this particular deal because I didn't have any "Sunday pants," which is what we called nice pants back then. The pair she got me was made of that old-timey wool that just ate you alive. You could walk across the street and the inside of your legs would be raw.

They held the carnival in June, so you can imagine how hot I was standing out there in my wool pants and white shirt and tie with my hair all slicked back. As the prince, I had to escort this girl out to the middle of the football field when Dick Hawley called our names. I was standing there getting hotter and hotter until he finally got to us and said, "From Collierville, here's Prince Jo Coats and Princess Lucille Harris!" You talk about breaking out into a sweat. I was already worn out with those pants, and if I would've had a shovel and could've dug a hole right there in the middle of that field, I would have. But I had to walk out all the way to the other side as the whole place laughed their behinds off.

Things like that have happened to me so many times that now whenever I go sit down in a waiting room, I just wait for the nurse or somebody to come out and call "Ms. Harris." And I say, "No ma'am, it's Mr. Harris. Do I look like a Lucille?"

SPORTS

School was a lot of fun – especially the sports part of it. I played basketball and football and was pretty good at them. Our basketball and football teams were better fighters than players, so we fought all the time. When we played somebody, our little gym or stadium would totally fill up with people who came just to watch the fights.

We'd fight before, during, and after the ball games. Germantown was about seven miles from Collierville, and we played them a couple of times a year. We couldn't wait until the ball games to fight, so we'd call over there and ask them if they wanted to meet us at the clubhouse at Forest Hill to rumble a while. They'd come out, we'd fight for an hour or two until everybody gave out, and then we'd all just go home. I see those guys all the time now. It was just a different kind of life.

Our town was so close-knit. On Saturday we would go right up the road to the black kids' school, where they had a dirt basketball court and just one old basket. We'd always play shirts and skins – like we couldn't tell who was on whose team.

I dressed out with the high-school football team when I was in the eighth grade. Mainly it was just to make our squad look bigger, because we didn't even have enough players to make two whole teams to scrimmage. Our football coach at Collierville was Fred Medling, and his brother Will came in to help him coach. They were two of the best offensive guards to ever come through Memphis State, so they really knew their football.

That year we went to Humboldt, Tennessee, and they had a senior named Doug Atkins, who was the baddest character that I ever was around. He was 6'8", 285 and had outstanding careers both in college at Tennessee and in the pros. Dick Butkus once said that Doug Atkins was the only player he was ever afraid of. What does that tell you?

Our first tackle that lined up against Doug was David Fitzgerald. Doug crippled him after a couple of plays, so Coach Medling had to move a guy named Pinky Russell over to David's spot. A couple of plays later, Doug put him out. We didn't have facemasks on our helmets, and Doug had scraped all the skin off Pinky's nose. I was sitting on the end of the bench, not really expecting to play, because I was in the eighth grade and only weighed a hundred and fifty pounds.

Will Medling came over to me and said, "Leechel, you ready?" He never called me Lecile. It was always Leechel.

"For what?"

"You need to go in and take Pinky's place."

"Coach, I didn't even bring my thigh pads and hip pads."

"Well, I bet you bring them next week."

I went in and thought I had to set a precedent with Doug to let him know right off the bat that he couldn't push me around. I don't think he paid much attention to me since I was so much smaller than the rest of them and especially him, so at the snap I went by him and popped him in the head with an elbow. I guess that got his attention, because he hit me everywhere you could be hit for the rest of the game. And just like Will Medling said, I never forgot my pads after that.

Coach Fred Medling had a huge impact on my life. I was big and all, but before I met him I couldn't chew gum and walk at the same time. I had a lot of natural athletic ability but no real athletic experience. Coach Medling was the turning point for me as to whether I was going to be a good athlete and really successful in anything. I've been laid out under bulls ready to give up, but then I'd think about Fred Medling and somehow come on out. There was no quit in him, and he instilled that attitude in me and a lot of other athletes. I credit Coach Medling for my ability to make all the right moves for bullfighting.

BASEBALL

I wanted to play baseball, but we were farming back then. In the spring, we had to plow and get everything ready to plant. My daddy didn't want me to play because I needed to be home to work the farm. But I wanted to play and Coach Medling really needed some more players, so he said, "Let me go talk to your daddy." He did, and Daddy finally gave in and let me go out for the team.

The first day of practice, Coach got me out there and said, "You know, you're big and tall and you've got a long stretch – I think you'll make a good pitcher." So he put me on the pitcher's mound.

I threw a little while and he said, "You know, as long as you are with that good reach and everything, maybe you'll make a good first baseman." So he put me over on first base.

That didn't work out too good either, so he said, "I'm going to put you out in left field – I think you can get around out there all right." It turned out that didn't work either, so he finally put me over in right field, where they don't ever hit anything.

At the end of practice, Coach Medling called me up to the dugout and said, "You know, Lecile, I think you need to help your daddy on the farm this spring."

DADDY

Daddy was rough. He would knock you on your butt in a heartbeat. Nobody messed with him. He was the kind of guy that laughed when a horse kicked you, or you fell in the mud, or something like that.

His family had a sawmill in the front yard over in Alabama, and he saw his daddy get shot in the back there. Two of the guys running the sawmill got into an argument, and one pulled a gun and shot at the other. The bullet went through the guy's ear and hit my granddaddy in the back and killed him as he was walking up to talk to my daddy. His blood stayed on the front steps for years as a constant reminder to my daddy.

The sawmill was a dangerous place just by the nature of the work. Daddy's granddaddy, my great-granddaddy, lost an arm to the saw. One of my uncles had a log roll off the top of a wagon and kill him. Daddy just had a rough life, and his step-dad used to whip him all the time with a bullwhip. He grew up rough, but he was a hard worker.

One time we were out in the field pulling corn, and I had to go to the bathroom really bad. I told Daddy, but he said, "Just hold it. We'll be a little closer to the end of the row in a minute." A little after that, I said, "Daddy, I got to go to the bathroom now." And he said, "Hang on, hang on, we're almost to the end." We got a little further, and I realized what was coming on, because I had gotten the cold sweats and started cramping. I thought whipping or not, I'm taking off. I hauled it to the bushes, did my business, and when I came back he said, "See? Don't take near as long when you're ready."

Nonconnah Creek came down the back side of our place. This old guy we called Buttermilk had a whiskey still down there.

One day the sheriff caught him and busted his still up, but he left a fifty-five-gallon barrel of corn mash there. The sheriff told Daddy about it since it was on the back side of our place, so we went down there with a wagon and hauled it back to feed to the hogs.

When we fed them that mash, they got so drunk they were stumbling around and could hardly walk. I thought that was hilarious, so I just kept throwing the mash to them, which got them even drunker. I ran and got my sister to show her, and by the time we got back, they had straightened up a bit, so I fed them some more mash. That really got them going nuts, and they got to running through the fence until there were drunk hogs all over the pasture. They would run a little ways and then fall over just like regular drunks!

One year Daddy decided I should have a share in the crop since I worked so hard on the farm, so he gave me a bale of cotton. Most people sold theirs at the gin right when they harvested in October, but Daddy said we should wait a few months until the price was higher. In the meantime, we lined up all our bales next to the road behind our house, and I wrote my name on my bale so we could keep up with it.

A few weeks after the harvest, somebody threw a cigarette out, and it burned a path right down the fencerow to the cotton. Daddy saw the smoke so we ran out and sprayed the bales down with water until we thought we had all the fire out. Well, when a cotton bale burns, it generally smolders from the inside. The best way to put it out, believe it or not, is to soak it in kerosene. That smothers the fire, while water just runs off the outer layer of the bale and leaves the inside burning.

That next spring my sister and I were playing on the cotton bales, jumping from one to another. When I jumped on mine, the whole thing just collapsed into a pile of ash. That bale of cotton had been sitting there all winter long burning up from the middle.

I went and told Daddy about it. He asked me, "Whose bale was it?"

"It was mine."

"Well, I'm glad it wasn't mine." And that was that.

Another time we were building a barn out back. I had played football the night before, so I was sore. I got up that morning, slipped my boots on with no socks, and went down to the barn. About the middle of the morning, I was up in the rafters working and my foot started itching, so I took my boot off and started scratching my foot. My daddy didn't put up with much foolishness at all, and he hollered, "What the hell's wrong with you?"

"My foot's itching."

"Well, that ain't no reason to take your boot off while you're sitting on top of the barn. Put it back on!"

I did, but my foot just kept on itching. By the time I got back down on the ground, my ankle had started hurting and I was limping around. Daddy hollered, "Now what the hell's wrong?"

"Well my ankle's sore, but I don't think I turned it or anything last night."

"Just hurting? Dammit, what else is gonna get wrong with you?"

A very few minutes later, my knee started hurting and my ankle quit hurting, so I'm thinking something's going wrong here and it must be all in my mind. Daddy saw me grimacing in pain and asked me, "By George, what's the matter now?"

"Well, Daddy, my knee's hurting."

"Yeah, you played football and ran around last night fighting, but when you come down here this morning, you can't even work because you're so sore. How come you were ripping and running around all night?"

I told him I didn't know what the deal was and tried to go back to work. A very short time later, my hip started hurting and my knee quit. I could hardly walk now, and that really ticked him off. "Go to the house then and see if your mother can take care of you!" When I left, my chest and stomach were hurting. By the time I got home and told mother what was going on, I was having a little trouble breathing.

Mother took me up to Dr. Kelsey's office, and I told him this long tale about what had happened. I didn't think he was going to believe all that, but he just nodded his head and asked, "Did you change shoes before you came up here?"

"Yes sir, I took my boots off."

He said to my mother, "Rubye, go home and get his boots." She brought my boots back, and when he turned one over and tapped on the sole, a smashed black widow fell out of it.

That spider had bitten me between my toes, and black-widow poison follows your nerve system. It'll take a joint at a time, and it can affect the nerves around your heart. That's why it hurt me in all those places. So the doctor gave me some shots around my chest and told me this was probably going to last a while. And it did: the pain lasted almost a week. It went up my back, into my neck, and then right to the top of my doggone head. After that, it worked its way back down to my foot. I never will forget, we had just bought our first TV, and Howdy Doody was on. The pain was so bad that I got to where I didn't even like Howdy Doody. I never could watch it after that.

I'M NOT A MUSICIAN, I'M A DRUMMER

Collierville High was small. There were only twenty-two in my graduating class, but the school had a band in addition to all the sports teams. The band needed some more members, so they got me to join up.

The first instrument they put me on was a viola, which is just a big violin. And obviously, knowing me, I'm not cut out for a viola. After that, they told me what they needed was a drummer. I was real glad to do that, even though most other musicians really don't consider us drummers to be real musicians. If they asked you if you were a musician, and you told them "Sure, I'm a drummer," then you started off on the wrong foot with them.

Shortly after I joined the marching band, the music teacher decided to put together a little jazz combo. That's when I first put together what we called a trap set, which was a drum set with a bass drum, snare, and cymbal. We had a little Dixieland jazz band going, and I started getting pretty good on the drums.

The music got me into the comedy thing. The school band concert had a big number called "Serenade to Insomniac." I was the dude lying on a bed trying to sleep until I'd get up and go kick the band into a rock n' roll song. They just wanted me to go out and have trouble sleeping, but that wasn't good enough for me. I'd get up out of bed and go get a glass of milk, and I had made this little refrigerator that had a hole in the door, so it looked like I slammed my finger in there and got it stuck. I just had to overdo it to be even funnier, and I've kept that up throughout my clowning career.

THE ECHOES AND THE MAYOS

Not too long after high school, some buddies and I started a rock n' roll band called The Echoes. I had already been playing around Memphis with one band or another. The Echoes played school dances, concerts, amateur contests, and so forth. The band was made up of John Wayne Garrison on lead guitar; his brother, Donald Garrison, on rhythm guitar; Charles McOwen on lead vocals; Lewis Baker on upright bass; and me on drums.

The year after I graduated high school, my sister's boyfriend was playing basketball for Collierville. He was pretty hot-headed and fought all the time. I had heard that this bunch of guys were going to jump on him at the ball game, so naturally I came home from college to be involved in that.

Everything was fine during the game until the end, when everybody on this other team came out and jumped on my sister's boyfriend. Back then they would have deputy sheriffs at the ball games to handle these things, so all of a sudden this deputy in a long detective-looking kind of overcoat appeared. He walked out in the middle of the court, threw his coat back to show off his pistol, and hollered, "Okay! Everybody shut it down right now, or I'm going to start taking you all in!"

He was looking right at me with his hand on his gun, so I said, "You know what? You need to take time to go home and file the sight off that pistol so it won't hurt when you pull it out of your butt in the morning." That kind of took him by surprise, but it did break the fight up, and he never had to pull his gun.

The Echoes were in battles of the bands all the time with this group called The Mayos. Their drummer quit and my band kind of fell apart because we were always arguing, so The Mayos wanted me to come play with them. I did, and all of them were Mayos except for me. There was a lead guitar, the bass guy, the piano player, and me. While I was setting my drums up at the first night of practice, the piano player, who was the daddy of these other Mayos, came up to me and asked, "By the way, do you know who I am?"

"No sir, I don't."

He laughed and said, "Well, one night at a ball game you told me I better file the sight off my pistol if I didn't want it to hurt when I pulled it out of my butt the next morning." The deputy and I were just fine after that, and we played music together for several years.

MY FIRST RODEO

That summer is when Bobby and I went across the river to Arlington to the rodeo. We had heard there were a lot of good-looking girls over there, so we went for the chicks mainly, but also to see what a rodeo was all about.

They had two sections of bulls. You could get in the first section that started the rodeo off or you could wait and get in the one on the end. It was a five-dollar entry fee for each. I watched that first section and told Bobby, "You know, I believe I could ride those bulls."

I had three dollars and he had two, with one left over for gas. So I paid the five dollars to get in that last section, but I didn't have anything I needed. I didn't have spurs. I didn't have a bull rope. I didn't have a glove. I didn't have anything! But the other bull riders were eager to loan me theirs because they knew they were fixing to get my five dollars. One said, "Oh hell, take my rope!" Another said, "No, take mine! Let me put it on there for you!" When I got on the bull, they opened the gate and *whap!* I didn't even make it out of the chute. That sucker reared up and tore my shirt off and skinned my back up, and that just really made me mad.

Next Sunday I told Bobby, "We're going back over there and I'm going to ride one of those bulls." I took my five dollars to get in the bull riding and drew one that wasn't very bad, and I rode him out of the chute before he bucked me off. I thought if I'd already made that much progress, then in a month or so I'd probably be a world champion or something.

We kept going every Sunday, until one day we got over there and the bullfighter hadn't shown up because his car had broken down somewhere over in Arkansas. I was still riding bulls, but had yet to *really* ride one, so I told the guy who owned the thing that I could fight the bulls for him too. He told me I could try it, and if I did all right, he would pay my entry fees for both sections of bulls. That was ten dollars, which was a pretty good deal back then. I figured there wasn't much to it, that I could just step around them and stiff-arm them like I was doing in football.

Once a bull rider makes a ride or gets bucked off, your job as a bullfighter is to move in there and make yourself a more desirable target than the cowboy on the ground so that the bull will come to you. Then you have to outmaneuver him and fight him well enough to keep his attention until the bull rider can get up and get out of the arena, and then you have to fight your way out of that. It can be a really hairy deal, but I did it for a couple of weeks there at Arlington and got pretty good at it.

One day the owner of the rodeo said, "You know, I like what you're doing. I like the way you're fighting bulls, but you need to develop a comedy act."

I had a '34 Chevrolet that I thought I could make an act out of. This car had a crank on the front of it that you could use to turn the engine over when the battery was dead, so I came up with a great act built around that feature.

I told Bobby we would go over there as a team. I'd fight the bulls and he'd help me with the comedy. We were going to get out in the middle of the arena with our car and pretend like it wouldn't start. He would get out, get a hold of the crank up front, and turn it a time or two to get it going. Then I'd crank it up like he started it and go forward immediately. He'd act like he couldn't get out from in front of it in time, and then he'd just fall back and catch the rear bumper as it passed over him. I thought that would be funny because I'd be dragging him along behind me on his back. We practiced it over and over in the pasture at home and it worked absolutely perfectly.

We needed some clown clothes for our act, so we stopped by this guy's house that we had played basketball with in high school. Jimmy Summers' daddy was about six-and-a-half-feet tall and weighed close to three hundred pounds. He was just a huge man. We asked him if he had some old overalls we could have, and he did. They were really sloppy and baggy on us, so they looked funny.

We went over the next Sunday and got ready to do the act. This fellow had put tons and tons of sand in the arena, so when we drove in there, the tires sank way down. I went out to the middle and cut the car off. Bobby jumped out, ran to the front to turn the crank, and after a couple of times I started her up. My little car was already in gear, so it just fired off frontward and right over him. The problem was that it had sunk down so deep in the sand that he couldn't wait for the back bumper. The car was so close to the ground that the front axle caught him under the chin and dragged him along like that.

Of course I didn't know it, so I went ahead with the act. I was driving around the arena and the crowd was just going crazy hollering and screaming. I heard all that and thought we were going over so good that I better make another lap. As I made the turn, I looked back and saw this slick spot dug out right in the middle of the tire tracks, but I couldn't figure out what that was. All I knew was the crowd was loving it, so I kept going. I made another lap and was getting ready to go around a third time when all the cowboys ran out and waved me down. I said, "Y'all need to get out of the way!"

"No, no, wait! Your buddy ain't come out from under that car yet!"

"Y'all got to be kidding."

When I got out and looked under there, I saw that not only was the car too low for him to totally get under there, but those overalls in the back were acting like a scoop and pulling sand in and building him up higher and higher. We couldn't even get him out from under there until all these cowboys got a hold of the front of the car and picked it up. When we were finally able to drag him out, Bobby stood up with his face red as a beet and said, "I quit!"

MEMPHIS STATE

When I graduated from high school, I had football scholarships from UT Martin and Memphis State. I chose Memphis. By then I had already been riding bulls right here at home in my own pasture, and right before football season started, I got bucked off and broke my tailbone.

I went on and reported to football camp anyway. One of the first things we did was a drill that put the freshman team against the varsity team. I played defensive end, so I lined up in a four-point stance for this drill. They had a young coach there who had played ball the year before and was real cocky. He was walking down the line kicking everybody in the butt as he went by. When he got to me, I didn't know what he was doing, and he kicked me in the butt too – right on my sore tailbone. I kind of flared up at him, but I went on and did whatever I was supposed to do. After we finished the drill, I told him, "Coach, if there's something you want me to do, just come and tell me if I'm not doing something right. But don't kick me in the butt anymore because I've got a sore tailbone."

We started the next drill and I got back down in my stance. I could see him coming down the line kicking everyone's butt, but I thought surely he wouldn't do that to me again. Well, sure enough, he once more kicked me right in the butt. That got me pretty hot, but I went on and got down in my stance for the next drill.

I watched him come down the line a third time. When he got behind me and drew back his foot, I stood up and knocked him colder than Cooter Brown.

Well, you just don't hit a coach, whether he's an assistant or whatever. They put me on this cinder track that went around the football field, running laps in full pads during football practice. This was a two-hour practice in August, and I ran the whole time.

The next day I went to where they posted the list of what everybody was supposed to do that day in practice, and they had me on the track again. So I ran that day too.

I did that all week long. We had Saturday and Sunday off, so on Friday I told the head coach, "I came here to play football, not to run track. I realize that I shouldn't have knocked the assistant coach out, but I had asked him not to kick me in the butt because I have a broken tailbone. I'm through running. If I'm on that track list Monday, I'm leaving."

"Well, you can't do that. You've signed a letter of intent, so you can't leave."

On Monday, I went down to look at the list and there I was on the track again. So I went ahead and ran that day – I don't know why. But when it was over, I got Bobby to help me load my stuff into my car and I went straight to UT Martin.

MAYBELLINE

I bought my '34 Chevrolet with another friend for eighty dollars. He paid his forty dollars, but I didn't have mine, so his daddy bought the car for us with the understanding that I was supposed to pay him back my half. I don't even know whether I ever gave him my part or not, but somehow I ended up with the car and took it off to college, where I took it to my shop class one day and cut the top off.

These other guys on campus had '57 Chevrolets and Corvettes and everything, but we'd ride around in that old '34 and pick up more girls than they could ever even think of in their new cars. For my first Christmas at UT Martin, I took a piece of pipe and built a Christmas tree holder behind the front seat. A normal Christmas tree holder might be about three inches across, but mine was more like six or eight inches across, and I welded it to the frame so it would really hold. We cut a tree that would just barely fit in it, about twelve feet tall, and we rode around campus with this tree sticking out of the car and a little guy named Guggenheimer hanging on to the top. The girls really loved that.

One day I was driving by this building on campus and saw a guy painting letters on it. I pulled up there to watch him, and I was just amazed at the way he could lay them out and fill them in. I got him to lay my name out in chalk on the hood of my car, so when I got time, I went and got me a little can of white paint and a brush and filled it in. It looked really good because all I had to do was color inside the lines where the fellow had laid it out.

Later on, people would autograph the car, and when I'd get time, I'd sit down with my little brush and a can of paint and go over the signature so it was permanent. I also ended up painting the fenders red and the headlights like eyes. Right in the middle of the grill was a great big smile, so it looked pretty wicked going down the road. I also had signs on it saying stuff like "You girls that smoke, throw your butts in here!" and "Passing side" on the back left fender and "Suicide" on the back right fender. Chuck Berry had a popular song back then called "Maybelline," so that's what I named my car.

My '34 Chevrolet and the painting on it is what got me interested in artwork and lettering. The engineering students at UT Martin would take drafting, and they had a book with lettering exercises in them that they had to fill up. I would charge the engineers to fill their books up and I got better and better at it. It worked out well for everybody because they were making A's on their books and I was learning how to letter.

There was a Dairy Freeze in Martin, and the owner wanted me to paint the menu on the board outside. He also wanted some characters on the building, like Popeye and Wimpy. I know most people probably don't even remember them, but Wimpy was always eating a hamburger, and of course Popeye was Popeye. I painted these huge characters on the building, trading my painting for food.

UT MARTIN

When I got to UT Martin that summer, football practice hadn't started yet, so some of the guys were selling bibles to get by. You had to go to salesman school, where they'd give you a little satchel with some samples in there – a Bible, dictionary, some children's books, things like that. These guys were going off up to different parts of the country selling bibles and making good money. Whatever you sold there, you kept the down payment to live on, and then later on you'd get paid for the rest of it.

John Maloney and I decided we wanted to do that. We had to go to Nashville to this salesman school, and I mean they taught you all kinds of stuff. They taught you how to hold your little satchel to keep a dog from biting your leg. They even taught you how to put your foot in the door to keep somebody from slamming it on you. We learned all that and more and then they sent us to Washington, Pennsylvania. That town was nothing but Catholic, and all we had was a Protestant Bible and kids' books, so that was a problem. The other problem was that we had to walk everywhere. My car wasn't running well enough at the time to drive up there, so we had hitchhiked. This was a hilly town, so we were walking up and down all these hills, and it was hot and I was tired and blistered. I had sold maybe one or two little books, and we were eating off that.

John and I were staying at a boarding house. He'd come in at night all sunburned and worn out, but he hadn't sold anything all week. I came in before he did one day, and I had some clothes and things on my bed, so I just flopped down on his. When I did, something hard hit me in the middle of the back. I looked under the mattress and there were all of his books that he was supposed to be showing and selling!

I just lay there and waited until he got back. He came in at dark huffing and puffing about how hot it had been all day carrying his bookcase up and down all those hills. I asked him how it had gone, and he said, "Oh man, I didn't sell nothing. Another bad day."

When he went to use the bathroom, I opened up his satchel and found a wet bathing suit in it. Come to find out, he was going to the swimming pool every day because he had met this pretty girl who worked in the concession stand there. She'd give him food all day while he was swimming and having a big time. At the end of the day, he'd put his wet suit in his case and come back to the room and tell me how bad it was. When I found out what he had been doing, I got mad and told him we were getting out of there right then.

We owed the landlady some rent, but we didn't have the money to cover it, so we crawled out the window, slid down the wall on a drain pipe, and slipped out of there. We caught a bus and rode it somewhere close to the edge of Tennessee, but we didn't have any more money, so we couldn't catch the next leg on into Martin. We had to hitchhike.

John and I finally got back to school, where my car was sitting in this pasture beside the athletic dorm. The guy that owned the Dairy Freeze had a son who wanted my car the whole time I was in school, but I never would sell it to him. John and I were starving, so we walked into the Dairy Freeze and I told the guy that ran the place, "You know, your son's been wanting to buy my car for a long time now."

"Yeah, I know, but it's broke down."

"I'll sell it to you cheap."

"How cheap?"

"For two cheeseburgers and two chocolate milkshakes."

"Tell you what. I'll give you two cheeseburgers and two chocolate milkshakes apiece, and I'll even throw in some french fries."

"You got a deal."

That was the last time I ever saw my car. Somebody later on told me it sat right there in that pasture and just rusted to the ground.

School hadn't started yet, so we were still trying to get to Collierville. After we ate, we hitchhiked to this little town a few miles out of Martin. There was a rail line that went through it, so we went to the depot to figure out our next move. We were sunburned, blistered, and tired, and I was ready to get home, but Martin was about one hundred and twenty miles from Collierville. I had a Samsonite suitcase that my folks had gotten me for graduation, John had his suitcase, and that's all we had. The train was stopped there, and when it was pulling off, I told John, "That train's going to Memphis. Let's jump it."

So, we did. We slipped on while it was just creeping off and jumped into a boxcar. We rode this train for hours, and I could kind of tell where we were, but not really. What we didn't know was that this train wasn't going to stop in Memphis. It went right on across the bridge over into Arkansas. The first time this train slowed up was on the other side of Little Rock, which is more than two hundred miles on the other side of Memphis. I saw a sign that said Benton, Arkansas and the train began to pick up speed again. I told John that we had to get off this thing or we were going to end up in California. I said, "Okay, we'll back up, throw our bags out, and run with the train and jump out the same way it's going. That way we won't hit as hard. We just got to get some speed up and be going with the train."

We backed up against the wall, I counted down, and we took off. John was supposed to jump out one side and me the other. The railroad bed was up on this rise, and there was sage grass all over the side of it. When I jumped, I hit that sage grass and I slid and I slid and I slid for what seemed like forever on that stuff until I rolled up against a fencepost and stopped. I waited until the train went by, figuring John was at the same place I was. Well, he wasn't. John had chickened out and not jumped. I couldn't see him anywhere until he finally did get nerve enough to jump way on up the track. While he was heading back to me, I was walking the other way to find the suitcases. I found his first, which was fine. Then I saw mine, which had hit that sage grass and slid and slid and slid until the hinged side of it hit a fence post and strewed my clothes and stuff everywhere.

I picked up some old barbed wire, tied my suitcase back together, and put my things in it. There was a cow standing near us in the pasture, and cows are just naturally nosy. If they think you have something in your hand, they'll come to you to check it out. So I finally got the old milk cow to come up close, and when she did, I took her by the horns and held her there. We took our suitcases and tied them together with another piece of barbed wire and strapped them over the cow's back like saddlebags. We led the cow down the railroad track toward Benton, trying to get back to where we had come from. We didn't know what we were going to do, but we were trying to find a road or something. When we finally came up on one, I pulled the suitcases off of the cow, slapped her on the butt, and sent her back to where she came from.

We started hitchhiking again, and it wasn't too long until this guy stopped and asked if either of us had a driver's license. I told him I did. He was coming from California and had to get to St. Louis. He said he'd haul us if we'd drive and let him get some sleep. So we did. He crawled in the back and slept while I drove his car from Benton, Arkansas, which is on the other side of Little Rock, to Memphis. We got to where you're supposed to turn off there at the river to go to St. Louis, and I hated to just get out and leave him there, so we went on across the river to the other side of Memphis. He was still asleep, so we just pulled over into a parking lot and left him there. Then we didn't have far to walk on into Collierville.

While I was on a football scholarship at UT Martin, I was slipping off up to Fulton, Kentucky and boxing at the local armory. I wasn't supposed to be boxing for money because that would ruin my eligibility for college football, but you could go up there and make seven dollars a round to lose and fourteen dollars a round to win. That was a lot of money back then. If you lost all three rounds you got twenty-one dollars, and if you won all three you got forty-two. I was winning almost every fight I had up there, so I was making good money.

One night this guy showed up who was just out of the Marines, and he had been his battalion's boxing champion. He was five or six years older than I was, but we were both about the same size at 6'5" and 235 or so. We thought this would be a good match because Fulton was the guy's hometown, so it was blown up really big and there was a little more money in it than usual. He was left-handed, and I hated fighting southpaws, but the first two rounds I had him beat. I was ahead on points because my arms were longer than his, so I was reaching in and tapping him again and again, but I knew that if he ever tagged me, it might well be lights out.

By the third round I had him worn out pretty good, and I thought, boy, if I could knock this guy out, it would really be a feather in my cap. So I set him up with a jab and started around with a right hook, but his left hook beat mine by a split second and it knocked me out and hung me up on the ropes. Back then they didn't stop the fight if you were just hung up like that: they let him beat you until you finally hit the mat, so that's what he did and that's what I did.

That was the first time I'd ever been knocked out boxing in my life. He busted my top lip loose from my gum, broke my nose, and blacked both my eyes. I also ended up colorblind. This guy had beat me so much around the head that the optic nerves, or whatever it is that gives you the color in your vision, were shot. The doctor told me that my color vision might come back in a week, or a month, or never.

I was still colorblind when I was going home a couple of weeks after that. Right outside of Martin, they had one red light on the highway back to Memphis. I had learned by then that the order of the lights on traffic signals was usually green, yellow, and red from bottom to top. Well, this little town had theirs backwards. When I went whistling through there, a cop pulled me over and did the small-town cop deal, giving me static for running a red light. It didn't set well with him when I told him that his lights were backwards, that the green was supposed to be here and the red was supposed to be there. I explained that since his were wrong, I misread them because I was colorblind. He listened to all that and said, "You know, I've been working here a long time, but that's the first time I've ever heard that one. You're colorblind and our lights are backwards." And he let me go.

The next weekend I was going home through this town again, and I still couldn't tell one color from another. Of course I remembered their lights were backwards, so I ran through them accordingly. The cop pulled me over again and said, "You know, we've been through this before."

"I don't understand what the deal is –

"We changed our lights."

He had gotten to talking to somebody about it, and come to find out, his lights really were wrong, so they changed them. But he gave me a ticket this time.

The next weekend I was passing through again, making sure to mind the lights, and the same cop pulled me over yet again. He asked me, "You haven't paid that ticket yet, have you?"

"No sir, I haven't."

"Give it back to me. I'm going to tear it up because your story really is the best I've ever heard."

I wasn't supposed to be boxing for money because that would ruin my eligibility for football, so they put me on probation when they caught me doing that. I was being real careful then not to get into any fights, but one day I got into it with a motorcycle gang that came along through school. That got me on double probation. The coach told me, "You're the first one we've ever had to put on that."

So I was being extra careful at this point, but one night some of the guys were planning a panty raid and wanted me to get in on it. A panty raid is when you rush into a women's dorm and steal all their panties. But most of the time the girls started it, because they'd be waving their panties out the window and all of that and you didn't even have to get them out of the drawers. They'd have them all laid out for you, and then holler out all dramatic like, "They got my panties!"

The guys couldn't get anybody to start this panty raid, so they kept after me to do it. I told them I wasn't getting in on it since I was already on double probation, but they kept on and kept on until they finally talked me into it. I went up a ladder to the second floor of this women's dorm, cut the screen out, went in through the window, and ran downstairs and out the front door.

I was headed back to the athletic dorm, but the guys had a ladder up on another girls' dorm, and they wanted me to start that one too. I thought I'd just do that one more and then go on back and stay out of trouble. I went up the ladder and the window was already open, so I should have known right then not to stick my damned head in there. This window was to the room where they stored the extra beds, and when I put one foot through and then stuck my head in, this little old dorm mother picked up a bed post from a bed that was taken apart and put a great big old knot on my head. That slowed me up enough so she could tell who I was, but I climbed on in and went down the stairs, out the front door, and back to the athletic dorm.

The next morning the coach called me in and said, "Lecile, there's no such thing as triple probation. Double probation was a stretch, so we sure can't do a triple probation. They're going to make you lay out a year and come back." Luckily I had gotten another offer from Northwest in Mississippi before this one, and I had a buddy playing down there, so I left.

NORTHWEST

Northwest was absolutely the rankest football I ever played. I never will forget the first day of practice. We were in shorts and shoulder pads, and our first exercise was to get around a light pole and do forearm practice on it. We did that for I don't know how long, so my arms were all blue and swollen and sore by the time we got finished.

Athletic tape used to come in these long, round cardboard tubes kind of like the cans that tennis balls come in. As soon as the trainers used the tape up, the seniors would cut those cans down the middle and tape them on their forearms. The cans didn't have any pads on them, but they helped, so eventually us first-year guys got some and made us some forearm protectors. We didn't have facemasks back then, so these things would also bust a lip.

Coach Jackson knew about my trouble up at UT Martin, so he thought I'd be a good candidate for the Wrecking Crew since I hadn't made first string yet. The coaches would give you a list before the game – the right tackle, he's hot-tempered; the quarterback's got a bad right ankle; the tight end has a bad left knee. And that's what the Wrecking Crew was sent in there to work on. You went in and put them out. If you got put out, fine: you didn't start anyway. If you went in and started a fight with their main guy and you both got put out, fine: you didn't start anyway, and now they lost their main dude. It was that kind of football.

One night we went down to Scooba to play East Mississippi. Bull Sullivan was the coach there, and I mean they were rank. This was wintertime and we had no hot water or heat in our dressing room, but of course theirs was working fine. We knew on the front end how things were going to go. We could've brought a pro team in there and obviously not won.

We got out on the field and there were fights breaking out left and right, but the referees just let it go unless Scooba was losing the fight. I was playing defensive end, so I lined up on this tackle with a big gap between his teeth. Whenever I got down into my stance, he'd hack up a wad and spit it on my hands. I got so mad about it that twice I fired off the ball early just trying to tear his head off. That was two five-yard penalties and they got on my butt about that, so I quit. It wasn't too long after that until the other defensive end got into it with one of their guys. So when they were all worried about what was going on over there, I found it was a good time to get this tackle down and just wear him out good. I had that tape can on my forearm and I was throwing it over and over. Of course he didn't have a facemask, so it was really workin'.

By the time they got all that straightened out, one of our guards had broken his ankle. The trainers took his shoe off and he was sitting on the bench with his helmet off and his foot in an ice bucket. About two minutes before the ball game was over with, the whole thing broke out into one great big fight. So this guard took the bucket, poured the ice out of it, put his helmet on, and hopped out there with the bucket in one hand and his shoe in the other. Back then our shoes had these long aluminum cleats, and they'd hurt you, so this guy came out there with his shoe and his bucket and was just whopping anybody he could with both hands as he hopped on one foot through this fracas.

Even the band came out of the stands and got in on it. The bandleader was trying to get the band to play the national anthem to shut everybody down, but it was just a flute player and clarinet player left and you couldn't even hear them.

We never did get to finish the game, because every time we'd start back, a fight would break out again. We were right down on the goal line, fixing to score and beat them, when the referees said, "No, y'all can't play without fighting, so Scooba wins."

Well, our coach had been down there before. He knew it was going to be rough getting out and we didn't have any business going back to the gym. So while all this fighting was going on, he sent the managers back to get all our clothes and put them on the bus. We were all really sweaty and it was really cold, but we went straight to the bus without changing. Scooba was building an addition onto their gym and they had a huge pile of bricks there, so their people threw those at us and knocked all the windows out of both buses. We had to ride home in the cold with no windows, so we just about froze, but we were glad to get out of there alive. That's the kind of ball Scooba played.

SCRATCH

About 1957 or so there was this bunch in Memphis called the Lamar Terrace Gang. Nobody much had guns back then, so they carried chains and switchblades. Switchblades had a button on the side of them, just like the ones you saw in the movies, that you mashed to make the blade flip out real quick.

We used to play a game called Scratch. You walked up to somebody who you knew had a knife and they knew you had a knife, and then you each tried to pull your knife quicker and slash the other guy. We didn't jab; we sliced. To make it burn a little more, we would take a file to our knife edgeways and make little jagged teeth on it. That way the guy knew it when you cut him, but it just tore the skin and didn't go too deep.

We'd go up to Memphis from Northwest on the weekends just to meet those Lamar Terrace guys and fight and play Scratch, and we found out real quick that they were much faster than us. We finally realized they weren't using the buttons on their switchblades because that was way too slow. So we did the same thing they did by taking the spring out of it, which made the blade just flop loose. Then it was all wrist action on your part. You just flipped it to lock it open.

You always carried your knife in your jacket pocket. I had a letter jacket from Northwest that I got as a football player, and it had a little slant pocket on the side that was perfect for pulling your knife real quick. You'd come out with it and come back toward them with a flick of the wrist to open the knife.

Well, it got to where that wasn't fast enough, so we'd put a little piece of wood in the knife so it wouldn't shut completely. That way, when you came out of your pocket, the blade caught on it and opened as you were coming back. So when you started coming forward, there was no flipping, no nothing – it was already open. I got so fast with it that I could be in a room with an eight-foot ceiling, take an empty beer can, throw it up with my right hand, reach in my pocket with that same hand, draw my knife, and stab the can before it hit the floor.

I still have scars on my arms from playing Scratch. I have more on my right one because it was the one that was always out. When my arms are tan, you can see the scars a lot better.

SARDIS

My rodeoing was getting popular around this time, so I started venturing out with that. I would work places like Sardis, Mississippi, which was about eighty miles or so from Collierville. That was a pretty good trip back then, so it was an overnighter for a two-day rodeo. I went down there one weekend to ride bulls with this bulldogger named Pete Russell. He was just a bad dude, and easily one of the toughest guys I ever met. I saw someone pull a double-barrel shotgun on him one time, but Pete just stuck his fingers in the end of it and told the guy he didn't have guts enough to pull the trigger.

They didn't have a clown for this particular rodeo at Sardis, so they asked me if I would fight bulls and clown too. Of course I said yes, because they were going to give me twenty-five dollars a night, which would have been fifty dollars total. I didn't have any makeup with me, so I went down to the drug store to get some. I bought a tube of lipstick for the red and a little bottle of Kiwi black shoe polish. That's the only color I could get, so I didn't have any white around my eyes. I put the lipstick on my nose and the liquid shoe polish on my face.

On the first night a bull hooked me out of the arena, over the fence, and into the crowd. I had on a pair of football cleats, which hit this older lady in the noggin, cut her forehead, and broke her glasses. I apologized to her and went back to the show.

After that first performance, I went to take my makeup off, but the black wouldn't come off very good at all. Well, Kiwi shoe polish and Kiwi shoe dye came in the same kind of little bottle and, unbeknownst to me, I had gotten the shoe dye. Shoe polish comes off pretty easy, but shoe dye doesn't. I rubbed my face raw trying to get it off with baby oil and rubbing alcohol until Pete finally told me to just leave it on there since I had to have it for the next night anyway. So all the next day, wherever we went, I had that stuff on.

We did the show the next night and I got hooked again really bad. When it was all over, we went into the office to pick up my check and the guy said, "They already came and got your money."

"Who came and got it?"

"The little old lady who had to pay for getting her head sewed up and her glasses fixed."

So I got hooked bad twice, didn't make anything, and took a week getting that shoe dye off my face.

DANCIN' WITH THE BULLS

I consider myself to be the original bull dancer. I started dancin' with the bulls back in 1955. I would work through the whole rodeo doing comedy, so by the time the bull riding came around, I needed something to pep me up. Some of the rodeos would have a record player on the announcer's stand, so I'd ask them to play me an uptempo song while I just danced by myself to whatever they played. The announcer's stand was usually right by the bull chutes, so inevitably the record would skip and scratch as the bulls got excited and started banging around to the music. That gave me the idea to try to dance with them.

When the sound guy started my record playing, I'd pair off with a bull and actually dance with him. If the bull was good and hot and really rank, he'd watch my moves and match them in rhythm to the music. Then every once in a while, right in the middle of the song, he'd blow towards me. When he did, I'd make a pass and step back out and start dancing again. I did that for over thirty years, and it got to be a feature.

In 1956 I started carrying around my own little 45RPM record player and record, which was "Tutti Frutti" by Little Richard. In 1957 I danced to "Searchin'" by The Coasters. In 1958 I used "Splish Splash" by Bobby Darin. In 1959 it was "What'd I Say" by Ray Charles. I danced to that for three years before I started using "Walkin' the Dog" by the Memphis musician Rufus Thomas in 1963. I did that for a couple of years and then went to "Wooly Bully" by Sam the Sham & The Pharaohs in 1965. Later that year, James Brown came out with "Papa's Got a Brand New Bag," so I danced with that for a couple of years. In 1967 I went to "Soul Man" by Sam & Dave. I switched to "Twenty-Five Miles" by Edwin Starr in 1969.

I danced to many different songs, but the one I did the longest was "Joy to the World (Jeremiah Was a Bullfrog)," which I started using in 1970. The last time I danced with a bull was back in 2002 or 2003, and I used that same song even then because that's the one that everybody remembered.

A lot of people thought you had to have a tame bull to dance with, but that really didn't work. You had to have a hot bull that wanted to get you and had the athletic ability to do so. Believe me, I got caught pretty often, but I got away even more often. When the bull was hot, he would move with me and it looked like we were dancin' to the same beat.

ETHEL

The owner of the Arlington rodeo, Davis Brockwell, had a good lookin' blonde daughter. I got interested in her, so I kept going back every Sunday to ride bulls and see her.

I was playing music with The Echoes back then, and the blonde wanted to come over to a concert we were doing in Collierville. Her best friend, a brunette, and the brunette's fiancé came over with the blonde. After the concert was over, we all went down to Joe's Drive-In, where I just couldn't take my eyes off this brunette for the whole night.

A few weeks later, the blonde asked me to go to her senior prom. I did, and a lot of the guys wanted to dance with the blonde. I wanted to dance with the brunette, and her fiancé didn't dance, so I danced with her a lot that night. I asked her for her phone number, but she wouldn't give it to me or tell me where she lived. She said she couldn't do that because I was her best friend's boyfriend. I told her the blonde and I had just dated a couple of times and that was it, but she wouldn't budge.

A couple of weeks later I finally found out where she lived and figured out how to get her phone number, so I called her and told her I was coming over to see her. She told me I couldn't do that because I was her friend's boyfriend, and besides, she had a date. I told her I was still coming over, and I did. We sat down in the front parlor, which is where folks used to court back then, and talked for hours. Finally, somebody knocked on the front door and she said, "That'll be my fiancé."

There was his picture on the piano that I had turned face down before I even sat down, and there was a teddy bear on the couch he had given her that I had put a pillow over. So when he knocked on the door, I said, "Let me get that," and I picked up the picture and the teddy bear. Then I looked at her and said, "Let me have that ring."

"My engagement ring?"

"Yes, let me have the engagement ring."

She took it off and handed it to me. I walked to the front door and opened it, and there was a screen door between us. He came up to about shoulder height on me, because back then I was 6'5". He asked, "Is Ethel here?"

"Yeah."

"Can I talk to her?"

"No."

"Can I see her?"

"No, I don't think so."

The screen door had a little latch on it, so I unlatched it, opened it up, and said, "Here's your teddy bear, your picture, and your ring. Ethel's with me now." Then I shut the screen door and the big door and just came back and sat down. She didn't say anything, I didn't say anything, and we just went on like he never even came to the door.

From then on, it was her and me. She's my friend, my lover, my wife, my kids' mother. We hardly go anywhere without going together, whether it's the grocery store or hardware store or wherever. We're probably the youngest old couple anybody knows.

SIDE JOBS

Soon after I started rodeoing, I carried with me what the old-timers used to call a snap box. That was just a tackle box that held my brushes, thinner, and three or four little pints of paint. It was called a snap box because the painters used to go around doing what we called snap painting. That's when you went around to stores or farms and asked them if they had anything you could paint. Those were snappers. Arkansas and Missouri both had a lot of snappers because they had a law that required all the farm vehicles to have a number and a name on them. So during the daytime I'd letter trucks and trailers and things like that, and then at night I'd go to rodeos and fight bulls and do comedy. Snapping was just a way for me to pick up extra money.

It seemed like I had a different side job every year, because I'd quit the job every spring when it came time to rodeo. Back then you didn't have rodeos year-round. They pretty much started in the spring and ended in the fall. Now you have them all year long because of the covered arenas and stadiums, but back then you didn't. So I had to get a day job every winter. I'd do something like work construction or pull parts in a warehouse. I'd also put my band back together, because all the good gigs were during Christmas with all the holiday parties. That's where the big money was. I was playing music six or seven nights a week with two tea dances on weekend afternoons, so I was busy. On top of all that, I was holding down a day job. But then spring would come and I'd smell the wild onions and right back to rodeo I would go.

Our band went through some lineup changes during this period. Sam Mayo had to drop out because of the traveling. That left Freddy, Billy, and Jack Mayo. We added Skip and Bubba and became The Capris.

One particular year, Freddy, Bubba, and I were working for Mills Morris pulling parts. Every Thursday, Friday, and Saturday we played in Little Rock at a place called Beverly Gardens. There wasn't a good interstate to Little Rock back then, so it was five hours or so across there on Highway 70. We'd get in our old station wagon, leave directly from work, pick up the other three members, and hit the road. We'd play the gig from 8PM until 1AM, drive back, and get home around daylight. That gave us just enough time to shower, change clothes, and go to work the next day.

We used to pick a lot of parts by Gates, which made belts and hoses of all sizes. They'd come packed in a big box about three by four, because they weren't heavy, so hundreds of belts and hoses fit into one of these big boxes. We emptied one of those, put it in the back of the warehouse, and slept in it. I'd nap for an hour while Freddy and Bubba pulled my parts, and then we'd switch out all day long. When we got off work we'd drive right back over to Little Rock again.

The two guys that owned Beverly Gardens had both been in the pen. One night one of their girlfriends showed up over there and was coming up to the bandstand with requests for songs. Her boyfriend thought she was coming up there to talk to me, so he was getting hotter and hotter. This was a Saturday night, so we were tearing down our equipment to take back home until the next week, and I saw the two guys headed our way. They each had a solid piece of lead, about a foot long and as big around as your thumb, wrapped in leather. Back before Bondo, they used to melt lead and pour it in the dents of cars, so that's where these lead bars came from. One of the band members popped off something to them, and they knocked him right off the stage. I jumped on them but they kept whopping me over the head with those lead bars until I was pretty much out. I felt my head later on and it was like one big knot, the knots were so many and so close together. I went home all beat up that night and told Ethel what happened. She called over there and talked to one of them, but of course they didn't care what she had to say. They said they didn't know which one it was that this guy's girlfriend was interested in, so they figured they'd just whip us all, which they pretty much did.

I came back one night from one of those gigs at the Beverly Gardens. Ethel's sister was staying with us at the time, and when I got home, it was just her there and not Ethel. This was 6AM or something like that. I asked my sister-in-law, "Where's Ethel?"

"Oh, Lecile, you didn't know? She had a baby last night." That was the night Matt was born, who went on to become a big part of my act. It was also the last time we played at Beverly Gardens.

I changed clothes and went to the hospital. St. Joseph's was a Catholic hospital that had a lot of nuns working as nurses. Ethel's room had two beds in it. She was asleep in one, and the other was empty, so I crawled up in that one and went to sleep.

I dozed off there for a while until I sort of halfway woke up and saw somebody in this black outfit slapping my wife. Reflexes took over, so I jumped up, grabbed him, stuck him up on the wall, and gave him a good cussing for slapping Ethel. While all this was going on, in came a doctor, who quickly pointed out that I was just about to whip a nun. I tried to explain to him what was going on, but the doctor said, "That's how we wake them up."

One winter a pipeline came through, so I went to work with them. They were paying five dollars an hour, which was really good, but it was one of the coldest winters we'd ever had. We were going across the Wolf River with the pipeline, and I was a snaker for a bulldozer. That meant I pulled the cables around and hooked them onto whatever they wanted them hooked on. It was so cold that the ground was frozen and everything would be frozen to it, so you'd have to take a pickaxe and chip the ice away just so you could move something. It was a really hard job, but I still stayed cold even though I was having to wear so many clothes that I could hardly move.

One day I was in an Army surplus store and saw a pilot suit. It was made of this really good lightweight material that was supposed to protect you from the cold. I thought it would be great to work in, so I bought it. This outfit was a suit of coveralls with straps around the cuffs to keep the sleeves and legs tight and a zipper to cinch the whole thing up. I could hardly wait for work the next day because I knew I was going to be so warm.

We always filled fifty-five-gallon drums with diesel fuel and limbs and lit them just to stay warm when we weren't doing something. We were standing around a barrel that morning and I backed up to it to get warm. I kept easing closer and closer to get warmer and warmer until my suit went *poof!* This nylon suit, or whatever it was made of, exploded just like that – *poof!* In a couple of seconds, I was standing there with nothing on but straps around my wrists and ankles and a zipper hanging straight down my front. It was gone just like that – melted clean off.

One morning I was just about to walk out the door to go to work when Ethel started having labor pains, so I took her to the hospital and that's when Chuck was born.

Chuck was a very quiet kid. In fact, he hardly said anything at all for the first twenty years. I could give him a whipping and he wouldn't even cry. When Chuck was little, he had a bad habit of opening the door to the truck before we got stopped. That happened a few times and he kept getting banged up, so I told him not to open the door for any reason until I cut the truck off. We had gone to town one day and were on the way back home when I noticed Chuck sitting over there whimpering. I asked him what his trouble was, and he said nothing was the matter. By the time we were pulling in the driveway, he was crying pretty good. I asked him again what was wrong, but he still wouldn't tell me. I reached up to turn the truck off, and when I did, he opened his door and said, "I shut my fingers in the door when we left town."

Chuck took after me on the drums. He was about three years old when he started, and I was still playing then. I had never seen a drummer play to the melody of a song, but that's what Chuck did. Most drummers play a rhythm to a backbeat, but Chuck played along to the melody. I almost never got him out of that habit, but once I did, he became one of the best drummers I ever heard. Chuck has been in many bands and still plays music today.

That next winter after Chuck was born, I came back from rodeoing and went to work at a Ford parts depot. There was a guy there who couldn't stand me, and I couldn't stand him. This guy would just raise hell at anything I did. He was an old referee that had worked my football games in high school, didn't like me then, and didn't like me now. I just bit my tongue and put up with him all winter because I needed this job, until one day my buddy John Maloney and I went outside to take a break. I said, "John, do you smell what I smell?"

"What's that?"

"The wild onions. They're coming up and somebody's cutting them. It's time for me to go back to the rodeo."

I was back at work that afternoon when this guy started in on me again. I was in front of a bin of kingpins, which is a part of an automobile's suspension that's about six inches long and as big around as a roll of quarters. He kept on chewing me out, so I just reached behind me into that bin, came from all the way back there with a kingpin in my hand, and knocked him cold as a cucumber. Then I threw the pin down there beside him and said to John, "When he comes to, tell him I quit."

In September of 1966, Ethel was due to have another baby. I was working the Wichita rodeo that fall and staying with Mr. Shepler of Shepler's Western Wear. He wasn't feeling very good that night, so he told me he'd just stick close to the phone in case the baby came while I was working the rodeo. By the end of the night, a bull had already gotten me down and worked me over pretty good. There were still a couple of bulls left when the announcer came on and said, "Lecile, we have something to tell you." I thought he was going to say something about the wreck, but instead he said, "You have a little baby girl that was born just a while ago." Ethel had called Mr. Shepler, and he had sent somebody over to the rodeo with the news. That's the night Christi was born. David Witzer, a Canadian songwriter, wrote a song about her being born – "Papa's Little Angel."

Christi was a really good athlete and she always played sports. She also took gymnastics and dance and was a cheerleader starting in the third grade. She got a scholarship to Memphis State, now the University of Memphis, as a pom-pom girl on their championship squad.

Maria Cook was on the pom-pom squad with Christi, so they were really good friends. One night they went to a Beach Boys concert, where they stood on the front row, and Maria and Christi did dance step for dance step what the Beach Boys dancers were doing, which got Mike Love's attention. He called them up on stage, told them that they were looking for two more dancers, and asked if Maria and Christi would like to go on the road with them. Maria wanted Christi to do it with her, but Christi wanted to graduate, so she didn't go until after graduation. Then she got to travel all over the world for three years with the Beach Boys and was treated like royalty everywhere she went.

The first time we saw Christi dancing with the Beach Boys was when they came to Mud Island Amphitheater in Memphis with the band Chicago. Our whole family went to the show, so it was me, Ethel, Matt, his wife, and Chuck. We had really good seats close to the front, and of course we were all sitting together. Chuck was still playing music at the time, so he had this really long pretty hair. A girl was sitting behind him and she just could not keep her hands out of his hair. She'd play with it, run her hands through it, and all that. Well, her boyfriend was sitting right next to her while she was doing all that, which didn't suit him too well. At the end of the show, he said something to Chuck and took a swing at him. Chuck ducked and the guy hit Matt's wife in the jaw instead. I jumped up and reached out and grabbed him by this stretchy sweater he had on, which was stretching even more as he ran toward the aisle. I didn't let go, of course, so I caught up to him by the time we got to the aisle, and I was really thumping him when the bouncers got there. They were all football players at Memphis State, where Christi had just graduated, so they knew me. One of them got between me and the guy and said, "Mr. Harris, just let him go and we'll take care of him," and they took him out.

The Beach Boys and Chicago were having an afterparty, so Christi came out and brought us back to a big hospitality tent full of food and drink. I used to wear a diamond and gold horseshoe ring on my right hand, and that's the one I was using to whip this guy. I was standing there next to the buffet line looking at my ring, when I noticed it had little flecks of the guy's skin in it, so I was cleaning that out with a toothpick. Robert Lamm, the keyboard player for Chicago who wrote "Saturday in the Park" and many other hits, came over to introduce himself to me and asked, "Aren't you going to have something to eat?"

"I am as soon as I get this stuff out of my ring."

He looked a little closer and said, "That sure is a pretty ring, but what's that in there?"

"That's somebody's skin."

"From that guy that messed with you during the show?"

"That's the one."

Robert laughed real big about that for a minute before he turned around and hollered, "Hey, everybody! From now on we're calling him LETHAL Harris!"

The Beach Boys were doing a show in Las Vegas and Donny Lalonde, who at the time was the light-heavyweight champion of the world, came to watch. He was in town training for the Sugar Ray Leonard fight. The Beach Boys had five girls dancing for them, and Christi was the "California Girl" dancing in the middle. Donny was really taken with her and, since he was friends with Mike Love, asked him after the show if he could introduce him to that California Girl. Mike said that first of all, she's from Tennessee, and second of all, even though he and Donny were friends, he was very protective of her and all the girls. Donny said he just wanted to take her to lunch, so Mike agreed that they would all go. Well, Donny and Christi ended up getting married and now they live in Costa Rica, where they honeymooned years ago. I always told Christi that whoever she dated and married would have to answer to me, so wouldn't you know she had to go off and marry the light heavyweight champion of the world for me to deal with.

I had a wife and three kids when I was thirty, and I knew that fighting bulls was dangerous. There was a good chance I could even be permanently crippled from it, so I always had other sources of income from side occupations. I thought since I had that painting ability, I could still sit and paint even if I ended up crippled. That would be a way to make a living for my family. So I ended up opening a sign company. I hired a fellow named Joe Allen, who I ended up becoming very close friends with, and he helped me out greatly with that. Joe's gone now, but I still paint signs today around town.

TOBY

Billy Bagby was a stock contractor and rodeo producer from Black Rock, Arkansas who did a lot of rodeos in Arkansas and Oklahoma in the late fifties and early sixties. He was a shade over five feet tall and just as feisty as a little banty rooster. He'd poormouth all the time, saying things like, "I owe so much money and get so many bills in my mailbox that the postman thinks my name is Ples Rimet."

Billy kept telling me I had to have a mule. You rode them in the grand entry, you had them in acts, you rode them in parades. You just had to have one, but I didn't. All I had was a burro named Hubert, and he wasn't worth a damn.

One night Billy came up to me and said he had bought me a mule that was supposed to be trained. I told him I didn't know if I could afford the hundred dollars for it, but he told me it was mine and he'd just take the money out of my check. So I didn't have a choice, and Toby and I worked together for a long time.

I knew Toby was supposed to be trained, which was good because I didn't know a thing about training a dog or horse or mule or anything. So I started working with Toby, and every once in a while I'd hit a certain cue and he'd do his thing. What was happening was that Toby was teaching me how to work him as I was learning all his cues.

I was going to a rodeo in Jackson, Mississippi with a friend of mine named Buddy Chapman. We were on the way down there when Buddy told me he wanted to go by his daddy-in-law's house and introduce me to him because he used to be a rodeo clown. When we got there, he asked me what I had in my trailer. I told him I had my little clown mule. He said, "I used to have a little clown mule, but I sold him. Could I see yours?" When I took Toby out, this guy hit a cue and that mule fell right into it. He hit another and Toby fell right into that one too. I said, "That's amazing!" And the guy said, "Not really – that was my mule. His name is Toby, right?" I told him it was, and that I wished I had known him a long time ago because he could have saved me a whole lot of time learning how to work with Toby.

I had a great act with this mule that I called "The Oatsmobile." I'd get him to roll over on his back, and then I'd straddle his stomach and sit there just like I was driving a car. I'd say I had power steering, and I'd move his front feet back and forth. I'd open his mouth for my ashtray. His tail was my windshield wiper. I had genuine mule-hide seat covers. Without fail, Toby performed this act to perfection.

That is, until he didn't. I got him out in the middle of the arena one night and tried to get him to roll over on his back, but he wouldn't do it. I just couldn't believe it, because he'd never failed to hit his cue. I tried again and he still wouldn't do it, so I figured he'd just decided he wasn't going to do that trick anymore.

I got back home with him, took him out, and when I started petting him and rubbing my hand down his back, all the hair came off. Come to find out, when I thought I was spraying him for flies before I left, I was really spraying him with herbicide. Daddy had gotten my sprayer, poured the insecticide out, and replaced it with Johnsongrass killer. That made Toby's back so sore that he wouldn't turn over, and I didn't blame him one bit. He was a good mule.

SPOOK

I was working for a veterinarian on the side who had a brother in Alabama that had a traveling donkey baseball team. He was getting out of that deal, so he was trying to sell his stock, which were little Shetland mules instead of donkeys. He had one white mule with a club foot, and that was the batter for the baseball team. They'd back him up to home plate, roll a basketball toward him, and he'd kick that sucker plum out of the park every time. The only problem was that he'd kick the heck out of whatever came up behind him, so you really had to watch out. I thought this mule would be great since I'd be the only one in the rodeo business with a solid white Shetland mule, so I bought him and named him Spook.

We were in Athens, Alabama one night. I had Spook tied to a post inside a little pen to keep him from kicking anybody. I even put a sign on the railing that said: "This mule will kick – Keep Out!"

I was gone during the day when this kid came up to Spook with a brand new bicycle and teased him by pushing the bike up behind him. Spook kicked at it and got his foot hung in the back wheel. By the time he got it out, he had kicked every spoke out of the wheel and bent it into an S shape. I didn't see any of it, but somebody else did and told me what had happened.

I was sitting there later that afternoon when this great big fellow came up with this kid and said, "You owe my boy a new bicycle."

"For what?"

"Your mule kicked my boy's bicycle all to pieces."

"Yeah, some guys out here told me that your boy ran that bicycle up behind him and was teasing him. You see that sign on the railing?"

"My boy said that mule got loose and kicked the bicycle out from under him."

"Well, that's not true. The mule is still in the pen and he's been in there the whole time. These cowboys told me what the kid did. He kept pestering my mule with the bicycle until he got sick of it."

"I tell you what. You can either buy my boy a new bicycle or I'm gonna whip your ass."

I never even said another word, because by then I had learned to get in the first lick, and I knocked him colder than a welldigger's ass. The boy ran off and left his daddy and bicycle laying there, and I never had any more trouble from them.

SWEET PEA

My next mule was a sorrel named Sweet Pea. I was working Franklin, Tennessee one weekend, and after the rodeo, I tied her to a tree while I hooked up my trailer and got ready to go. I was about to leave when I noticed a bunch of guys across the way throwing knives for money. I was pretty good at playing Scratch with a knife in college, and I also learned to throw them pretty well. I had a real throwing knife that was balanced and everything.

I asked them if I could get in on this contest deal, and they said sure. After I ended up winning all the money they had, they were doing everything they could to get it back. Things were fixing to get rough because they had been drinking and weren't happy about being cleaned out like that. I told them I had to go to the bathroom and that I'd be right back, so I left and got in my truck and hauled ass out of there.

I had gone a hundred miles or so when I started running out of gas, so I pulled over to this service station and told the fellow to fill 'er up. I went in and got me a cup of coffee, and when I came back out he asked me what I had in the trailer. I told him I had a little mule in there, and he asked if he could take a look. I said he could, and when he looked in the trailer he said, "Must be damn little because I can't even see him." Sure enough, I had left Sweet Pea tied to the tree back at Franklin.

So I turned around and drove all the way back to get her. The knife guys had all gone, and there she was still tied to the tree. I put her in the trailer and started home again. Of course I ran low on gas at about the same place, and when I stopped, the same guy came out. I asked him if he remembered me, and he said he did because I'd told him I had a mule in the trailer when I really didn't. I said, "I do now, so you better take your happy ass around and look at her!"

One night Bishop Arnold and I were traveling through Iowa. We had to stop to use the bathroom, so we let Sweet Pea out to do her business too. It looked like a million acres of corn all around us, and while we turned our backs to do our business, Sweet Pea disappeared. We didn't know what to do, so we just lit out through the cornfield trying to track her. We'd find a track and then we'd lose it. I'd see where she'd stopped and pulled an ear of corn off a stalk, but there would be no hoof prints. We did that all night until we had no idea where we were, so by then we didn't have a clue where the truck was either. Once it got light, we sort of figured out where we were, and when we got back to the truck, there was Sweet Pea standing at the trailer waiting on us.

Another time we were in Bangor, Maine, and somebody knocked on our motel door at about two o'clock in the morning. I opened the door and a policeman asked me if I owned a little red mule. I told him I did, and he said, "Well, you need to come with us. Your mule's downtown and we can't catch her." I had put her in a stall at the fairgrounds, but she had pretty much picked the lock on the stall and headed downtown. So I hooked up the trailer and headed downtown myself. When I got there, I saw six squad cars in a circle in front of a beer joint, and there was my little mule right in the middle of it. I just went over to her, slipped a halter over her head, and led her into the trailer.

Sweet Pea was pretty much a Houdini – she could get out of anything.

Another time, Bob Witte and I were going west on I-30 around Mount Pleasant, Texas in the middle of the night. Bob was driving, I was asleep in the camper, and Sweet Pea was in the trailer behind the truck. All of a sudden, I woke up and felt the camper jumping around under me like we were going on and off the road. I looked out the window and saw the side of the trailer beside us. Then it straightened out and I couldn't see it. Then I saw it on the other side. We jackknifed several times until we went backwards off a concrete wall at a river. This thing was deep; at least twenty feet. The trailer went first, with Sweet Pea inside. It went over the concrete ledge, but the bottom of the trailer hitch hung up on that ledge, so that's what kept us all from going over into the water. The trailer was pointed straight down, so Sweet Pea had slid down and was sitting on her butt on the rear gate. The front end of the truck was up off the ground, and we were balanced on that ledge like a teeter-totter.

Bob was scared to death, so he opened his door and put one foot out. When he did, that took some weight off and made the front end of the truck start to raise up. I was crawling through the window between the camper and the cab, so when I saw him do that and felt that front end come up, I told him to get back in and stay right where he was. Then I crawled out the side window and wrapped myself around the windshield and hood just like a snake. I got to the front bumper and stood down on it so that the truck wheels came down and just barely touched the ground. Then I told Bob to ease out, which he did. The truck raised back up a little bit, but I could hold onto the grille, lean back out in front, and get it to settle down again. It was that close.

Bob and I were on the front of the truck, but it was the middle of the night and nobody was stopping, so I figured I'd have to go for help and leave Bob to counterbalance the whole deal. About then a farmer from the area pulled up. I explained the situation, so he left to get his friend, who had a wrecker. Bob and I sat on the front bumper of the truck until that guy got there. He winched the truck forward and the trailer just kind of raised up until it leveled out and came on over that ledge. When we got it all out onto the grass, I went around, opened the trailer gate, and Sweet Pea stepped out and started eating grass. The whole situation never fazed her a lick, but we were lucky – really lucky.

Ed Cole was the president of General Motors back in the seventies. He and his wife, Dollie, who was from Texas, were big rodeo fans. One year we came to do the Longhorn rodeo in Detroit and they wanted to have a party in the arena to kick it off. They invited all these upper-crust people and, right there on the dirt, they put out tables with white tablecloths, silver place settings, candelabras, and the finest food. Dollie loved Sweet Pea, so when she made her introduction, this high-society lady rode out on my mule. In fact, she rode her around all night as she went around to all the tables and visited with folks.

George Taylor and I were laying over in Texas one time between rodeos. George knew of a race track around there where they ran little Welsh ponies. They had one called Cadillac Gal that nobody could beat. George thought Sweet Pea could beat that horse, so he got us a race for a fifty-dollar pot. Sweet Pea wouldn't run with anybody else like she would with me, but I weighed over two hundred pounds. A little jockey was riding Cadillac Gal, so that was a disadvantage for us right off the bat.

They put us in the chutes, dropped the gates, and we were off. Sweet Pea didn't like to run behind anything, and she didn't like anything passing her, so she broke out in front of Cadillac Gal and would not let that pony pass us. We were about to win the race, by less than a length, when she saw a shadow on the ground right in front of the finish line.

Sweet Pea had a fear of anything dark on the ground. When we were in parades, if she saw a manhole or a black patch of asphalt on the ground, she would dodge it or jump it. Or, like in this case, she'd check up. When she shut it down on the track, I went right over her head. To keep from going all the way off, I reflexively locked my knees around her head, which took her on over with me. Of course Cadillac Gal went on across the finish line and won the race.

Years later I was talking to Vaughn Wilson, who was writing a book called "My Favorite Horse," and he asked me about a story for it. I told him I didn't have one about a horse, but I did have a favorite mule story. That gave him the idea to write the kids' book, "Lecile and the Racing Rodeo Mule."

DING-A-LING

Phil Steward was a guy from Springdale, Arkansas who worked the barrel for me. I told him right off the bat that Phil just wasn't a good clown name. At the time, the song "My Ding-a-Ling" was popular, so I thought that would be a good name for him. Of course we ended up calling him Ding for short. Phil was really good on the other end of my acts because he never said anything and he never wanted to say anything, so he adopted a Harpo Marx type of character with a lot of body language. We even tried him with an old bicycle horn, but that got to be too irritating, so we threw the horn away.

Ding was dating the daughter of a stock contractor we knew. One day we went by her house to pick her up and take her to the rodeo. I was building a stone wall for my house at the time and needed a certain type of rock for a cornerstone, and I just could not find it anywhere. We pulled up to this girl's house and right out in the middle of their yard was a rock just like what I needed. I asked her father what the deal with it was, and he said, "That damn thing's in my way. I have to cut around it with the lawn mower and I'm always hitting it and tearing something up."

"Well, it'd fit just right in a wall I'm building."

"You can have it. Back the trailer up and we'll load it."

It took all three of us to get it in there because this thing was about three feet square and heavy. I then hauled it home, put it in the wall, and finished my project. It looked really good there.

The next time we went by to see Phil's girlfriend, her mother came running out of the house straight over to me and said, "I know you came up in the middle of my yard and stole the tombstone off my little dog's grave! My husband said he saw you!"

"Ma'am, your husband helped me put it in the trailer."

"I don't believe that and I want it back!"

"Well, I hate to tell you this, but that rock is a cornerstone in a wall in Tennessee now. We'll replace it with one that looks just like it."

Phil and I looked the rest of the season for a replacement. This was Arkansas, so we walked all over pastures and hillsides looking for the perfect match. Finally we found one, so we took it back to the lady's house and placed it where it was supposed to go. We were standing there admiring our work when she came out and said, "You all load that rock back up and take it off. I don't like it! You just keep on until you find one that I like."

We got in the truck and I told Phil, "If you ever want to see your girlfriend again, you just go by yourself, because I'm not going back." That rock is still in my wall.

TIMEX

I was working a rodeo in Yazoo City, Mississippi for Billy Bagby. Some ad agency from New York sent a crew down there to do a Timex watch commercial. Why they picked Yazoo City, I don't know. John Cameron Swayze, a prominent newscaster of that era, came with them because he was their spokesman.

Billy's rodeo company had a horse named Sunny, which was a real old horse that had bucked in rodeos back in the days before they had pens to buck in. The early rodeos just had a set of chutes out in the middle of the field with no fence around them. The horses bucked on the end of a rope, and they'd buck until they hit the end of that rope. To keep the horses from hurting themselves, the cowboys would holler at the horse just before he was about to hit the end of the rope. The horse learned after a while that he'd better stop or he was fixing to get jerked down. Sunny was that old, but he was still a good bucking horse. When eight seconds were up, you could holler "Sunny!" and he'd just lock it up right there.

They put a watch around Sunny's leg and turned him out with a rider. After they blew eight seconds, I hollered, "Whoa, Sunny, whoa!" When Sunny stopped, I went out and grabbed a hold of his halter while another guy came out and picked his foot up – a bucking horse, now – and took the watch off his leg. The guy cleaned the watch off and handed it to John Cameron Swayze, who looked into the camera and said, "Timex: it takes a licking and keeps on ticking!"

MIDAS TOUCH

I was working a rodeo in Columbia, Tennessee when a guy came up to me and said, "I've got something you may be interested in that might go good in your act. I've got a goat that walks on his front feet." He wanted to sell him for twenty-five dollars, which I thought was a good deal, so I told him to come by the next day and let me see what he could do.

The deal with the goat was that he was born without the use of his back legs. When he stood up, he'd throw his butt over his head, balance himself, and go everywhere on his front feet. He walked around and did whatever he wanted to do, but when he stopped – *plop* – he flopped down butt-first.

I thought it could be a pretty good act, so I gave the guy twenty-five dollars. For the next performance, I made up a story about training the goat and dressed up like a lion tamer. I even got a whip and chair to complete the look. When I popped the whip to give him a cue, he'd jump up on his front feet and run around. The crowd really liked it, so I was pleased with my investment.

After the rodeo, a lady came up to me and said, "You ought to be ashamed of yourself. That goat is handicapped and doesn't have any other way to get around but on his front feet. You're out there making money off a handicapped goat!" She just went on and on and on until I realized that everywhere I went, somebody would be thinking that.

The guy who sold me the goat happened by shortly thereafter and asked me how I liked it. When I told him why I couldn't take it and asked for my twenty-five dollars back, he looked at me and said he'd give me ten. I thought ten dollars was better than nothing since I wasn't going to be able to use the goat, so I took his offer. After all that, what actually ended up happening was that I rented the goat for fifteen dollars for one performance.

A month or so later, I was thumbing through a LIFE magazine in the barber shop. The centerfold showed a man and this goat that walked on his front feet. It was a full story, with pictures and everything, about this guy and the goat that I had rented.

I called a buddy of mine from Columbia and asked if he knew that guy. He said he did, so I asked him to find out if the guy had gotten paid for that story. My buddy was a bareback rider, so I saw him at a rodeo a couple of weeks later, and he said the guy got paid a thousand dollars for his story in LIFE magazine about the goat I sold back to him for ten. So it was kind of like that old saying about the Midas touch that the muffler shop of the same name used in their advertisements: everything I touched just turned into a muffler, not gold.

STATE LINE RODEO

There was a big rodeo on the Arkansas and Missouri border, up around Hayti, Missouri, called the State Line Rodeo. I'd hitchhike up there with my snap box and little tin suitcase, which said "LECILE HARRIS – RODEO CLOWN, BULLFIGHTER" on the side, so I usually didn't have too much trouble catching rides. We did Saturday night and Sunday afternoon performances, and at some point during each one, they'd ask the crowd to pass a hat for my pay. I'd usually do well enough to catch a bus back home, which was big time.

The bus station was at a truck stop, where you could rent a bed for a dollar a night. We'd go in there, take a shower, and grab a little shut-eye until it was time to catch the bus home. I would make this trip every week. I'd paint with my snap box in the morning, rodeo that afternoon, catch the bus home that night, and hitchhike back up the next week.

I was asleep in my room one night when a drunk came busting in wanting to fight. I got him by the back of the neck and the seat of his pants and just picked him straight up into the air and then put him straight down onto the concrete floor. Well, it almost killed him. Somebody called the police, who took him to the hospital and me to the station. They knew me because I was around there all the time with the rodeo, so they didn't lock me up right then. But the chief said, "If this fellow don't make it, you're gonna be in trouble. And it looks bad."

I laid awake all night long wondering if this dude, whose name was Hank, was going to make it. The police came in the next morning and told me he would, but he swore a warrant against me saying he wanted to press charges and have me arrested. This was in Missouri, so the chief told me the best thing to do was to leave and not come back to Missouri for a while.

The reason they called this rodeo the State Line Rodeo was because the arena straddled the state line. The calf-roping chute was on the Missouri end and the bucking chute was on the Arkansas end. There were two posts on each side of the arena that sat right on the state line, so the production company, knowing about the trouble I had gotten into, painted the tops of them white. This way I would know where I was and could stay on the Arkansas side. I told the bull riders, "You all better get off before the other end because I'm not going into Missouri with you." I'd follow the bull down to the white posts and then turn around and go back.

A buddy of mine had a spare tire stolen off his truck one night. Somebody told him they saw the guy who did it at The Butt and Ball, which was a club out in the middle of a cotton field on the Missouri side, so I went over there with him to help get his tire back. When we told the owner who we were looking for, he wouldn't let us in because he didn't want any trouble. He had a water pistol full of household ammonia that he'd shoot you in the face with. That's what they used instead of pepper spray or mace back then, and it'd knock you on your ass. Since we couldn't go in the B & B, we just waited in the parking lot until my buddy said, "There's the guy." We went after him and the whole club spilled out for a big fight right there in the middle of the parking lot. We were getting after it pretty good when I heard somebody holler, "There's the guy that put Hank in the hospital last week!"

They all came after me at that point. I knew I couldn't be caught on the Missouri side, so we hauled it back across the state line to that same truck stop. As soon as we pulled in, there came the state police right behind us. But I was about ten yards into Arkansas by then, so I was safe.

State Line had a one-eyed bull called Seventy. You'd think that the best thing to do with a one-eyed bull would be to go to his blind side to fight him, but I knew he knew he was blind. Therefore he knew which way most bullfighters would go, and he set a trap for them every time.

They set up a bullfighting match between this other guy and me and took up a collection for the prize money. Whoever won the match got the whole pot. This other guy and I both knew that Seventy was blind in one eye, but I'd fought this bull before and knew that he knew. The other bullfighter didn't, so he went to his blind side, and Seventy just ate his lunch. When it was my turn, I went to his good side. He had his head right but his feet crossed up because he was expecting me to go to his blind side, so when I made my pass at him, he tripped himself up and went down to his knees. Then I just kept on turning him inside out until we got back to the gate.

When Seventy went back in the chute, this other guy came up to me and told me that even though the judges had said I won the match, he didn't believe it and wasn't going to let me have the money. "The only way you get that money is you're gonna have to whip my ass for it."

So we went out back to settle things. He got in my face, took a big swing at me, and missed. I hit him with a big left hook and knocked him cold as a mackerel. But I hadn't been paying attention to where I was, and I looked up to see a Missouri deputy and me both standing on his side of the line. He was about to take me to jail but I said, "Let me get my money and I'll go wherever y'all want me to go." He agreed, so I got my money and they escorted me back to the truck stop. The deputy told me if I just stayed there and stayed out of trouble until it was time for me to leave, then everything would be fine. I nodded and headed right inside because by that point all I wanted to do was catch a bus home the next morning, which couldn't come soon enough.

MUSIC OR RODEO?

I had a lot going on then. In the summer, I fought bulls and played music. During the winter, when the rodeo season shut down, I worked day jobs and still played music. We had a lot of club gigs, and some of these places were pretty rough, so they'd give me an extra ten dollars a night to help the bouncer. We'd be playing and I'd hear the chairs scoot back all of a sudden, and that's when I knew there was a fight somewhere. It's a very distinctive sound when those chairs scoot back on the floor. We'd usually be right in the middle of a song when that happened, so I'd just lay my sticks down and go help the bouncer. We'd get the guy, take him outside, throw him out, whip him, whatever we needed to do. Then I'd come back in and start playing drums again. With my extra ten dollars a night, I was getting forty dollars a night to play. This was when people working forty hours a week were making seventy dollars a week if they had a real good job. So playing music six nights a week with a day job on top of that – I was making good money.

One night there was a really pretty lady with long hair sitting at the bar. Her husband came in, grabbed her by the hair, and dragged her out the front door. I saw what was going on, so I put down my sticks and came off the bandstand. By the time I got out the door, this guy was slinging his wife around by the hair in the parking lot, so I went up and knocked the crap out of him. He fell onto the back of a car and the license plate almost cut his ear off. The girl was skinned from one end to the other and most of her hair was pulled out, so he had messed her up pretty good.

A little while after we made them leave and went back inside ourselves, the cops came in and tried to take me to jail because the wife had filed a complaint on me for whipping her husband. That's when I learned that if it was a man and woman fighting, or two brothers, you just let them go.

I had jobs with different bands because back then you didn't work all the time for one particular band. You were just a musician on a list, and if some rock-and-roll band came to town and wanted a drummer, they called you and you went and worked it. If it was a country band, you did the same thing. Whatever it was, you'd learn it. That way you learned every kind of music there was to play.

I even played for strippers. A piano player called me and said he needed a drummer for a private party he was working for some airline pilots at a hotel in Memphis. It was just him and me playing a bump-and-grind thing until daylight while the strippers did their thing. That's the night I found out what a "mucket" is.

I was non-union because the best jobs were non-union. There was another drummer in Memphis who was union, so when he wanted to play a non-union gig, he used my name. When I wanted to do a union thing, I used his name. I helped write a bunch of songs, but if you were non-union, they wouldn't credit you for it. That didn't matter to me, though, because I was after the money.

I spent a lot of time at Sun Studios after Ray Harris hired me as a drummer to do a song called "Greenback Dollar." There were all these folks like Sam Phillips, Charlie Rich, and many other famous people around, but they were just regular guys in there. I guess I have so much more appreciation for Sun today. Back then it was just another job, but now I can see it for what it became.

Later on I was the drummer for a guy named Carl McVoy. Carl, Jerry Lee Lewis, Jimmy Swaggart, and Mickey Gilley were all cousins from Ferriday, Louisiana. Carl's real last name was Glascock, so he obviously had to change that.

Carl was the first one to do a really good version of "You Are My Sunshine." He had this certain style of playing piano and singing that Jerry Lee, Swaggart, and Gilley all kind of had. Carl's band had himself playing piano, Tiny Dixon on guitar, Bill Black playing bass, Johnny "Ace" Cannon on saxophone, and me on drums. We played with Carl almost every night, so we were pretty much a band of our own then. We recorded some at Sun and Hi in Memphis and RCA in Nashville.

Hi, owned by Willie Mitchell, was just an old theater that had been stripped out and made into a recording studio. Ace and I built the echo chamber there, which might have been the first one in Memphis. We took the bathroom and put chicken wire and plaster in it and set the microphone right in the middle. This setup gave Ace that echo sound, which is what you especially wanted with a saxophone.

I also played with Charlie Feathers. We did a session at this studio called Starlight that I think eventually became Stax. It was by a railroad track, so every time a train would get anywhere close, you'd have to shut down and wait until it went by. The most famous one I did with Charlie was "Jungle Fever." I remember doing that one real well, because I had to switch sticks in it, but I kept dropping my sticks and you could hear that on the recording.

The first time I saw Elvis Presley was at a performance he was doing one night at the Clearpool entertainment complex in 1954. I wanted to see his drummer's bass drum, because I had heard it was made of unborn calfskin. Being a country boy, I thought that was cool, so I figured if it looked good and sounded good then maybe I'd do the same thing.

Another time, Tiny Dixon, an outstanding guitar player, and I were in Sun Studios recording something for somebody when this guy came in to talk to Sam Phillips, the owner. We were all dressed in blue jeans and white t-shirts, with flat-top haircuts, but this guy had on a shiny black shirt and pants, and he had his long black hair pulled back in a ducktail. Tiny told me the guy was Elvis Presley, who he had played with at the Eagle's Nest in 1954. I sort of sized him up and said, "I don't think he's going to make it."

In January of 1956, Tiny and I were back at Sun to record something else. We had a break, so we went next door to eat. There was a little black-and-white TV up in the corner behind me, and Tiny was facing it. While we were sitting there eating, "The Dorsey Brothers Stage Show" was on. They started introducing somebody and Tiny said, "You know what, I think that's Elvis Presley."

I turned around and looked and said, "Yep, I believe it is."

"You're right, Lecile, I don't think he's gonna make it!" Tiny never let me forget that "brilliant" statement.

The next time I saw Elvis, he had called me about some horses he wanted to buy. He was just a plain, ordinary guy – one of us – except he was Elvis. I asked Chuck if he wanted to go over there with me, but he didn't. He has since become an Elvis fan. Ethel, of course, wanted to go, but I didn't think that was a good idea to take my wife around Elvis, so I didn't take her. She has never forgotten that to this day, and I still hear about it from time to time.

Along about that time is when I had to make a decision of which way I was going. My rodeoing popularity was growing and my music was going good too, but one night in particular helped me reach a clear decision.

I was working the Airways club one night, and I'd had too much to drink. When you're in a band, people in the crowd are constantly buying you drinks to play them a song or just because. Not being much of a drinker, I was pretty messed up.

I came out of that club and had no business whatsoever driving, but I did and ended up at my friend Bobby's house. My wife and I lived in a second-floor apartment at the time, and for some reason I thought I was going to our house. Bobby's mother had some little sticks and papers over her flower bed, and I thought those were the steps to our apartment, so I was just tromping right through those from one end to the other and tearing them up. Finally I found my way around to the back of the house and went in and got in bed with Bobby.

I lay there and got halfway straight until I realized I was at the wrong place and had to go home. I knew my wife was going to smell the alcohol on my breath, so I went to the bathroom trying to find something to gargle with. I ended up swallowing half a bottle of Old Spice aftershave. I left Bobby's, made it to our house, staggered up the stairs, and passed out on the landing in front of the door.

When I came around the next day, I told Ethel, "That's it. If that's what music life is going to be, I quit." So I stopped playing music on a regular basis and started focusing on my rodeoing.

A BRIEF HISTORY OF RODEO

Rodeo began as a competition between ranches to see who could break horses better. Then somebody said, "Well, I can ride anything with a hair on it," so they started riding bulls. Then they started these events that were based around skills involved with everyday cattle working, like bulldogging and calf roping. In the early days, a rodeo cowboy would do all the events. But as they started having more rodeos in different places and it got to be an organized sport, the cowboys started specializing.

It got to be the same way with clowns. When I first started out bullfighting, I had to do comedy also or I didn't work. Nowadays, most bullfighters don't clown and most clowns don't fight bulls. Everybody specializes because of the travel, time constraints, rules, and money.

Naturally, my favorite era was when I was both fighting bulls and clowning. I'd walk and talk during the rodeo and do a couple of comedy acts, so when the bull riding started, I was all warmed up and loose and relaxed. I did that until I was 52, which was really old to be fighting bulls.

It was so laid back then. I'd spend five dollars for a hotel room or fill the truck up with gas for thirty cents a gallon and sleep in the back under my camper. I have really good memories of those days. I still really miss fighting bulls. That's one reason I try to help out young bullfighters all I can: it's like I'm fighting bulls through them.

Before the associations like the IRA and RCA, there were mostly "open" rodeos, like the ones run by Preston and John Fowlkes, that weren't sanctioned by anybody. The Fowlkes brothers were both ropers, so they entered the roping event at their own rodeos. Since they were great big guys, they brought big calves that they knew the other cowboys would have trouble with. That gave them an edge and doesn't seem right, but there was no rule telling them they couldn't do that.

Rodeos today have a lot of spectacle and showmanship to them. Many of them are indoors, which has really helped with the production values. Take my rodeo here in Southaven, Mississippi. The Landers Center is a state-of-the-art coliseum with huge video screens, ribbon boards, spotlights, and a great sound system. The arena seating arrangement puts the crowd right on top of all the action, so they enjoy it. You don't have to worry about it raining or anything like that, so it works well for the production. When you go into a building like that, you don't go in there with a plain old rodeo – you go in there with a production. Coliseums are great, but they're expensive.

It doesn't matter if the coliseum is used for other things. When we go into the Landers Center, there's a good chance that the hockey team will still be in the playoffs, so there might be ice on the floor. We'll put plastic down over the ice, lay plywood on top of that, and dump over a hundred truckloads of dirt to make a layer up to a foot thick. Then we put our chutes and pens and the whole nine yards on top of all that.

The opposite of a big coliseum production is an outdoor rodeo like Ralph Morgan's in Lauderdale, Mississippi. They have an arena with bleachers that are covered, but the dirt itself is not. I've worked that rodeo during tornadoes. When one came down the road, everybody just sat there and watched until it went past; then we'd all go back to what we were doing. Other times it'd rain so hard you couldn't see your hand in front of your face, but the show went on anyway. The people there are used to that kind of thing, and they like it.

What they don't like at Ralph's is a lot of change. There's never been any replay screens, spotlights, or big production, and that's the way the people want it. If you change something, it makes them mad, so you don't change anything. You don't add anything. You don't subtract anything. You don't change the sound system. You don't change the bleacher boards. You don't change the food. You don't even change the clown. I've been going there for over thirty years, and if I miss a year on occasion, they get mad at me. Sometimes they even get mad if you change your jokes, because they might have told their brother-in-law about Lecile and his wife at Wal-Mart, but I didn't tell it at the rodeo.

When I walk through the gate at Ralph Morgan's and say hello to the crowd, it's a totally different feeling than walking into Madison Square Garden or some other coliseum because I hear the people say hello back to me. At Lauderdale I don't have to worry about somebody thinking, "Okay, I paid twelve dollars for a ticket. You just try and make me laugh, buddy." They're thinking, "I paid twelve dollars for a ticket. Let's have fun!"

At a little place like Lauderdale, I can break the rule of not doing inside jokes. When I tell one about the constable pulling me over, I can call him by name and say, "Buck pulled me over." That's because everybody knows that Buck's the constable there, so that would be funny as hell. In a place like Denver, I couldn't do that because nobody knows anybody. But at the smaller places like Lauderdale, I can tell the inside jokes. They're a part of it and the people expect them.

FOWLKES' RODEO COMPANY

As I started concentrating on my rodeoing, it was really picking up good. I went to work for Preston and John Fowlkes of Fowlkes' Rodeo Company, which was the first big outfit I got with. Preston and John were brothers from Marfa, Texas, and they fought all the time. I mean they were real cowboys. If they had a bull that kept jumping the fence, one that could flatfoot jump a six-foot fence with no problem, they'd turn him out in the pen and run him until he wanted to jump out. They were good enough ropers and had good enough horses that they would wait until the bull left the ground, and then they'd throw a rope over his horns – not his head, nothing but his horns – and turn their horses and ride the other way and bust him. They were that sure of themselves and that good.

When I went to work for them, Preston told me that I had to make up my mind whether I wanted to ride bulls or fight bulls and clown, because he couldn't take the chance of me getting hurt riding bulls and fighting bulls too. I was going to get hurt if I did both of them, and he just didn't want to worry about it. I wasn't a very good bull rider because I was long and tall: my center of gravity was too high and I got slung off a lot. That wasn't paying for much more than my entry fees, which wasn't very good, so I chose to fight bulls instead of ride them. When you were a bullfighter back then, you were a rodeo clown and did the comedy too. You didn't have a choice: if you weren't funny, you didn't work. So that was the beginning of my seriousness about comedy.

I had a real funny joke that I told back in those days. I would ask the announcer, Tex Townsend, "Do you know how many bones is in a rooster's neck?" Tex would say he didn't, and I'd say, "Just enough to hold his pecker up." So back then you could say a whole lot more stuff in the arena than you can now. I had told John that joke, and he thought it was real funny. I had also told it to Preston, but he didn't like it at all.

This particular afternoon we were in Mountain Cove, Georgia. The Fowlkes brothers were pickup men, so they were both in the arena with me. We were in the middle of an event there when John rode up to me and told me to tell that story about the rooster. When I asked Tex how many bones were in a rooster's neck, Preston came roaring up on his gray stud and said, "Son, you tell that joke and you ain't going to be working my rodeos no more." So I quit right there.

When I did, John rode up and told me if I didn't tell it then I wouldn't be working his rodeos anymore. So I started it up again, and here came Preston, and then here came John, and they got into this big argument right there in the middle of the rodeo.

They started duking it out, so I just stepped off to one side and watched. After they stopped, John told me to tell it, but Preston told me not to. I asked Tex the question, and he said he didn't know. I thought about it for a second and said, "Just enough to hold..." I stopped right there, so everybody quit what they were doing, leaned forward, and listened. Tex said, "Well?" I looked at Preston and John and then looked back at him and said, "That's it. I told half of it and that's all I'm going to tell. You tell the other half."

Preston and John had several bulls that were good fighters. One was a big Brahma called Blue. He wouldn't come to you that much to fight you, but he loved to get a rider down and make you come in there. Then it was a wreck. He'd work you and the bull rider over until you both got out.

There was another one called Swindler, and he was the first bull I ever knew that I thought was mentally off. He just didn't have good sense. He was hard to fight because he never did the same thing twice, so you never knew what he was going to do.

Then there was another bull called Raggedy Bob. He was a muley bull: one of the only ones there that didn't have any horns. If a horned bull got you down and you worked yourself between the horns, they got stuck in the ground and kept his head from going right through you. Of course, you had to make sure you were in between the horns because it was tough when you got a little off and they stuck you. I have a hernia to this day from a horned bull that pinned my arm down with one horn and stuck the other horn in my chest. He also broke my sternum and even held me down until the cowboys finally got him off of me. As bad as all that sounds, a muley bull has an advantage that horned bulls don't have: when they get you down, they can mash you flat as a piece of paper because there are no horns to stop them.

Raggedy Bob was the last bull out every night. He wasn't a very good bucking bull, but he loved to fight. We paired off every night, so I got to know him and he got to know me. It was a battle of wits and maneuvers and we both kept trying different things to keep the other off balance. One of my newest tricks at the time was to jump over him. He would come at me real fast and drop his head, and when he did, I'd jump right over him. Then he'd run right under me and I'd come down at his backside.

I was in Athens, Alabama one night when Raggedy Bob caught me. I had been jumping him way too often, so I could tell he was getting used to it. He'd run at me and just before I jumped, he'd check up a little bit. On this particular night in Athens, I didn't have enough momentum to jump over him with any forward motion, so I jumped straight up, hoping he'd run under me far enough to let me get away. But Raggedy Bob threw on the brakes, and I came back down on my feet with his head against my stomach. When he jerked his head up and hit me under the chin, I had my tongue out, so I bit it clean in two except for a little piece of skin that barely kept it hanging in there.

Earlier that night, a bull had knocked me into the fence, and a piece of the wire broke and slipped in behind my fingernail where the cuticle is. It made a little hook and pulled the fingernail out from the bottom, so my finger was in bad shape too. I showed it to Dr. Guffey, who was at all the rodeos, and he made a splint out of a Coke cup, taped it up, and sent me back out.

After the rodeo, Dr. Guffey told me to come to a clinic so he could do something about my tongue. They had just come out with this new kind of glue that was activated by saliva, so he smeared it on my tongue like contact cement and stuck it back together.

Athens is only about four hours from Collierville, so I left that night to go home. I could hardly drive with that one hand because of my bad finger. Every time my heart beat, my finger throbbed, and it was just killing me. A couple of hours into the trip, the feeling came back to my tongue and it started swelling. It got to the point where I could hardly breathe, so I stopped at a truck stop and ordered a Coca-Cola in a to-go cup. Then I dumped the drink out and put the ice in my mouth to keep the swelling down. By the time I got home, I had a mouth full of tongue and my finger was swelled up to three times its usual size. If I started to complain to myself about it, I'd think about what Preston would say whenever a cowboy was having trouble getting down on a bull or something like that: "You're just trying to make a big deal out of it!" But until my tongue came down from the size of a baseball, I was thinking that it really *was* a pretty big deal.

LEON ADAMS

Some of my problems with bulls were my own doing, which was the case when I worked with an extremely talented Roman rider named Leon Adams. Roman riding is usually when the rider stands atop a pair of horses with one foot on each horse, but Leon did this trick with a pair of trained identical Brahma bulls. When he was in a parade, however, he rode one the regular way and his partner rode the other. Leon asked me one day if I'd ride one of them in a parade with him because his traveling partner wasn't available, so of course I said I would.

The bulls were named Geronimo and Apache. I knew that one was hot and hard to control, and the other was better behaved and easy to handle, but I couldn't tell them apart so I couldn't tell which was which. When I told him I wanted the tamer one, he said, "OK, that's Geronimo."

I couldn't really tell them apart, but I thought that was the hot one, so I said, "No, I don't think so. I'll take Apache."

"No, no, Apache is the hot one. Geronimo is the easy one."

I thought Leon was trying to trick me, so I said, "I'll tell you what. You just take Geronimo then, and I'll take Apache," thinking I would really be getting the easy one.

It came time to do the parade. I was on Apache and Leon was on Geronimo. When the marching band started up, Apache took off running from the back of the line all the way to the front, where he then turned around and ran all the way back to the arena. I couldn't do a thing with this bull in all that commotion, so I just hung on for dear life.

Apache finally settled down enough for me to get off and start tying him up. I was pretty sweaty from all the excitement, so I had pulled my shirt off to try and cool down. I turned my back to Apache for a second to say something to Leon, and when I did, that bull smelled the salt from all my sweat and licked me from my belt line to my shoulder blades. A bull's tongue feels like sandpaper or dozens of little knives, so I thought for sure Apache had hooked me and cut me right in two. I dropped the rope, took off running, and got halfway across the pens before I realized what had really happened. Leon just busted out laughing and hollered, "I told you that was the hot one!"

CLYDE CRENSHAW

There was a guy named Clyde Crenshaw who was doing a rodeo in Benton, Arkansas, and he had a bull called Speedy Gonzalez. I'd been hearing a lot about this bull because nobody would fight him anymore: they were all just too scared of him. Somebody called me and told me they were going to do "Money the Hard Way" with him, so I took Bobby Ballard over there with me to try to make some money the hard way. That was when they would take a twenty-dollar bill and fasten it to the bull's horn with a rubber band. Whoever got the money off got to keep it.

The last thing at every rodeo is the bull riding, and after that they had "Money the Hard Way." All the clowns and bullfighters got up on the fence and out of the way, so I was the only one who went out there. I was in the middle of the arena when I called for Speedy, and the door to the chute was barely cracked when he wormed his way through it and came at me wide open. I was standing there thinking if I didn't move quick enough, he'd run me right over. Then again, if I moved too quick, he'd see that, cut me off, and run me over anyway. While I was thinking about all that, he was on me quick as a flash. He hit me right in the stomach and just white-eyed me – knocked me out for a second. He didn't even check up until he got to the other end of the arena. Then he stopped, turned around, and stood there looking at me. Back then we didn't wear protective vests and all the pads they wear now, so I was really hurtin'.

I was all wadded up on the ground coming to when I heard the announcer tell the audience that I'd dance with the bull if they played some music. I didn't think I could do that because my chest and stomach were burning, and when I felt down around my ribs, they were all moving around like a beanbag. I made it over to the fence and Bobby came and got me and took me to this hospital that was right across the river. They put me on a slab and I laid there and laid there waiting on X-rays or something until I finally told Bobby to get me out of there. Unless you've got a punctured lung, there's nothing they can do for broken ribs. You just have to live with it. So we left and went back home.

I went back to that rodeo to work it the next year, and a reporter who was interviewing me for the local paper told me this rodeo wasn't a very good one for bullfighters. I asked him why not, and he told me that last year a bull had run over a bullfighter, and when they took him to the hospital, he walked out of there and right into the river, and they hadn't seen him since.

When Clyde found out I had survived the Benton rodeo, he hired me the next year for one in Bogota, Texas. By this time they were riding Speedy Gonzalez, who didn't buck much, but was a real good spinning bull. Johnny Clark drew this bull for his first ride. When they came out of the gate, Speedy started spinning and threw Johnny right off. At that point it was me and Speedy, with me trying to keep him off of Johnny, so I kept right against Speedy's shoulder and just spun with him. We went around and around and I finally just screwed him right into the ground until he got dizzy and gave out.

I was headed back to the chutes when Clyde waved me over, put a pistol between my eyes, and said, "If you ever do that again to one of my bulls, I'll blow your damn head off." Clyde and I ended up being really good friends, and I worked many, many rodeos for him, but he was one tough dude.

Today rodeo is a professional sport, so we have rules and regulations to keep things like that from happening. If you get into a fight in the arena, they'll suspend you or ban you. But back then, it was rough. I've gotten into fistfights several times right in the middle of the arena.

OLD BAILEY

Clyde Crenshaw had another bull named Old Bailey. I mean this bull was hot. If you left to go to the bathroom, he'd be pissing in the stall right next to you. We were doing an IRA final in Chicago in the late sixties, and we had a specialty act who was a Mexican matador. This guy wanted each of us to fight one of the other's bulls. He had been going on and on about how our bulls were tame, until we finally got so tired of it that we agreed to a match.

Mexican bulls fight one time and one time only. When they're trained, they never see a man on the ground. The trainer is always on a horse, so they think a horse and a man are one animal. They don't see anything different until they come into the ring for the first time to fight, and then they really don't know what to do.

I fought the Mexican matador's black bull. He didn't know what I was, I don't guess, so he was pretty easy. I just put him in a spin that turned him pretty much wrong side out with no problem at all.

Next it was time for the matador to fight Old Bailey. This guy pranced out there with his bright suit and cape and called for the bull. Well, Mexican bulls see a cape and go for it. They pay no attention to the man, since they were trained with a man on a horse the whole time. But Old Bailey knew there was a piece of cloth right here and a piece of meat right over there holding it. The matador hollered "Olé!" and Bailey headed straight for that cape. He got about three feet from it and then cut over into the meat. When Bailey hit that matador, he just wiped him out. I remember the announcer talking about what a valiant effort that had been, trying to get him out of there with a little grace, but the cowboys ended up having to drag him out of the arena and prop him against a fence while he came to.

A couple of years later in Milwaukee, once again we had a matador who wanted to do a match fight. There was a lot of money on it with some side bets that the producer was holding. I had already fought a Mexican bull and I knew how they worked, so it didn't bother me at all. Just before the match, though, the matador came over and asked where his bull was. I pointed to a bull in a pen with the other ones. He asked me why his bull was in the pen with the other bulls, and I told him that was where the fighting bulls were kept. He asked me if the bull had ever been fought, and I said, "Oh yeah, lots of times." He jumped back and said, "Whoa, he's been fought? I don't fight bulls that have been fought before." Then he conceded. Come to find out, he was the same guy who had fought Old Bailey in Chicago, gotten ironed out, and now didn't want any more of it. So I got my money and never even had to fight his bull.

NORMAN ADAMS

I used to work with a guy named Norman Adams. Norman was a Cajun from Baton Rouge, so naturally he was Catholic. He loved hamburger steaks, but Catholics weren't supposed to eat any meat on Friday: they were supposed to eat fish. Norman didn't like fish, so he would order a hamburger steak, take his hat off, put his hand over the meat, and say, "Hereafter thou art fish." Then he'd eat the hamburger steak just like it was fish. He did this every Friday.

Norman and I traveled in a pickup truck with a camper on it. One of us would drive while the other would sleep. We were up in Wisconsin one time and Norman was driving. He pulled over at a service station, woke me up, and said he was going to bed. I got out, went in and got a cup of coffee, and came back out and left.

That particular truck had a range of about three hundred miles, so I drove until I was about out of gas. When I pulled into a truck stop and went to fuel up, a guy walked out of the garage there and said, "I see your name's Harris there on that trailer."

"Yes sir."

"Well, I got a phone number for you to call."

"I don't understand. What's the deal?"

"All I know is that somebody called and said to give this phone number to anybody who came in with a trailer that said Harris on the side."

So I went inside and called the number. The guy answered and I said, "Somebody there called and told Harris to call."

"Yeah, I got somebody here who wants to talk to you."

There was a pause, and the voice said, "Lecile?"

"Norman?"

"Yeah, you run off and left me when I got out to go to the bathroom."

This was all before cell phones, of course. What he had done was talk to the people at the service station and called six or eight truck stops down the line where I'd be most likely to stop. I told him where I was and that he needed to catch a ride, because I was going to sleep in the meantime.

About six hours later I heard a knock on my camper door. I opened it and Norman said, "Lecile, I need five dollars." He had told a truck driver that he'd pay him to catch a ride to where I was, but he didn't have the money, so I had to pay the trucker. I guarantee you from then on, every time we gassed up, Norman beat me back in the truck.

IZZY SHARP

Norman and I were working a rodeo in Franklin, Louisiana. The guy that ran this rodeo had a fellow working for him named Izzy Sharp. Izzy cleaned the stands in the arena and all that. He wore overalls with creases pressed sharp as a knife and a shirt so white it'd hurt your eyes. The owner of the rodeo told me that Izzy just loved me and had asked him several times if he could ask me if I'd come to his house. I told him that Norman and I would do that, so we followed him home that night deeper and deeper into the swamps until we had no idea where we were. Finally we got to his house, which was just a little shack built on stilts out over the bayou.

When we pulled up, Norman looked at me and told me he didn't like it out there because it was kind of spooky. I told him that everything would be fine, and we followed Izzy inside. The house was made of cypress boards sixteen inches wide and spaced a couple of inches apart, so you could see the moon through the cracks in the wall or the water through the cracks in the floor. It was all pretty rough looking, but the whole thing was just as clean as his clothes. The threshold to the front door was worn down almost to nothing where he swept the dirt out with his homemade broom. He had a strand of barbed wire stretched across the kitchen with another pair of overalls and another white shirt hanging on it, both just as clean as they could be and pressed to the nines.

Izzy had a beautiful bed in there that didn't fit anything in the house. It had all these ornate gargoyles carved in the headboard and footboard, so it was pretty scary looking. Norman took one look at that and said, "Lecile, I can't sleep in that bed with them awful looking things on it." I said, "Well, we ain't got no choice. Just cool it and let's get settled in. It'll be all right." We got ready for bed, and Izzy left us there while he went to another room to sleep. I don't know if he was in another bed or in a chair or on the floor, but I guess he just wanted us to be comfortable.

We laid there for a while just staring at the stars through the cracks in the ceiling. Every now and then the moonlight would shine through the trees and light up the gargoyles on the bed, which had their teeth and claws bared. Norman was obviously having a hard time going to sleep, but we finally dozed off after a couple of hours of tossing and turning.

Early the next morning, before it was even daylight, I felt that something wasn't quite right, so I opened my eyes and saw Izzy leaning over me. Norman was looking at him too, scared half to death, but he never moved a muscle. I didn't know what the deal was, so I didn't move either. What Izzy was doing was reaching for a rifle he had in the corner behind the headboard. When he pulled it out, Norman stopped breathing. I thought, "Well, he's fixing to kill us now. That's why we're out here." But Izzy just took the rifle and slipped out the front door, leaving Norman and me lying there wondering what was going to happen. After a few minutes, we heard *POW! POW!* Izzy came in shortly after with two squirrels. When he put the rifle back over in the corner, Norman played like he was asleep. I asked Izzy if everything was all right, and he said, "Yeah, I got us a couple of squirrels for breakfast. I'll call y'all in a little bit after I get everything ready."

A kitchen went all the way across the back of the house. Izzy had a wood stove that he cooked on when a rooster wasn't sitting on top of it. He fried up the squirrels, scrambled some eggs, and made up some cathead biscuits. The walls didn't come down all the way to the floors, so there was a gap of a couple of inches where Izzy would just kick the scraps from his cooking. When he did that, you could hear the gators splashing to get whatever had fallen into the water below.

The main course of our breakfast was armadillo sausage balls out of a big pickle jar. They were about the size of a golf ball, and there's nothing in the world that smells like armadillo sausage. He put our meal on tin plates for us, and when I'd try to stick my fork in that armadillo sausage, I just couldn't get it in there. I kept on trying to poke it until it finally jumped off my plate and rolled across the floor and into the water, where we heard the gators chowing down on it. Other than the sausage, it was a fine breakfast

The guy who owned the rodeo told us the next afternoon that we had made Izzy so happy by going out there to spend the night with him. I had thoroughly enjoyed myself too, but I'm not so sure about Norman.

CRANKY CORNERS

I once had a match bullfight with another bullfighter in Franklinton, Louisiana. That was when we both fought the same bull at the same time. The bull they chose for us was Alley Oop from the Cranky Corners herd, and he was a bad dude. He wiped the other bullfighter out right quick, but I was still going when he got me on his head and ran across the arena with me. He got to the fence, stuck me on top of it, and backed off to hit me. I flipped on over the fence and he tore a hole in it not quite big enough to squeeze through and get me. Alley Oop was one of the baddest bulls I had ever seen. He was just a crazy swamp bull.

That was the first time I had heard of Cranky Corners, but shortly thereafter I got a call to go work a rodeo down there. The arena at Cranky Corners was pretty rough. When they cleared the land for the arena, they left stumps right out there in the middle of the dirt. Bulldoggers had to make sure they got to the steers before they reached the stumps because otherwise they weren't going to win anything. It was the same thing with the calf ropers, but it worked out well for the bull riders because it gave them a place to hide if a bull got after them. It was just a strange deal.

There was even a beer joint that backed up to this arena. It had a cage made of chicken wire that went out the back door and butted up against the rodeo arena. If there was a fight, they'd put the guys out the back door into this cage, and they'd scrap until one came back in. The winner would get to stay and the loser would have to go home. So the rodeo would be going on as usual, but when a fight broke out in the beer joint and they put them in the cage, the rodeo would shut down so everybody could watch the fight. When that was done, they'd pick the rodeo back up just like nothing had happened.

Little Jimmy Dickens was playing the Cranky Corners rodeo one night. They didn't have a bandstand, so they just took some boards and laid them across the pen where the bulls were. The band was up there jumping with the rhythm when all of a sudden one of the boards broke and Little Jimmy and his guitar went right down into the bullpen. Cranky Corners didn't have just one Alley Oop: they had a pen full of them that were all just as bad. It didn't matter if they bucked or not at Cranky Corners, but they really had to fight. When Little Jimmy fell in, his bass player reached down there and caught him by the sleeve and pulled him out just as quick as he could. Little Jimmy always wore these bright suits, and the yellow one he had on that night was covered with mud and crap from one end to the other, but not a single bull had touched him. The band shut down for a minute while they pulled that board out and replaced it, and when that was done, Little Jimmy got back up there and went right on back to picking.

RACELAND

The people in Louisiana would either like you and accept you, or they would try to kill you; there wasn't much middle ground. I used to work a rodeo in Raceland, and there was a guy down there who pretty much whipped everybody around. Of course, I liked to fight, so naturally my buddy told me about him and said that if I wanted to get along with everybody down there, then I needed to fight this guy.

I met him in the parking lot of a restaurant. He was a little taller than I was and probably had forty pounds on me. I wanted to box, but he wanted to wrestle, so I tried to keep my distance and land big shots on him. He kept charging me until he finally got me in a headlock. It felt like he was about to pop my head right off, when I saw his thumb out of the corner of my eye. I got a hold of that and he told me if I didn't let it go, he'd either choke me to death or break my neck. I said, "If you don't turn me loose, I'm going to break this thumb off and hand it to you." He kept on choking me and I felt like I could go out at any second, so I showered down on his thumb and broke it so it was just flopping around. That made him turn me loose. But then we squared up and started throwing haymakers at each other, him with that thumb flopping all around. This went on for a few more minutes until he finally stopped and said, "I've had enough." I told him I had too, so that was that.

The next day he came to the rodeo with a cast on his hand and told me he wanted to buy me some beers. After the rodeo, we went behind the chutes, drank a case of Schlitz ponies, and got along just fine. When word of that fight got around, the people down there thought so much of me that two years later the Louisiana Secretary of Agriculture gave me a plaque that says "Honorary Coonass." Not Cajun – Coonass.

DOUBLE AUGHT

I was working a rodeo in Hopkinsville, Kentucky with a bunch of green bulls that liked to come out and run right through the arena instead of coming out and spinning and all that. The rodeo liked for them to come out, turn back, and spin because that was more exciting. Since these bulls were young and didn't do that naturally, it was up to us clowns to turn them back. We'd bait them and get them to spinning.

We had a couple more bulls in the round when this bull rider came up to me and said, "Clown, if you turn my bull back, I'm gonna whip your ass." He was a paratrooper or something at the Army base and thought he was pretty hot stuff. I looked right at him and said, "Well, you better get ready, because I'm sure going to do it."

He got on a bull called Double Aught that I had seen many times, so I knew he was going to turn and spin whether I was on the arena floor or up in the stands. I wasn't really going to turn him back, but I was going to act like I did. After Double Aught came out and spun the rider off, this guy jumped up, ran over to me, and drew back with a big punch. I had been boxing for quite a while by that time, so when he did that, I just thumped him. He staggered off and came back after me, so I grabbed him by his shirt to hold him off and see if he wanted to change his mind. But he kept on trying to whack at me as I told him he needed to settle down. He didn't, so I hit him with a big right hand and down he went. I broke my hand on his head and gave him a brain concussion right there in the middle of the arena.

I got back home and my hand wouldn't stop swelling, so I went to the doctor and got a plaster cast put on it. The doctor knew I fought bulls, so he put a big heavy one on my hand to keep me from breaking it again. Well, over the next few weeks, I found out that the cast came in handy fighting bulls. If they got too close, I'd crack them over the head with that cast. Then I'd have to go back to the doctor to get some more plaster put on it. I did that until it just about got too big to carry around.

A month or so later I was at a rodeo in southern Arkansas with two friends of mine, Bud and Dub Grant, who were trick riders, ropers, and bulldoggers. We were sitting there against a cyclone fence that afternoon before the rodeo. This cast was so heavy that I didn't know what to do with it, so I just kind of stuck it behind my back to sort of prop up on. We were shooting the breeze when this paratrooper walked up and said, "Hey, do any of you happen to know where that damn clown is that was at Hopkinsville?"

Bud said, "We might. Why?"

"Because I'm ready to give him an ass whippin'."

Dub said, "You better get ready to start then, because he's sitting right there."

I jumped up with that cast behind my back as he ran up to me and tried to do the same thing as before, so I caught him by the collar again and said, "You really don't want to do this." He kept whacking at me until I had finally had enough, so I took that cast and gave him just one lick with it. I guarantee it weighed at least fifteen pounds at that point, so when I did, he hit the ground like a sack of hammers. The EMTs came and carted him off, and that was that.

SHARK ROUNDUP

Albert Pewitt, the other end of my act at the time, and I used to make a winter run down to Florida. We'd do two rodeos at a time down there, so we'd stay for two weeks. Since we usually had a little time on our hands between shows, we were always getting into something.

One time Albert, Johnny Clark, Glen Bird, and a guy from Florida went with me to the beach. Johnny and Glen were world champion bull riders, but Johnny was scared of the water, so he just sat up on a sand dune with the Florida guy while Albert, Glen, and I went swimming. Pretty soon we heard Johnny holler, "Hey, there's a porpoise right over there! See if you can catch it!"

We started herding it into a little cove and could see the one fin, but then another one popped up, so now we were herding two porpoises. We just about had them hemmed up into that cove when another fin jumped up, so there were three of them at that point. We'd get them sort of penned up but then they'd slip by us and turn around and come right back, so we'd just try to herd them back in there again. They were making some pretty good passes because they were going pretty fast and bumping up against us as we tried to corral them.

We were working them into what I guess you would almost call a frenzy, when the guy from Florida started jumping up and down and hollering and waving and all of that. We thought he was trying to tell us where to go to catch these porpoises, so we just kept on doing what we were doing. Finally he came running down the sand dune and hollered, "Let them alone! They're sharks!" Johnny, being from Dallas-Fort Worth, didn't know anything about the ocean, but thankfully the guy from Florida did.

CHURCH KEY

Albert and I were in Palatka, Florida for a rodeo. The night before the last performance, we went to a club to get a beer and chill out. My buddies and I were standing around outside when some guy came up from behind us and knocked one of my friends colder than a wedge. I turned around and knocked him flat, but another guy came and jumped on me. I got him down and was working on his head when all of a sudden I felt a burning in my leg. I was later told that a friend of theirs had come up behind me with a bottle opener, the kind we used to call a church key, and stuck it in the back of my leg.

The next day, I was bullfighting and Johnny Clark came up. He always used what we called a suicide wrap. I knew when he got on his bull that if he made the whistle, which he did an awful lot, he wouldn't be able to get off. I'd have to go in there and untie him, or there'd be a wreck and then I'd have to get the bull off him. Sure enough, Johnny made it eight seconds and was hung up, so I went in to get him out. I jerked his hand loose but stayed on the inside a little too long, and the bull came around, hit me in the back with one of his horns, and broke several ribs.

They took me to the hospital and let the doctor examine me. He rolled me over to look at my ribs and asked, "What in the world is this on the back of your leg?"

"That's where a guy stuck me with a church key."

"Do you know it pulled a big chunk of meat out?"

"Well, my buddy put a bandage on it, and I haven't really looked at it."

"You've got a hole in the back of your leg that's so big we can't even sew it up. It's going to have to just fill in. You need to go on back to a room and rest for a few days and heal well enough to leave."

The doctor left and I told Albert, "We're going home tonight." We slipped out and he put me in the camper on the back of the truck. Albert got the prescription for my pain pills filled at some all-night drugstore, and that stuff really knocked me out, so I was sleeping pretty good on a mattress we had in the camper.

We had an intercom system connecting the cab with the camper. Albert had my end locked on so he could hear me moaning and groaning when I came to. About every four hours he'd have to stop and give me another pill. He did that all the way home, from Palatka to Collierville. When we got there, I was so sore I couldn't get out, so Albert and Ethel pulled the mattress out of the camper, with me on it, and dragged me into the house. Albert brought me back from a bunch of rodeos like that.

JOHNNY CLARK

Johnny Clark used to wear one black boot and one brown boot. When he first started doing that, I asked him why he was wearing a pair of boots that didn't match. He said they were a matching pair, but one of them had turned black. I didn't understand how that could happen, so he explained it to me. He said he went out on his back porch to use the bathroom one day, and a wasp stung him on his private part. It swelled up on one side and made a knot that never went down, so it made his thing crooked. Every time he went to pee after that, he peed on his left boot and turned it black.

One year Johnny and I had a one-night performance in Indiantown. We decided to overnight it, which meant we'd drive straight through to Florida early the night before, work the rodeo, and turn around and drive right back home. I started out driving and got us to Atlanta, where Johnny took over.

He had barely made it to Valdosta before he asked me, "Lecile, do you have any driving pills?" Johnny would take these little white pills to drive.

"No, I don't."

"I need a driving pill."

"Well, I don't have any."

"Are you sure you don't have any?"

I had on a Western shirt, of course, and a button had come off the cuff. I had put the button in my pocket so I could get it sewn back on later. I was feeling around in my shirt pocket and felt that button, so I pulled it out and said, "This is all I've got."

Johnny snatched it out of my hand and swallowed it without even taking a drink of water. Then he drove us all the way to Indiantown, worked the rodeo, and drove us all the way back home – on a button.

INDIANTOWN

One year I was working the rodeo at Indiantown and staying on a dentist's ranch, which was named "Tooth Acres." I got this dentist to make me a false set of teeth, kind of like the redneck teeth you can get at costume shops, to fit over my regular teeth. This was a really nice version of that. They stuck out real bad and had one gold tooth right up front.

Bud and Dub Grant came down from Arkansas to work this rodeo, and they brought their daddy, Wes. A bull had run over me at the last Florida rodeo, and it got all over the country that he had hit me pretty good and fractured my jaw. Well, it had gotten up to Arkansas that I'd been hit in the face and was all messed up.

I put those joke teeth in my mouth and went up to Mr. Wes and asked, "How are you doing?"

"Oh my God, Lecile, I heard you got hit in the face."

"Yeah, I did, but I'm doing fine. This dentist that we're staying with gave me a really good deal on some new teeth."

Mr. Wes just looked at me with a pained expression, but he didn't say anything bad about my teeth. He wasn't one to have a lot of empathy for anything much, but this really got to him for some reason. When I walked off, he went over to Bud and Dub and said, "Did you all see Lecile? I don't know what that dentist charged him for his teeth, but he's really got his mouth messed up. Somebody needs to whip that dentist's ass for giving Lecile such a dirty deal."

I went on out to my trailer to get ready, took my teeth out, and forgot about my little joke. When it came time to head into the arena, I passed Wes' trailer. He was about to take a saddle pad off a horse, and he said something to me. When I answered him back, he saw my regular teeth.

"Where's your other teeth?"

"Aw, I was just kidding you, Mr. Wes."

A saddle pad is pretty solid, but he snatched that one off the horse, whirled around, and hit me right in the face with it. So I got a busted lip and a really good cussing for my teeth gag.

The cowboys down there at Indiantown all played a card game called Pitch. I didn't know anything about Pitch, but they got me into a game. I lucked up against these pros and won four hundred dollars. This was about 1970, so that was a lot of money back then.

They tried to get it back the next day, and I mean these cowboys would bet on anything. There were a bunch of birds sitting on a power line, so we each picked a bird for a hundred dollars. Whoever picked the last one to leave got everybody's money. I picked right and won another four hundred dollars that day, so I took my eight hundred dollars back home to Collierville and bought our first color television.

FLOYD RUMFORD

Floyd Rumford was a rodeo producer and stock contractor from Olathe, Kansas. If you looked in the dictionary for the word "gentleman," Floyd's picture could have been beside it. He put on the Benjamin Stables Fourth of July Rodeo, with his stock, in Kansas City.

The Kansas City Chiefs football team was really popular about this time, and a lot of them would come hang out with us at the rodeo. They also had Indians who came in with their tents and put on a big pow-wow. Back then we were sleeping in campers on the fairgrounds, so we'd hear the Indians chanting and playing drums all night long. Sometimes we'd have a few drinks and go chant and play with them. It was a great atmosphere and a very entertaining rodeo.

One of the specialty contractors was Johnny Rivers, who had a different act every year. One of them was the high-diving mules. There was a ramp that led to a platform that was probably forty feet above a pool of water, and the mules would run up that ramp and dive right off into that pool.

He also had racing ostriches. The kick of an ostrich is much worse than that of a horse, so they were big enough and strong enough to ride. It was usually me and the other bullfighter, Joey Steverson, as the jockeys. We didn't have anything like reins or bridles, so we used a little broom to guide them. If you wanted them to go right, you'd put it over their left eye, and vice-versa for the other way. They'd do close to thirty miles an hour, and they didn't stop on command. Once they got to the other end of the arena, they just turned around and kept running. You eventually had to bail off and hope they didn't kick you on the way down.

Johnny's wildest act was his chariot race. He had two chariots made up just like the ones from "Ben Hur," except these had a special rigging on them you could trip to unhook from the bull. They always picked the hottest fighting bulls of the rodeo, and the way they were harnessed to the chariots with a swivel arrangement, they could turn around and face you. Half the time you were going backwards because they'd see you, turn around, and come after you. The other half of the time, if the bulls weren't fighting each other, the other guy's bull would try to get up in the chariot with you. The back of it was open, so he could jump right in. After this went on for a while, they'd blow a whistle and we'd trip that latch and turn the bull loose. Then we had to fight the bulls until we got to the fence. To call this whole experience wild would be an understatement.

Floyd's wife, Lola, pretty much ran the rodeo behind the scenes. She was very nice, but she was demanding. She was a real professional, so she expected that from everybody else.

One day I was standing in front of the chutes during an intermission. I smoked at the time, so I lit up a cigarette. Mind you, everybody smoked back then. Miss Lola was sitting in the crow's nest above us, so she could see what I was doing. I was just puffing away when I heard her say, "Lecile, come up here, please." I took that long walk up the steps to the announcer's stand feeling like I had been called to Mr. Osteen's office and said, "Yes ma'am?"

"Let me tell you something, son. I don't know whether you know it or not, but kids are out there watching you, and if they see you smoking a cigarette, they'll think that's all right. You have a choice. You can either put that cigarette out and never let me see you smoke another cigarette where the crowd can see you, or you can find a job with somebody else."

I was probably thirty years old then, and I smoked until I was fifty, but I never smoked in anybody's arena after that. Every time I see Miss Lola now, she just smiles and asks me first thing, "You still haven't smoked in that arena, have you, Lecile?" And I say, "No ma'am, I surely haven't."

MEL TELLIS AND THE BUFFALO FIGHT

Ken Lance had a rodeo arena in Ada, Oklahoma with a dance hall beside it. That was the first place I ever saw Mel Tillis, who sang beautifully but stuttered terribly when he talked. Mel had heard I was a bullfighter so he wanted to talk to me about that, but he stuttered so bad he could hardly say a thing. He finally managed to ask me about a buffalo I was going to fight that night. I told him that Ken wanted me to fight one, and I didn't know of anyone who had fought one before, so I told him I would.

Fighting a buffalo was much different than fighting a bull. First of all was his size. I don't know what that buffalo weighed, but I was 6'5" at the time, and his hump was even with the top of my head. Their front end is huge because that's where all their power is, but they have hardly any rear end.

The other difference was in the way they moved. When you fight a bull, you do what we call breaking them down. You go to their head and then you come around it and get inside, next to his shoulder. That makes the bull bend and slows him up. You break him down by keeping him in that bend, so it's hard for him to get to you because he's having to make that circle. Well, a buffalo doesn't work that way. They plant their front feet and their butt flies around, so they just pivot instead of bend. This makes them much trickier to fight.

My first pass at this buffalo was beautiful. I came to his head and went to where his shoulder should be, but his head was still there. I felt really good, but you can't break a buffalo down: they just swivel. So the next pass I made, he cut the shirt right off my back. On the next pass, he caught my suspenders and popped them loose. On the last one, he cut a hole in my pants and whirled me around a couple of times until he slung me right out of my britches. That put me in good enough shape that I could get on out of there.

When I came out of the arena, Mel was standing next to the gate and said, "Buh-buh-buh-buh-buffalo almost c-c-cut all your clothes off, didn't he, buddy?"

BUDDY HEATON

I was good friends with a guy named Buddy Heaton, who was a sure-enough cowboy. Buddy was really tough and was always getting into trouble. He was a pretty good bullfighter, but he was an excellent animal trainer. He mainly worked with buffalo, and I have a picture of him riding one in the inaugural parade for Kennedy. Somehow he got into it and rode right in front of the podium and tipped his hat to the President, who waved back. When he got to the end of the route, he jumped his buffalo into the back of his truck and just drove off.

I was working Snyder, Texas one year when they asked me to go do a farm show with Buddy on an AM radio station at 5 o'clock one morning. We had never met each other, but I had heard about him and he had heard about me. We were sitting there together being interviewed when the announcer said, "Buddy, I hear you're pretty tough."

He said, "I am."

"Lecile, I hear you're pretty tough too."

I said, "I am."

"Which one of y'all is the toughest?"

We both said, "I am!"

We got done with the interview and headed out to our trucks. Buddy was just about to climb into his when he turned to me and said, "You're pretty tough, huh?"

"Yeah, I am."

"You think you can whip me?"

"Yeah, I do."

So we commenced to fighting right there in the parking lot at six in the morning. We rolled around in the gravel until we'd skinned all the hide off our elbows and knees. Finally we both had enough and just quit.

We were friends after that, and we both worked the rodeo that day. It was a Sunday afternoon, and it was really hot. We had two sections of bulls that day. I had worked the first section and broken my hand on a bull's topknot, so it was really hurting.

I asked the veterinarian if he had anything for me, and he gave me some DMSO, which is a liniment you put on animals. It gets in your system very quickly. You can rub it on the back of your hand and in a matter of seconds you'll taste it in your mouth. I was in the shade next to my trailer rubbing this stuff on my hand when I heard a woman scream in a section of the stands next to me. I looked that way and saw another woman jump up and do the same thing, and then another, and another.

Buddy had taken a bag of ice from the concession stand and was up to his usual mischief. Years ago, rodeos would buy chipped ice from ice plants. That ice would come in canvas bags with a metal bottom and a drawstring top. Buddy had taken a sack of ice under the stands and was throwing handfuls of it at women's' crotches. He did that all the way down the stands until the cops got after him.

Buddy came running my way dragging his sack behind him. When he ran by my trailer, he just threw the sack in the back of it and kept on going. They never saw him do that and never did catch him. I still have that sack to this day. Now it carries my oil, chains, wedges, and all the things I use to cut wood.

Buddy came up with a stunt one year for the Fort Worth Stock Show. He climbed up in the rafters of the coliseum, tied a rope off so it hung down about halfway, and attached an inner tube to it. Between events he was going to let out a yell and throw himself off the catwalk. He had calculated his weight and measured the rope to where he thought it and the inner tube would be just about right to give him some spring but keep him from hitting the ground. Nobody knew anything about it: not the cowboys, not the management, not anybody.

They had just finished the barrel racing, so everything was quiet, when all of a sudden Buddy screamed at the top of his lungs and bailed off the catwalk. The inner tube stretched and stretched and stretched until he hit the ground with a *whop!* Then he bounced right back up and right back down, up and down, up and down, until he finally came to a rest just above the ground.

Well, women were fainting, men were yelling, kids were getting sick, and all that kind of stuff. Buddy simply untied himself, walked out of the arena, and left his rope and inner tube hanging there. Management met him at the gate and told him to pack his stuff. He was out. They couldn't have him getting the people all stirred up like that.

KID MARLEY AND SPUTNIK MONROE

Sputnik Monroe was a very famous professional wrestler from Memphis. He had a shoeshine operation at all the events that were held at the Mid-South Coliseum. Sputnik had a bunch of little kids following him around who did the work for him while he strutted around in a tuxedo and top hat. When he saw somebody with dress shoes on, he'd point at them and tell the kids to give that guy a shine. Most people just went ahead and paid them and didn't argue with him because he was so big and mean looking.

We were doing a rodeo there one year when Sputnik came around behind the chutes raising Cain, cussing and telling the boys to get the crap off the cowboys' boots and get them shined up. The cowboys didn't want their boots to be shiny, but Sputnik kept on hollering and talking ugly. We were all getting pretty irritated with him until Kid Marley, who was one of the toughest cowboys I was ever around, had enough. He walked up to Sputnik and said, "Mister, these guys don't want no boot shine, and don't be cussing around our ladies if you want to stay back here." Sputnik just kept on bellowing until Kid came over to him and said, "Mister, I've told you once, and this is the second time. I'm not going to tell you three times." When Sputnik started up again with the same thing, Kid came back and clobbered him upside the head, which knocked him colder than a witch's tit. Kid hit him so hard that Sputnik went up under the front end of a truck and there wasn't anything but his feet sticking out. He laid there and laid there and laid there until somebody finally pulled him out. His forehead was laid open to the skull where Kid had hit him over his eye.

Sputnik was bleeding like a stuck hog, so the paramedics took him to the hospital to get sewed up. He made sure the press found out about the whole deal because he thought he could make some money from it. He wrestled in Memphis every Monday night, so in the newspaper article he challenged Kid to a fight in the ring. He even said he'd pay Kid's way back down to Memphis if he showed up. The press then went to interview Kid for the story and told him about Sputnik's offer. Kid told them he wasn't going to come down and fight him in the ring, but he'd pay Sputnik's bus ticket to Paris, Tennessee, Kid's hometown, if Sputnik would come up and fight him in his pasture. Needless to say, Sputnik Monroe did not take Kid up on his offer.

Kid went on to be the only mounted policeman the city of Franklin, Tennessee ever had. He rode around town on his horse, and if anybody caused him any trouble, he'd rope them and drag them right off to jail.

BARREL IN THE GROUND ACT

One of my early acts was common to a lot of clowns and we all had the same problem with it at one time or another: somebody would play a trick on us and get us into a tight spot that could end up pretty rank.

I'd go out in the middle of the arena the afternoon before the rodeo and dig a hole big enough to hold a 55-gallon drum. I'd drop that in and put a top over it, which had to be strong enough for the bulls and other animals to stomp on and not go through. I'd lay that over the top of the drum, cover it with dirt, and mentally mark the location of it. Then I'd go to town and get a big refrigerator box made of cardboard. I'd cut a door in that, bring it back to the arena, and set it up over the barrel.

The whole arrangement was meant to replicate an outhouse. When the announcer saw me walking around funny during the rodeo, he'd ask me what my problem was. I'd tell him I needed to go to the bathroom real often, so I just brought one out with me to make it easier to get to. We'd talk a little more until the urge would strike me, and then I'd run to the outhouse and shut the door. When I did that, a pickup truck would come out the other end of the arena, hit that box wide open, and flatten it. I had to drop down in the barrel before they crashed into the box, so my timing had to be pretty good, obviously.

After they ran over me, they'd bring an ambulance out with a bunch of guys in white doctors' coats. They'd gather around the box and fret about how bad it was until they decided they had to load me up. But what really happened was they would hold their coats open and block everybody's view so I could slip into a white coat too. Then I'd hold my head down and slip into the ambulance with them and we'd ride out. When we got out back, I'd pull off the coat and show back up in the arena all ragged as hell. People thought that was just hilarious.

One weekend I was working the Schugtown, Arkansas rodeo, which was just outside of Paragould. I had done this act Saturday and was going to do it again Sunday. Unbeknownst to me, some of the guys went out there after Saturday's performance and filled the barrel with water and a fifty-pound block of ice, so it sat there all night just getting colder and colder.

It came time to do the deal on Sunday. I heard them revving up the engine at the other end of the arena, so I got ready to jump in the barrel. Usually I just jumped in without looking, but for some reason I looked in there this time. When I did, I saw the barrel almost full of water. They hadn't allowed for the ice melting, so when it did, I only had about three inches of air between me and the top of the barrel when I jumped in. I had to hold my head straight up to keep my nose above water. I was freezing to death and thinking they needed to hurry up and smash this thing, but they just kept sitting there revving the engine. The driver was in on it, and he told me later he was giving me time to come on out. There was no way I was coming out, but I just wished he had come on and done his part. When they finally ran over it and pulled me out, I was absolutely blue and so stiff I could hardly move.

A lot of clowns did an act like this one, so I wanted to put a new twist on it. I figured out how they could come after me and I wouldn't be there at all.

We were at Athens, Alabama for a rodeo, and I knew that the guy who was putting it on owned a construction company. I told him I'd like to try something new if he'd pay the expense of doing it. I would dig a hole and drop the drum in it as usual, but then we'd dig an underground tunnel all the way out of the arena where nobody could see me get out. He loved this idea, so he went to a whole lot of trouble to do it. We cut a hole in the side of the drum so I could go down in there and turn and get out.

Then he cut the bottoms out of a bunch of drums to line the tunnel with. He figured that way we could just leave it all down there so I could do this act every year.

We finally got it all done and it came time to try it. The first time I dropped down in there, I went feet first. The bend was a little sharp, but I could make it. The problem was that I would have had to crawl through the tunnel feet first, which would have taken forever. I didn't want to do it that way, so I came back out and went headfirst. That was a little spooky because when you got down there, you'd have to bend backwards before you could crawl out.

It came an absolute flood the night before the next day's performance. When it came time to do the act, I ran into the toilet and dropped in headfirst. I twisted and turned and went frontwards through the first two barrels before I had to stop. The rain from the previous night had seeped down in between where the barrels weren't joined very tight together, so it had pushed mud through those cracks and filled the drums up to the point where I couldn't get through. I was stuck.

Of course, they didn't know that. They were waiting for me to come out but I never did. I couldn't come back out feet first, so I couldn't get out. They finally realized I was hung when I stuck my feet out of the hole, and then they panicked and called an intermission. A whole bunch of them tied a rope around my feet and pulled while I just bent the reverse of the way I had bent when I went in. The claustrophobia of the situation was awful, and I would never try that again. It was the rankest.

INTERNATIONAL RODEO ASSOCIATION

I joined the IRA because I thought they had an insurance program, but it turned out they didn't. I got real involved with the association leadership because my theory was that the association had to grow if I was going to grow. There weren't many cowboys east of the Mississippi River, so it was pretty easy to start out as a spokesman for our area. People would bring problems to me and I would take them before the board to make sure they were heard. I was getting things done so well in that capacity that they made me the Contract Acts Director, which put me on the Board of Directors. There were also directors of steer wrestling, bull riding, calf roping, barrel racing, and other events in the rodeo. I was trying to build my act, so the association had to grow first, but I knew the contract acts were going to be the last ones to get any part of that growth. With all that in mind, I decided to run for President of the IRA.

No clown had ever been president of a cowboy association. I was a bullfighter and a clown, but back then you hardly ever used the word "bullfighter." You said "clown," and that meant you were also a bullfighter. It was all one thing, but people thought of me as mostly a clown.

I had an act at the time that involved an exploding toilet, and at the end of it I'd wind up with a toilet seat around my neck. One of the directors, who was a good friend of mine, told me, "Lecile, I'd really like to vote for you because I think you'd make a good president. But every time I think about voting for you, I see you standing there with that toilet seat around your neck. Then what would the rest of the rodeo world say about our president?"

I knew it was a longshot, but I won anyway. Most people knew I was trying to get everyone moving in the same direction and operating in everyone's best interest, but there were still a few that said, "We don't need no damn clown for president," so right after the election I ran an ad in our "Rodeo News" magazine with a picture of me standing there with that toilet seat around my neck.

One of the first things I did was start looking for endorsements for the cowboys. Athletes in other sports like NASCAR were starting to do it, so I thought the cowboys deserved that too. I went to an oil company and got them to donate so many gallons of gas. I also went to an insurance company and got them to cover us. The return to the sponsors was that the cowboys would wear the companies' patches on their shirts.

In conjunction with this sponsorship program and the patches, I designed new shirts to help identify the top fifteen cowboys in each event. They'd have their number on the back signifying their rank, and they'd have on a particular color shirt that identified what event they participated in. For instance, the audience could look and see that Joe Bob was the number six bulldogger in the nation because he had on a gold shirt with a 6 on the back.

When I presented this plan to the Board, one of the directors held his hand up and said, "I ain't for that."

"What do you mean you ain't for that?"

"If I wanted to wear a uniform to work, I'd get me a regular job. I ain't wearin' no uniform."

Then another one threw his hand up, and another one, and another one. I said, "Guys, listen. We're going to get so many hundreds of gallons of gasoline. We're going to get insurance. And we're going to have our own shirts." But they voted it down, which tells you a lot about how some cowboys thought back then. Obviously they don't think that way now.

Another big idea I had was to have a Super Bowl of rodeo. We were going to have the Canadian Rodeo Association, the Rodeo Cowboys Association, and the International Rodeo Association all compete. A beer company out of Milwaukee was going to throw in a lot of money to pay for it. I proposed the deal to my board and they were for it. I pitched it to the Canadians and they were for it. But the RCA turned it down.

I had been president for about eight years by then. I had managed to implement a couple of successful things, like the first National Finals for the IRA and a blanket insurance policy for the cowboys, but I started feeling like I needed to worry more about my own business. I wasn't getting anywhere with the cowboys. I was getting into their business, and they didn't want any part of business, so I decided to start my own business and not run again.

LORETTA LYNN'S LONGHORN RODEO

I was working a lot of rodeos in Louisiana, Arkansas, and Missouri with an announcer named Bruce Lehrke. Bruce was a newspaperman from Milwaukee, but he had also been a calf roper. He had a great voice and great timing. Of course, being from Milwaukee, he spoke proper English. We made a good team because I talked redneck and he spoke English.

Somehow Bruce got connected with Loretta Lynn and her husband, Mooney, who everybody called Doolittle. They decided they wanted to have a rodeo company, so they started one and called it the Loretta Lynn Longhorn Rodeo Company. We started out having them at her place in Goodlettsville, Tennessee, and then we branched out to places like Monroe, Huntsville, Winston-Salem, Detroit, Minneapolis, and Milwaukee. We went all over the East, and it just grew and grew because it was such a good production. Bruce Lehrke was a perfectionist, and being from the newspaper business, he was extremely good at promotion. Loretta performed at the shows, and Doolittle would just come hang out. It was fun for everybody.

Doolittle and Loretta had an office in Nashville, and their home was about seventy-five miles away in Hurricane Mills. I was in Nashville one night when he and I ended up in their office. We sat there passing a fifth of whiskey back and forth until he decided he wanted to go home. He wanted me to come along, so I did. Neither one of us was in any shape to drive, but we went outside to look for his truck. We couldn't find his, and mine was at the hotel, so Doolittle decided we'd just take Loretta's tour bus.

Somehow he got it all the way to Hurricane Mills without causing an accident, but when he got there, he was trying to turn it around next to the house and ended up running off into a creek. We decided we couldn't do anything about it that night, so he said we'd just go on into the house and take care of it the next day.

I knew Loretta and I sure didn't want to hear her chew his ass out about that, so when I saw one of their guys leaving to go back to his house in Nashville, I caught a ride with him and left Doolittle to get his ass eat up by himself. Well, I found out the next day that he had told Loretta he wasn't in any shape to drive, so I was the one who had driven the bus home and backed it off into the creek. I wasn't too mad at him, though, because I would've done the same thing had the situation been reversed.

MY KIND OF COMEDY

Like Davis Brockwell told me over at Arlington when I first started out, a bullfighter also had to do comedy. That came easy to me because I liked it, so I started to study comedy early on. I loved W.C. Fields, Laurel & Hardy, Red Skelton, Abbott & Costello, and the Pink Panther. Nowadays bullfighters are specialized. They wear bright clothes and pads and vests but hardly any of them wear makeup anymore. They don't want to be funny – they're athletes. What they don't understand is that they can be athletes and also be comedians too – plus it pays a hell of a lot more.

If you weren't funny, you didn't work back then. That answers the question as to why bullfighters dressed as clowns. Of course, your main job was to take care of the cowboys, so the makeup and the clown part of it was to make it easier for the crowd to watch. If a bullfighter dressed up as a regular cowboy got hit, the audience would say, "Oh my goodness! A cowboy got hit!" But if you're a clown and you have makeup on, that takes a little bit of the edge off, so they laugh and say, "Oh, look at that. Wasn't that funny. The clown got run over." Of course it hurt just as bad for us whether we had the makeup on or not, but it was better for the crowd if we did. So that's how the makeup part came about.

Emmett Kelly was an old circus clown who played a tramp character, and I always loved him. I didn't want to copy his makeup, but ever since I was eighteen years old, I wanted to portray an old clown. Now I am one. I used to have to study where to put a wrinkle when I drew on my makeup, but now I just follow the trenches.

People ask me how long it takes to get my makeup on. It pretty much depends on how much time I have. Sometimes I'm messing around with my acts or talking to somebody and I forget the time. Then I look up and see that I have fifteen minutes to get ready. Other times I can relax and take thirty minutes or so to do it. In those cases I'll get in my rig, close the doors and shut the outside world out, turn on a little Pink Floyd, Eagles, or Alabama, and sit there and relax and get ready and think about what I'm going to do that night. It's my little bit of time to have by myself.

The funny clothes came about because bulls are colorblind, but they know bright from dark. Anything with a lot of contrast gets their attention. That's why the cowboys usually wear dark colors and the bullfighters wear bright colors. But I wore dark pants, dark shoes, and a red and white checkered shirt because when you're throwing your fakes, you throw them with the upper part of your body. You don't want to attract attention to your legs because that's what's going to take you where you want to go. You don't want the bull to know that. So now that I'm just doing comedy, I wear Wrangler jeans that are too big in the waist and pretty much worn out. My shoes are white oversized tennis shoes made by Justin Boots. I don't know where my red wig came from; I just thought I needed a red wig. And my hat is just a small version of a regular cowboy hat that makes me look a little different.

Most people can recognize me from a long way off because I wear the red and white checkered shirt. It's become so associated with me that nobody else will wear one since that would just make people think of Lecile. I had a good friend back in the late sixties who was a salesman for Purina. The red and white checkerboard pattern was their trademark, and this guy told me they would furnish the material and have some shirts made for me if I would wear them. So that was sort of my first sponsor, before there even were any sponsorships. Believe it or not, that particular checkerboard pattern is patented by Purina. You can't get it anywhere else but from them.

My approach to comedy is similar to that of a shotgun: when you shoot it up there, you have to hit everybody. If the kid isn't entertained, he isn't going to want to come to the rodeo. And if the kid doesn't want to come to the rodeo, the parents aren't going to bring him. So you need to have comedy that reaches everybody. I have the slapstick and things like that for the kids, but then some of the edgier stuff goes right over the kids' heads and the adults catch it.

People often ask me if it's harder to fight bulls or be funny. Without a doubt, comedy is much more difficult. I learned to fight bulls well enough in three years to go to the circuit finals. I've been working on comedy now for over sixty years, and I'm still learning.

If you're fighting bulls and you make a mistake, and they have to haul you out of the arena on a stretcher, at least you go out of there with a little bit of dignity. But if a piece of comedy goes sour in the middle of the arena, you just want to dig a hole and crawl in it because there ain't no way out: you have to stand there and listen to the arena get quiet as a tomb.

I always tried to put two things in my acts: the elements of expectation and surprise. They're really two sides of the same coin, and one depends on the other. For instance, if I come out into the arena with a little bitty gun, you expect it to have a little pop sound. But the element of surprise would be if it has a really loud bang. The expectation is the setup, and the surprise is the payoff.

When I build my acts, I come up with the beginning and ending first, and then I put filler in the middle. It's got to have a good start, but it's got to have an even better end. You have to get their attention on the front end, but you have to blow them away on the back end. Ideally the filler will also be funny all the way through. You can make the act longer or shorter, depending on your mood and the time available, by adding to or subtracting from the filler. My approach to building an act is similar to something I heard one time about making a speech: you have a good opening and a good closing, and you keep them close together.

My early acts made use of only a few props and a lot of physical comedy. I later developed flashier acts that took advantage of the spotlights and sound systems that Bruce Lehrke's Longhorn Rodeo used to such great effect.

CAMERA ACT

The first big act I can remember doing with Loretta Lynn's Longhorn Rodeo Company was the camera act. It became a calling card for me because I did it for so many years. There was a really popular TV program back then called "The Ed Sullivan Show," and they had a bit on there with these two acrobats and a camera. One of them would go to take the other guy's picture, and when he'd unscrew the lens cap, all this confetti and this colored spring that looked like a snake would jump out. The other clown would be so startled that he'd turn three or four back flips, and that was the act.

I liked the concept and I liked the old camera as a prop, but I thought it really needed to blow up. I built a camera and put an explosive in it so that when I went to take a picture of the other clown, it'd blow up, he'd fall over backwards, and I'd grab the camera and run out.

Later on I thought it'd be neat if I could get a woman out of the stands to take her picture, so I'd dress a clown as a woman, plant him in the audience, and call him out there to do the deal. The camera act evolved until it was my first act, really, that I built myself.

TOWN PUMP ACT

The next one I came up with was the town pump act, and in it I pumped water out of my mule. I came up with that one when I saw a magician on TV who kept pouring water out of a pitcher even after he had supposedly emptied it all out. I thought that was really neat, so I studied on it until I came up with something that worked. Back then you couldn't just Google something like that and find it: you had to figure it out yourself. So I rigged up my water bucket that I still use today after more than fifty years. It rusted years ago and got holes all in it, but I patched them with chewing gum and painted over that, so it's just like J.B. Weld on there after all this time.

AMBULANCE ACT

The next one was an ambulance act. I got the idea for that one night when a bull rider got hurt, and they brought the ambulance out to pick him up with the siren, lights, and the whole nine yards. I thought it would be good if I had my own ambulance, so I built one. Mine was a box with bicycle wheels on it and plow handles on the side, and it was about the size of a wheelbarrow. I had a twelve-volt battery in the bottom to run my siren and light. Of course I wasn't going to fool with any riders who were really hurt, but I had to have somebody, so I'd come out and stage an "accident." I'd shoot somebody, he'd fall down, and then I'd haul him out.

LEVITATION ACT

The levitation act was after that. I'd take my partner and set him up on two brooms. Then I'd raise him up on the brooms until I accidentally kicked one of them out from under him. When I did that, he'd just be on one broom, levitating in thin air. I got the idea for this act from a tent show I saw as a kid.

BASEBALL ACT

I came up with so many of my acts just by watching what was going on in the world at the time. There was a big World Series going on one summer that people were especially excited about, so I decided to do a baseball act. The first one I built didn't have a really great ending, so I kept thinking about how I could make it better.

Hadley Barrett and I were at the Canadian Western Agribition in Regina, Saskatchewan when we heard the theme song to the movie "Chariots of Fire." I had heard the song when I watched the movie because it played during a really dramatic scene when the guys were running down the beach in slow motion. When I heard it again, I thought I might be able to work it into the baseball act to get the blockbuster ending I lacked. We got to the rodeo and I asked the sound man if he had the song. He said he didn't but could get it by the time of the performance, so I decided I would go ahead and work it in that night.

It came time to do the act, so I got up to bat and hit the ball. I ran the bases at normal speed to begin with, but when I got to second base, we all went into slow motion as "Chariots of Fire" played. I ran the bases in slow motion and the other guys moved at the same speed as they tried to field the ball. We kept that pace until right before I got around to home plate and scored a home run. Right before I got to the plate, "Chariots of Fire" stopped, we all went back to normal speed, and the catcher jerked home plate up before I could step on it. That song took the act from just okay to a real feature.

MEMORIES OF LECILE BY HADLEY BARRETT

I first met Lecile in Bertrand, Nebraska when he was fighting bulls and clowning. I recognized quickly that he was extremely good at both, but I had no idea that our first meeting would be the beginning of a lifelong friendship and working relationship that I will cherish forever. He and I came from similar backgrounds, having both been musicians working on stages and entertaining people long before our rodeo careers began. I rarely call him by his real name; usually I call him something like Pencil, Whistle, Nichol, or Lysol. He usually calls me Badley. Most people think we're just two old dudes who can't remember each other's name. One of the things I love about working with Lecile is that while we will stick to an overall structure during an act, we don't get locked into a script, so that invites a lot of ad lib. We seem to feed off each other and we both enjoy putting the other guy on the ropes to watch him fight his way off. Sometimes he might give me a card beforehand with some subjects on it, like drunks or cops, and we will just go from there. Many times he will bring a CD to my motor home so we can go over an act we haven't done in a long while, and usually we will die laughing at some of the things we didn't realize we had done the last time.

One of Lecile's most popular acts came about in Casper, Wyoming, where Lori and Hank Franzen were the stock contractors. During the bronc riding one night, Lori hollered to Lecile that we had a broken gate and needed a filler act. Lecile went to the entry gate, where he had some props stashed, and found a couple of pieces of rope, a rubber chicken, a Tide soap box, some colored bandanas, and a few rubber balloons. He grabbed a plastic trash bag out of a barrel, put all his stuff in it, and came into the arena claiming to be a magician. I had no idea what he was about to do, and neither did he. So after he made the ropes come out "Tide" and changed the colors of the bandanas (he always liked to challenge me with colors knowing I was color blind), he proceeded to tell me how he could turn a balloon into a chicken. He blew up a balloon and put it into the bag. Then, after an extended vocal performance of magician's babble, he reached into the bag, pulled out the chicken, and said, "Ta-da! How do you like that, dude?" I said, "That's not so great. That's just a rubber chicken." He paused a moment and proudly replied, "Well, what did you expect? It was a rubber balloon." Thus the act was born.

We were at the Colorado State Fair a few years ago doing Lecile's famous baseball act. I was on a huge stage over the chutes with Bill Falkner's brass band seated beside me. I was the umpire and Lecile was at bat. After two or three bad pitches that I had called strikes on, he was getting on me about how bad the calls were. So after the next pitch he was supposed to start objecting violently, ending with the remark: "Here I stand with my bat in my hand, cocked and ready to go." When he got to that line, he got it mixed up and (yes, you guessed it) said, "Here I stand with my cock in my hand..." and stopped. The band fell out of their chairs laughing while I tried to stay at the mic, knowing he needed some help, but I couldn't keep it together, so I ran to the back of the stage and hid. Lecile, being the professional he is, said, "I think we should erase that and do it over." Then he made the sound of a tape rewinding, like he does so well, and said, "Here I stand with my BAT in my hand, cocked and ready to go!" and the place just exploded.

(NOTE FROM LECILE: When the show was over, Hadley walked up to me wearing his Announcer of the Year buckle. He pulled it off his belt, handed it to me, and said, "Here. Until we can get a Screwup of the Year buckle, keep this one. You earned it." I gave that buckle up the next year to Randy Corley, who screwed up even worse than I had, if you can imagine that.)

I could write a book of my own about my experiences with Lecile, but I will simply say here to go see him live at your first opportunity, for it will be one of your great memories.

HANK COCHRAN

I got to meet a lot of neat people through Loretta and Mooney during the Longhorn years. One of my favorites was Hank Cochran, a great songwriter who wrote many hits. I was in Nashville for the rodeo one year when he came by and told me he had a song he wanted me to hear. I asked him if it was one he had written, and he said it wasn't, but it was one of the greatest songs he'd ever heard. I thought to myself, if Hank Cochran says it's great, then it must really be something. He wanted me to ride with him up to this little place and listen to it on their jukebox.

So we left Nashville and went up I-65, driving all afternoon long, until we got to Kentucky. I kept asking Hank where we were going, but he never would tell me. A few hours later, he finally said, "It's this place here," and pulled into a little beer joint. We walked in, he put a quarter in the jukebox, and it started playing "Folsom Prison Blues" by Johnny Cash. After it was done, he said, "I just wanted you to hear it," and we got up and left and drove half the night back to Nashville. That was just Hank Cochran.

Another time, Ethel, Hank, and I were going to go out, but Hank wanted to stop by his place first so he could change shirts. He invited us in to see his apartment, which was right next to Jeannie Seely's. She's a big-time country singer-songwriter who Hank was dating at the time. He wanted Jeannie to move in with him, but she refused to do so and maintained her own apartment right next door to Hank's. We were walking around his place looking at it when I saw a great big hole in the wall between his apartment and Jeannie's. While she was on tour, he had taken a chain saw and cut out a raggedy archway. It was nothing you could frame in, but it basically had them living in the same place, so it served its purpose. I always wondered what Jeannie said about it when she got home from her tour.

Right next to that hole was a stack of papers at least two feet tall. I leaned over to look at the one on top, and it was a song he had written. I flipped through a few of them, and they were all songs. I said, "Hank, you've got to be the most prolific songwriter there is."

"No I'm not. My buddy is. You don't know him yet because he has a ponytail and the Nashville guys don't like that, but he is without a doubt the most prolific songwriter there is." The name didn't ring a bell at the time, but not too long after that, here came Willie Nelson on his way to stardom.

JOE WALSH

One winter at the rodeo in Lafayette, a band called the James Gang was the entertainment there. They had a guitar player named Joe Walsh who was really good. After the rodeo was over with, Joe asked me if I knew somewhere he could go sit in and pick. I didn't, but I asked one of the local guys, who said he knew of a little juke joint way out in the boonies.

Joe didn't have a way to get around, so he rode out there with this other guy and me. It was just us three white guys among a huge crowd of black folks way out here at this club in the middle of a cotton field. They were surprised to see us but invited us in and were just as friendly as they could be. We hadn't eaten after the rodeo, so we filled up on fried fish, gar balls, and beer, and then we asked if we could sit in with the band. They were more than happy for us to join them, but eventually all of them left to go out and eat and drink until it was just Joe Walsh picking guitar with me on drums. We did that until daylight.

I knew he had a pretty good name by himself, but I didn't realize I had done something really special until a few years later when I saw him playing with the Eagles on TV.

BOXCAR WILLIE

One time I was on "The Ralph Emery Show" with Jerry Clower and Boxcar Willie. We were all sitting there talking about the rodeo, telling jokes and that sort of thing, when Ralph asked Boxcar Willie what his real name was. Boxcar said, "It's Lecile." I figured they were just pulling something on me, but Jerry looked at me and said, "No, his name is Lecile." Boxcar said his name was Lecile too. Ralph asked him how he got the name, and Boxcar said, "It was a mistake on my birth certificate." When I heard that, I said, "Now wait a minute, that's what happened to me. My name's Lecile." Jerry knew my name was Lecile, but he said he didn't know if he believed Boxcar, so Ralph asked to see his driver's license. Sure enough we had the same name, but he spelled his "L-E-C-I-L."

That's the only other person I've heard of with the same name, but many people have named their dogs after me. Preston Fowlkes had a lazy old dog that he named Lecile. This dog laid on the porch outside the door and was always in the way, so Preston named him after me just so he could holler at him, "Get the hell off the porch, Lecile!"

Dr. Lester Spell, the long-time Mississippi Commissioner of Agriculture, had a daughter who also named her dog Lecile. One year a snake bit the dog and they thought he might die, so people were sending all these text messages and emails back and forth saying stuff like, "Lecile's not doing good. He might not make it." And so I started getting calls from all over the world asking me if I was about to die. Finally I got a call from Dr. Spell's son, Jason, and found out what the deal was, but it took a while to get all that straightened out.

HEE HAW

Longhorn was really taking off and so was Loretta's singing career. Around this same time, a new TV show called 'Hee Haw" had just started, and they got Loretta to come down and tape an episode while we were in town for the Nashville rodeo. Doolittle asked Sam Lovullo, the producer of the show at the time, if he wanted to come see the rodeo. He did, so after it was over, Doolittle brought him back to the dressing room and introduced me to him. Sam said, "I really like what you do. How would you like to be on the show?" I told him I'd love to, and he told me he'd call me.

We've all heard that before, so I didn't think much more about it until I was in Tulsa working the IRA finals and got a call from Sam. He asked me if I could do two comedy bits per show, for a total of twenty-six bits for the season. They were all silent and outdoors, and they were all undercranked, meaning they were filmed at a slower speed. Then when they were played back at normal speed, they actually went faster. It was fast, jerky stuff like Benny Hill used to do, which gave them the old-timey look and made them that much funnier.

They paired me up with a guy named Jimmy Moore from Lawrenceburg, Tennessee. He and I clicked right off the bat. We went to Nashville and they gave us a deadline of a week to come up with the twenty-six bits before the season even started filming, because we had to go ahead and give them a prop list so the prop people could get those ready. We kept putting off the writing every night until it finally came down to us having to turn them in the next morning, so we went up to our room, set the TV out in the hall, and sat there all night long writing comedy bits.

Jimmy and I would go out with our own cameraman and prop truck to scout for locations. Most of our bits involved a barn, so we'd go way out in the hills and try to find corn cribs and sheds and buildings that were built like little barns. If it was a normal-sized barn, you just got lumber when you filmed it: you never got an idea of the scale or what it really looked like. So we always tried to find what was essentially a little barn just to give people a good idea of where we were.

When we found a suitable place, we'd go up to the house and ask the people what they were going to do with it. Usually it would be just a piece of a shed or something that was about to fall to pieces, so we knew they probably weren't going to do anything with it. They'd usually say something like, "Oh, not much. We'll probably get around to tearing it down one day." We'd tell them we were from "Hee Haw," which they were familiar with, and we'd ask them if we could tear it down for them. At the end of our bits, we'd usually destroy the barn. We might cut it in all the right places and hook a tractor up to it to pull it down. Sometimes we'd even burn them down, so we'd have to borrow the fire truck from the community's volunteer fire department. The owners would almost always agree to it because they wanted to tell their friends, "Watch 'Hee Haw' tonight! They're going to tear my barn down and burn it up!" So it usually didn't cost anything to do all that.

When the show got so big that they brought in a bunch of producers from California to do everything, they'd go out and scout our locations for us. They'd ask the farmer if they could burn it down or tear it down, and the owner would say, "Sure, I'll take a thousand dollars for it." The farmers knew the producers were from California, and those guys couldn't talk to the country people like we could. Come to find out, the people out in the sticks weren't as dumb as the people from the West Coast thought they were. It was just a matter of the way we talked to them. They could tell the difference between us and the Hollywood dudes.

The most common question I get asked about "Hee Haw" is if the girls were really that pretty, to which I answer, yes they were. But the second most common question I get asked is if Junior Samples was really like that in real life, to which I answer, yes he was.

Junior was a pulpwooder from south Georgia. The state highway department would go along the interstate and cut down the trees that they said were too close to the road. Then Junior and his brother would come along and cut them up, haul them off, and sell them to the chipping mill.

The story goes that one day he was way out in the boonies picking up pulpwood on the side of the road, when he found a giant fish head. It was from a great big old bass, bigger than Junior had ever seen, so he picked it up and took it with him. On his way home from the mill, he stopped by the country store where they all sat around and whittled and spit and drank coffee. When Junior walked in with that bass head, none of the guys could believe how big it was. Naturally they wanted to know where he got it, so he said he caught it in the little pond behind his house. He told them this big story of how he fought this bass for hours, and when he finally pulled it in, he saw it wasn't fit to eat because it was so big. He said he knew the fellows wouldn't believe him, so he just cut the head off and brought it up to show them for proof. And it worked: they all believed him.

Somebody at the store called the TV station in Atlanta, got in touch with the producer of their fishing show, and told him about this gigantic bass this guy had caught out of the pond behind his house. They sent a TV crew down there and Junior told them the whole story. When they took the tape back to the station, somebody with the show realized that this thing was a sea bass. It was a saltwater fish that somebody had probably caught down in Florida, and it had gone sour on them or something, so evidently they had just thrown it out on the side of the highway.

The guys at the TV station got such a big laugh out of Junior's fish tale that they sent it to some friends at the Nashville TV station, which happened to be helping out with the filming of "Hee Haw" there in town. The guys in Nashville were sitting around watching this thing and laughing when Sam Lovullo, the producer of "Hee Haw," walked in. He took one look at Junior and said, "Find him." And they did.

The "Hee Haw" company was producing a series for Loretta Lynn called "The Orange Blossom Special." Jimmy Moore and I went out to California to shoot it. I was Lecile and played the trombone, and he was Becile and played the guitar. We were supposed to be two hillbillies who went to California to hit it big.

We got out there and were walking down Hollywood Boulevard, wearing our hillbilly outfits and carrying our instruments, when this guy came up to us and asked, "Are you two in California to make a record?"

"Why yes we are."

"Well I just happen to be the one you're looking for."

"Is that right? Well how much does it cost?"

"How much do you have?"

"Four hundred dollars. Is that enough?"

"As a matter of fact, that's exactly how much it is."

We gave him the money and he took us to something that looked just like an old-timey photo booth sitting on the sidewalk, but it was an audio-recording booth. I don't remember much about the session, but I do remember having all kinds of trouble trying to get out of Hollywood alive in our hillbilly costumes.

George Lindsey, who played Goober, was also out in California with us. George just did not have an Off button. He was always on, so you had to always be ready. One morning before a shoot for Loretta's show, we were eating breakfast at the Hollywood Hotel, where we were staying. Dean Martin was sitting with his uncle in the booth next to us. The waiter came around and George ordered two eggs – one scrambled and one over easy – bacon, and toast. When the waiter came back and set our meals down in front of us, George started ranting and raving and just about scared this guy to death. We didn't know what was wrong with him until he turned to the waiter and hollered, "You scrambled the wrong egg!" When Dean Martin heard that, he stood up and asked me, "Where are you fellows from?"

"Tennessee."

Dean said, "That figures," and just shook his head and walked off.

I was doing a rodeo at the state fairgrounds in Billings, Montana, where Roy Clark was performing. He invited Bob Witte, my traveling buddy at the time, and me backstage after one of his shows, where we had a few drinks and visited. We got hungry after a while, so we headed out to the midway to get a bite to eat.

Bob and I had walked around the midway for the last three or four days, and we got interested in this hypnotist that had a really good act. When we passed by his show on the way to eat, I told Roy we should check it out, because I thought he'd really like it. He agreed, so we went in and sat down.

The hypnotist started pulling people out of the audience to hypnotize. He had them acting like horses, cows, and all kinds of crazy things. Roy and I were really enjoying it, but Bob just scowled and said, "I don't believe none of that stuff. All them people was just planted in the audience to go along with his act."

Roy turned to him and asked, "Well, why don't you get up there and try it then?"

Bob looked at me to see what I thought, so I said, "Go on up there and show him."

When the guy called for the next batch of volunteers, Bob jumped up and ran down front. They got up on stage, the hypnotist did his deal, and Bob's chin was the first to hit his chest. They say if you don't believe in hypnotism then that just puts you out quicker, which was certainly the case with Bob.

The hypnotist said to the first guy, "When I snap my fingers, you're going to act like a dog, running around barking and sniffing people's butts."

He looked at the second person and said, "When I snap my fingers, you're going to act like a cat, running around meowing and climbing trees."

Then he said to the third person, who was a woman, "When I snap my fingers, you're going to act like a hen, running around clucking and scratching. And you don't like roosters."

He finally got to Bob and said, "When I snap my fingers, you're going to act like a rooster, running around crowing and chasing hens."

When the hypnotist snapped his fingers, the whole stage erupted into bedlam. The guy who was the dog was chasing the guy who was the cat, and Bob was running around like a rooster chasing the hen. He'd pop his neck out, squat down, crow, and light out after her. I mean it was a wild scene.

The hypnotist let that go on for a while, and then he snapped his fingers again. When he did, everybody quit what they were doing and sat back down. Then he told them all, "When I snap my fingers again, you're going to wake up and not remember any of this. But the first time you hear the word 'hamburger,' you're going to jump right into your animal act." Then he snapped his fingers and everybody left.

Bob came down and Roy asked him, "Well, do you believe in it now?"

"Nah, I didn't go to sleep or anything."

I said, "What about you running around like a rooster?"

"I didn't do that. I saw those other folks running around acting crazy, but it didn't work on me." He didn't remember a thing.

We headed back out to the midway after it was over, and right off the bat we passed a vendor who was hawking hamburgers. When Bob heard that, he dropped right down and went to crowing and scratching just like a rooster. He kept on until he heard the word again, and then he was back to normal.

I asked him, "What about it now, Bob?"

"Naw, I don't believe it. He couldn't make it work on me."

Bob never did believe he'd done all that, but every time Roy and I met up in Nashville to do "Hee Haw," he'd ask me about my rooster friend.

My rodeo acts helped me get onto "Hee Haw," but the show also helped me in my rodeo acts. I never liked the fact that in rodeo you had to keep the audience waiting while you got out to the middle of the arena with all your props and set them up. Then you'd do the act, break it all down, and haul it back out. I never liked that, because I felt like it was awkward and took the audience out of it. "Hee Haw" was different. We'd get our props, get into position, and they'd roll cameras. Then they'd edit the bit and do the fades from and to black when they put the whole thing together.

I liked that way of doing things, so I decided I needed to take that into the rodeo arena. It was easy for me to do that when I was working with Loretta Lynn's Longhorn Rodeo because they had mostly indoor arenas and such high production values. They would turn the house lights off and make it go dark while I got into position and got my props set up. When they brought the lights back up, I was ready to go. When I was done, they would go dark. So what I did was make the arena my screen: the arena would go black just like on television and it made the whole thing a lot more professional and funnier.

That experience also helped my acts in the outdoor rodeos because I started doing something on the way into the arena and on the way out of it. Sometimes I'd even start it before I got out there, so you could hear me before you could see me. And when the act was over, I'd do something all the way to the gate on my way out, even if it was just mumbling comedy bits. Or if I got shot in the butt, I'd wait until I was almost to the gate before I got shot. I take it in doing something and I take it out doing something to keep from having those awkward transitions.

MOVIES

"Hee Haw" got me my first movie, which was "W.W. and the Dixie Dance Kings" with Burt Reynolds. It just so happened that one of the ladies working for the show had been asked by the movie's producer to cast some actors for it. I even had a speaking part in it, which is rare for a first movie. It was good that it was filmed in Tennessee, because here we have a "Right to

Work" law. A lot of states don't have that, so in order to get into the Screen Actors' Guild, you have to have done a movie with a speaking part. The problem with that is that you have to be in the Guild to get a speaking part. So it was a chicken and egg kind of deal. But since we were in Tennessee and I had a speaking part, I got right into SAG.

Burt and I hit it off really well, so we got to knocking around together. He was interested in rodeo, and I obviously learned a lot from him about acting. He was very down to earth. Some actors were real prima donnas, but if you didn't know Burt, you would have thought he was just a grip or something working on the set. At one time he was going to make a movie called "The Original Bull Dancer," which is how I was billed, but unfortunately it never got made. Maybe somebody will want to make a movie out of this book.

Shortly after that, I got cast in "Walking Tall: The Final Chapter," which was the story of the killing of Buford Pusser. I had gotten to know him back around fifteen years before that when I was working for an amusement company. I did rodeos on the weekend, but during the week I'd go out to beer joints and nightclubs to service jukeboxes, pinball machines, and things like that. One of my routes was up in Hardeman County, which was Sheriff Pusser's beat, so I saw him almost every week.

There were several movies that I could have done but had to turn down for one reason or another. I was cast in two or three John Grisham movies but had to turn them down due to my rodeo schedule. I had a part in the Larry Flynt movie, but the language in it was so rough that I didn't want to do it. Not to say that I never cuss, but this movie had some rank lines in it. I turned down the movie "21 Grams" because I thought it was a drug movie. Come to find out, it wasn't at all. I could have done a movie with a nude scene that would've been really easy: all I had to do was lie there naked with a naked woman on the bank of the Mississippi River. I really wanted to do that one, but my wife wouldn't let me. So I missed out on a few movies because I was too picky or too dumb, but I'm satisfied with the ones I've been in.

KRIS KRISTOFFERSON

I was working a California rodeo in the early seventies, and I had to go back and forth to my trailer to change costumes or acts and things of that nature. Every time I went back to my trailer, this hippie-looking guy would come up and just talk and talk and talk to me. He had long hair and was wearing blue jean shorts, a tank top, and sandals. I didn't know who he was, but I kept seeing him all afternoon.

That night a bunch of us went out to eat. A friend of mine, who was an executive with the MCA record company, joined us. We all went in to sit down and here was this longhaired guy again. I couldn't figure out what his deal was, but he was obviously connected somehow. At some point during dinner he got up to go to the bathroom, so I asked my friend who the guy was. He told me, "That's Kris Kristofferson. He's a singer-songwriter."

I was talking to Kris that night and he was telling me about a friend of his who had written a great song. I thought to myself, well, this guy must know a good songwriter when he hears one. Come to find out it was Johnny Paycheck, who wrote "Take This Job and Shove It."

I got back home from the rodeo and was telling Ethel about this guy I met who knew Johnny Paycheck. She asked me who it was, and I said, "It was Burt Bacharach." I don't know where that came from, but that's what I said. She seemed kind of doubtful, but I told her I sure had, and that he had long hair and wore sandals, shorts, and a tank top. She said, "That doesn't sound like Burt Bacharach." Later that winter we were watching television and I told Ethel, "There's that Burt Bacharach fellow I had dinner with." She then informed me that he was really Kris Kristofferson.

Years later, on into the seventies, I was cast in the movie "The Last Days of Frank and Jesse James." Kris was also in it, so we did a lot of scenes together. One day on the lot I pulled him aside and said, "Kris, I got a funny story to tell you. For years I thought your name was Burt Bacharach. I don't know if you remember or not, but we met once before and even had dinner together." He didn't really remember, so I tried to jog his memory a little bit, and he asked, "You're a rodeo clown?" I said I was, and he said, "Oh yeah! For years and years I told everybody that I knew a rodeo clown named Lucille."

SOUTH AFRICA

In 1966, twenty-five of the top cowboys and cowgirls from the United States were selected to travel to the Republic of South Africa for about two months on a rodeo tour. I was honored by being chosen the rodeo clown and bullfighter for this tour, which was the first American rodeo to ever be booked in South Africa. I was also responsible for the cowboys, while the producer's wife was to supervise the cowgirls, which left the producer free to handle business problems as they might arise.

I left Memphis the morning of November 22 and arrived at Kennedy International Airport around noon. The cowboys, cowgirl barrel racers, and trick riders were arriving from all over the country and gathering at the Sabena Belgian World Airlines area for the flight to Africa. All the Western outfits caused somewhat of a stir even in busy New York.

We flew from there to Brussels, Belgium and had an eight-hour layover. Some of the most beautiful buildings I saw on the entire trip were in the historic Grand Place, which was the heart of the old town. The buildings and statuary were trimmed in fourteen-karat gold leaf. The fronts of the buildings, which are hundreds of years old, were owned by the town. They could not be changed in any way by the people who owned the buildings, and the gold leaf had to be replaced every ten years because of the weather conditions. I also saw the permanent structures left from the Brussels World's Fair of 1958, which were awe-inspiring.

Our next stop was Leopoldville in the Congo. This was one of the most frightening experiences of the trip. We landed at a small airstrip, which was seemingly deserted, and were warned not to take cameras or any writing equipment out of the plane. Everyone had to disembark at this point, and when the door was opened, we saw a crowd of natives standing around the plane. Some of them had the elongated earlobes with coins inserted in them, and others had the protruding lower lip that is stretched from infancy. Some had coils of metal around their necks, making them much longer as more coils were added over the years. Others had decorative scars on their faces that looked as though they were bad cuts which had been left to heal by themselves. Most all of them had things hanging from or inserted in their ears and noses.

We were ushered into a room of the small terminal by the French police, all of whom carried automatic machine guns at the ready. On all sides, as we walked to the terminal, were the natives clamoring to get at us. Only the producer and I knew they had been told by political agitators that we were mercenaries sent there to help overthrow their government. We found out later that a compounding factor to the natives being so upset in Leopoldville, now known by the name Kinshasa as one of the most dangerous cities in the world, was that we happened to land there on the first anniversary of their new government. The others with us thought they were just excited to see Americans.

The room we were escorted to had a small patio from which you could see the landing strip. While in there, we watched about twenty-five small fighter planes and one large bomber land, reload, refuel, and leave. These observations, and one in which a trick rider was accused by a native of taking pictures, made me mighty glad to leave the Congo.

In about three hours we made it to Johannesburg, the largest city and industrial center of South Africa. As we approached for landing, I saw huge mounds of dirt that we were told had been dug from the gold mine. These mounds of dirt were very close to the business district of the city and were no trouble to see from almost any section of Johannesburg.

When we went through customs at the airport, our health and immunization records were checked along with our passports and other official documents. I was detained longer than the other cowboys because of the clown shotgun, pistol, and explosives I used in my acts. A special permit from Pretoria, the administrative capital of South Africa, had to be obtained for the entry and use of this equipment.

The rodeos had been well publicized in Johannesburg so there were many people at the airport to see real American cowboys. I suppose we were almost as much of an oddity as some of their natives in their loincloths with the huge rings in their ears and noses would be arriving at the Memphis airport.

An advance team of cowboys had gone over to Johannesburg to get the stock assembled and green-break some horses for the riders to use as mounts in the steer wrestling and other events. These cowboys were certainly happy to see us, and we were glad to know everything had been going so well. They told us how readily they had been accepted and how nice people were to them.

The American Consul was there to meet us, along with the local press. After many pictures and much information was given to the newspapers, we started out for our hotel. I was disappointed not to be able to see any native huts or wild animals, but we were in downtown Johannesburg, which was a relatively modern city with a population of well over a million people. It was a rather strange trip through the city in the small station wagon. We drove on the left side of the street, and the steering wheel was on the right side of the cars.

The driving conventions and the food were two of the hardest things to get used to while we were there. It was Thanksgiving, and I was thinking of the delicious dinner my family was having at home. At the hotel, which was very nice by European standards but without many of the conveniences we take for granted when staying in a large hotel, we were served what they considered to be the best meals available. The bread there was very hard, and they drank hot tea, warm beer, and lukewarm milk. Water was never served with a meal unless you insisted on it, and you paid extra for it. Ice was a rarity. Salads were mostly cabbage and other local vegetables with which we were not familiar, and they always seemed to be wilted.

My diet on the trip seldom varied. Eggs were frequently served, which I loved, but I just did not trust these eggs. I could easily imagine them coming from an ostrich or emu or even a buzzard, but I was reassured that they came from a regular chicken. I couldn't be convinced, however, so I stayed away from the eggs. For almost the whole week I dined on roast beef, which they also served frequently, hard bread, and warm beer.

Towards the end of the trip, I saw a guy in the hotel lobby playing Louis Armstrong songs on his trumpet. I was still curious about those eggs, because I was really tired of all that roast beef. I asked him, "What kind of eggs are those they keep serving here?"

"Those are chicken eggs."

"Yeah, but what kind of chicken?"

"Just a regular chicken like you have at home."

I believed this guy for whatever reason, so I said, "Well, I sure wish I had known that earlier in the trip. I haven't eaten anything but roast beef, bread, and beer all week long."

He looked at me funny and said, "That's not roast beef."

I looked at him quizzically and said, "It's not?"

"That's monkey rump steak, with monkey gland sauce on it."

My stomach did a flip and I took a few seconds to process this revelation before I asked, "What kind of monkey are you talking about?"

"The one with the big red rump."

So I ate baboon butts the whole time instead of chicken eggs. I found that out, however, near the end of our stay; let me go back to the beginning.

We were very tired from the trip over, so we all went to bed early. Johannesburg is situated at an altitude of about 6000 feet, while Memphis is at an elevation of 335 feet. It seemed as though I couldn't get enough oxygen, so just going up a short flight of steps tired me out. The sleep I got was even different. I slept very soundly but in the morning I never felt refreshed, and even felt almost as tired as I did the night before.

Friday morning we got an opportunity to meet some of the people and see some of the town. Everyone was very curious and wanted to talk and find out all about America and being a cowboy. Our clothes attracted quite a lot of attention and the people were constantly asking if they could buy our hats or boots, as they just didn't have Western clothes there. In the lobby of our hotel, a man offered to buy my hat for several hundred rand. I later figured out that what he had offered me equaled about $175 in American dollars. I wished right then I had filled a trunk full of cowboys hats and brought them with me.

I met a South African of English descent named Clive who spoke very proper English. He was staying in our hotel while his band played a local engagement. He was a jazz drummer, so we found that we had much to talk about. We became very close friends while I was there and he took me around the city and helped me find props and things that I needed for some of my acts. He also told me a lot about the local customs, which made me understand the people more and made my stay much more enjoyable.

The people carried almost everything on their heads, which was a most peculiar sight. I saw native women walking down the street with large packages on their heads and perhaps two or three more on top of that. If they were strolling along and the bundle became slightly unbalanced, they would move their necks and heads around to balance it all back up and just keep on going along without ever missing a step.

The rodeo was held at the stadium which they used for polo and soccer. It seated about 20,000 people, and at each performance, even the standing room was sold out. Just before the show started on Friday night, the South African national anthem was played and they drew their flag up the poles that were at each end of the stadium as the people stood in silence. When their anthem was finished, the American national anthem began playing and the American flags were raised on their poles. As they unfurled, we were all astonished to realize that both flags were flying upside down. The music was stopped and the cowboys all put back on their hats and went out in a body and righted the flags. Our national anthem was played again and then the rodeo proceeded. There were many apologies from the stadium management for the error. The boys who handled our equipment swore they had done everything just as they had been shown to do it. It was suspected that some agitators had reversed the flags while there was so much confusion and hurry before the rodeo. It was obvious that the people in the stands were very dismayed and shocked that someone had done something to try to embarrass us in their country.

Ever since I had been approached about going to South Africa, I had wondered about the bulls I would have to fight and how they would differ from the ones I was used to in the United States. I found that they fought pretty much the same way. The only real problem I had was getting used to the bulls' horns, which came straight out in front of their heads, unlike the ones to the sides on the bulls in our country. I also had to make mostly right-hand passes at their bulls instead of the left-hand passes that

I mostly use on ours. The main problem I had was tiring out very easily because of the thinner air and reduced oxygen.

The Friday performances were very well accepted, and the people would flock around us after each one to talk and ask us for autographs. They had never seen a real rodeo, and only in movie theaters had they seen cowboys. There were no televisions because it was against the law to own one.

After the last Saturday night performance, we were all very tired and went to bed as soon as we could, which was about 12:30 AM. I was awakened by the producer at 4:30 AM, who had been told by the American Consul of a plot by some underworld characters who had somehow gained partial control of the production of the rodeo. They saw it was a money-making venture, and they wanted to get their hands on the money.

We learned they had planned to serve us with legal papers on some trumped-up charge to hold us in South Africa. This situation, along with the trouble brewing in Rhodesia, were the two main factors for the cancellation of the rest of the tour. The producer stayed in his room to answer the phone and give the appearance that things were going normally. I had two hours to get twenty-five cowboys and all our gear from the hotel and arena to the airport.

After the producer woke me up at 4:30 AM and explained our situation, I checked the rooms to see who was missing. After Saturday night's rodeo, most of the cowboys had gone directly to bed. Some of them, however, knowing we wouldn't have a rodeo on Sunday, had gone out to see some of the Johannesburg night life. I figured that the missing cowboys wouldn't have ventured too far from the hotel at that time of night, or morning as it was, since they weren't familiar with the town. There were two bars, one cocktail lounge, and one nightclub in our hotel. Out of these four places, I found all but one of my missing cowboys. To these I found, I told them there was going to be a bed check in five minutes. Well, if you know anything of the rough way a cowboy makes his living, you'd know that they think they're old enough and tough enough to take care of themselves. It was rather difficult to impress upon them that a bed check was necessary without arousing the suspicion of the hotel management or anyone else in Johannesburg, but I must have spoken strongly enough to convince them because I got them all to the large room where I had told them to assemble. I then had to go out and find the missing cowboy. I went out the back entrance of our hotel, hoping not to be noticed, and found my cowboy walking down the street not far away.

I got back and told the cowboys of our situation and that we only had a short while to get out of South Africa. As you can imagine, there were mixed emotions in the group, disappointment and fright among them. I picked out six cowboys who had the least amount of gear in their rooms and told them to get packed and be ready to leave for the stadium in fifteen minutes. Once there, they had the job of assembling all the equipment and packing and labeling it for New York, where we would sort it out when we had more time. This task was not insignificant. It had taken the cowboys and cowgirls perhaps months to assemble all of it. Every piece of equipment it took to produce a full-scale rodeo, except for the arena and stock, plus the personal gear of the individuals, had to be packed and shipped.

One of the lawyers representing our company while we were in South Africa loaned us a truck to transfer the people and equipment from the arena, where we were all going to assemble, to the airport. The people working at the arena were told to get the gear to the airport without going through downtown Johannesburg, as we could not arouse any suspicion whatsoever at this stage. As they got a load ready, a couple of them would take it to the airport and return for another load.

I waited until the last possible moment to tell the cowgirls the situation because for one thing, I wanted them to be so busy getting their things packed that they didn't have time to be frightened. Also, I knew from experience with my wife that if they thought they had time, they would try to fix their hair just so, select the proper traveling clothes, and so on. We didn't have time to wait for that, because they naturally had more luggage than the men did because of all their outfits, make-up, hair rollers, and a hundred other things women seem to think they need.

We had been given the use of one small station wagon by the hotel, and I knew we would never get all the people and their luggage out of the hotel and to the arena on time using just this one small vehicle. I awakened Clive, my friend I had met there, and asked if he would help us get some of the equipment to the arena. Without asking for any explanation from me as to what was going on, he offered his station wagon and his services.

When we would get a load ready, we would take it down the back stairs of the hotel and load the two wagons to capacity. All the cowgirls were taken to the arena first and when they had all been gotten out, the cowboys started going in threes and fours piled atop luggage and hanging onto any place they could get a hold of. Clive and I kept returning in his car until all the equipment was out and everyone was at the arena except the producer, his wife, and me. I went around checking the rooms to see that they were empty of belongings and remembered then, that in all the confusion, I had forgotten to pack my own gear. I rushed to the room and found it empty. I hoped that the cowboy I had been rooming with had packed it and that it was at the arena or on its way to the airport.

From this time on, we had more things to worry about. The producer left with the American Consul for the American Embassy to get our money and tickets out of the safe there. If any of the production management, who were at a huge celebration party, called and couldn't reach the producer, inquiries would be made. We were also scheduled to be at breakfast at 8:00 AM, and at 9:00 AM a bus was to pick us up and take us on a tour of a gold mine. If the hotel staff discovered we were gone, this would lead to our discovery and detainment. After leaving the hotel for the last time and arriving at the arena, I learned that two trips had already been made to the airport.

About fifteen people were left at the arena who hadn't been able to pile on top of the gear as the truck traveled to the airport.

We were going to call taxis to take the remaining people to the airport, but nobody wanted to wait for the taxis and we thought there might be a possibility that the drivers might inform some of the production staff that we were trying to get out of the country. We had the two small station wagons and the truck loaded to overflowing. People piled all over the luggage and gear and the station wagons pulled away. We had to secure a rope around the luggage on the truck, as it kept falling off, and we finally left the arena behind. Somehow in all the commotion, the cowboy who had been driving the truck was in one of the station wagons that had already left, and I didn't know the route they had been using. One of the guys with us did know the way, so we took off.

We were already behind schedule when we left the arena around 7:30. The lawyers of these underworld characters were supposed to serve us with the legal papers at 7:00 that morning, we had been told. As luck would have it, we got lost. We stopped to ask a fellow for directions, and all he could do was point and say, "Too far." I didn't know if he meant it was too far to drive or too far to go without getting caught, but I floored it in the direction he pointed.

The truck we were using ran solely from a battery; it had no generator and the battery was weak. The truck wouldn't run very fast, and every time we stopped at an intersection, it would go dead. We would all have to get out and push it until it started again. It was probably a good thing it wouldn't go very fast because once we started picking up speed as we were going down the first hill, one of the ropes broke that was holding the luggage and a trunk bounced off with a cowboy atop it. It was certainly providential that he was one of the best bareback bronc riders in the country and that he had something under him to break his fall. We stopped and gathered everything up, including the cowboy, who was relatively unhurt considering the spill he had taken. We secured the luggage, hopped aboard, and continued on.

When we got to the airport, we unloaded everything by what seemed to be a mountain of luggage and equipment.

I went to the Sabena Belgium World Airlines counter to see when we could get a flight out, but they were closed. People had to be called, awakened, and gotten down to the airport. The next flight out of Johannesburg was 9:00 AM on Air France to Paris. Even though the prospect of an encounter with an unfriendly DeGaulle loomed in my mind, I felt that we would at least be closer to home. A call had to be made to Sabena in New York to get the tickets endorsed. We had almost an hour to wait until boarding time, and this time dragged on as if it would never end. I didn't know so many thoughts could go through a person's head in such a short time. The American Consul arrived and told us that even though we were at the airport and ready to leave that there was still the possibility that we could be detained. He assured us that he would do everything in his power to hold these underworld characters at bay by legal means until we had the opportunity to board the plane and get away. As we were waiting, we told the pilot of the Air France 707 jet what had transpired. He was very sympathetic toward us and said that he would help us in every way he possibly could.

We boarded fifteen minutes early, and as we were getting on the plane, eight cars full of the promoters, lawyers, and underworld characters arrived. Without further delay, the pilot slammed the door shut, not waiting for the boarding device that was attached to the terminal to be removed from the plane. A man ran out of the terminal waving a ticket in his hand, but he could catch the next plane to Paris because the pilot thought this might be our only chance to leave. He opened the jet engines to what seemed to be wide open, and without waiting for the long jet runway to clear, taxied down the only available runway and put the pedal to the floor. I knew it would be too short, because I had only seen prop planes using it, and there were buildings on either end of it. We got almost to the end of the runway before the pilot turned that huge jet almost straight up, and we knew then we'd made it. Once we were at cruising altitude, the pilot turned the controls over to the co-pilot and came back to where we were. He told us that if we knew as much as he did about aircraft and flying that we would have been as frightened as he was on that takeoff. When I heard that, I told him we were pretty well frightened anyway.

We had a layover in Brussels, Belgium on the way back, and Johnny Clark was rooming with me. The stipulation was that he was my responsibility, so he sat beside me on the plane, next to me at dinner, and roomed with me. I had to watch him the whole time because he was wild as a March hare.

Our hotel in Brussels was really nice, and we went up to our room to rest before dinner because the jet lag was getting to us. I was about to lie down so I went to the bathroom first, where I noticed we had a bidet. I didn't know a whole lot about them, but I knew how they worked and what they were for. When I got done and went to lie down, Johnny went in to take his turn. Right away he came back in and asked, "Lecile, what's this thing in the commode here?"

"That's a bidet."

"What's a bidet?"

"Well, when you were a kid, didn't your momma make you wash your feet after you ran around all day barefoot and got your feet dirty? That's for when you don't want to take a bath and you just want to wash your feet."

I turned back over to go to sleep and in a minute I heard him holler, "Hot damn!" What Johnny had done was stand up in the commode in his bare feet and bend over to turn the thing on. When he did, a stream of water hit him right in the face and soaked him. He came walking out of the bathroom just as wet as a rag and said, "Lecile, you need to tell them to turn the volume down on that foot washer."

Before this trip, I had never traveled so far, laughed as much, been frightened as often, prayed as hard, and been as thankful to be an American citizen.

LONGHORN RODEO COMPANY

Eventually Loretta's career got to the point where she couldn't afford to play at all the rodeos because she was filling buildings by herself, so Bruce bought the business and it became strictly the Longhorn Rodeo Company. When Bruce got it, he really turned up the production aspect of things, and it surpassed any company going at the time. It was a real show, with dramatic openings and grand closings. The opening pageants would have a theme, like "Ghost Riders in the Sky," and tell a story. They had trick riders. It looked pretty. They used a full live orchestra at every event. Almost all of the shows were indoors, so we had spotlights for lighting effects during the events and comedy routines.

These big productions were necessary in the East for the simple reason that they didn't know rodeo. Out West you had people who rode horses and roped cattle and did that for a living, so rodeos were like backyard basketball games: they were everywhere. But in the East, they had only seen cowboys on TV, so you had to have a great big production around the rodeo. These days, even out West you have to have the big productions, because there are more rodeos. The competition for the entertainment dollar is so fierce that even they must have the total package.

Some of the places we went with Longhorn included Richfield OH; Huntsville AL; Huntington WV; Charleston WV; Lexington KY; Frankfort KY; Louisville KY; Cincinnati OH; Columbus OH; Winston-Salem NC; Madison WI; Milwaukee WI; Hampton VA; Greenville SC; Lakeland FL; San Antonio TX; Houston TX; Nashville TN; Washington DC; Detroit MI; Monroe LA; Bangor ME; Portland ME; Saint Paul MN; Cleveland OH; Cape Girardeau MO; Daytona Beach FL; Jacksonville FL; Augusta GA; Texarkana TX; Davisburg MI; Sparta MI. Out of all those rodeos, only the last three were outdoors.

I was fighting bulls and doing comedy with Longhorn for about twenty years. Every year I had to have a new act, which had to fit that year's production, so it was a challenge. That's one reason I have so many acts. Most clowns don't have as many as I do – they mostly use the same three or four over and over again and can do that because they're working different rodeos. I had over seventy-five performances with that one rodeo company every year, so I had to build a lot of acts. Fortunately I liked that because I liked change and looked forward to doing something different every year.

Longhorn got so big that Bruce was too busy to announce the shows, so he hired a fellow from Florida named Jerry Belles to take that over. Jerry had been a bull rider, so he knew rodeo. He also had a really smooth voice, so he had kind of a calming effect.

Jerry and I clicked immediately, mostly because of our ad-libs. We were really sharp together. He'd pop off something to me and I'd pop off something right back at him. I tell all the announcers who work with me that I'm the kid in class that can't behave. They have to be constantly saying, "Lecile! Don't say that! Don't do that!" Jerry loved to play that teacher role and I loved to play the kid that he always had to fuss at, so we worked really well together.

THURMAN MULLINS

Thurman Mullins is the manager of Charlie Daniels' Twin Pines Ranch in Lebanon, Tennessee. The last time I talked to Thurman, he told me that he had gone to buy a fertilizer spreader at an equipment auction but came home instead with a fifty-thousand-pound train caboose. As far as I know, Charlie still doesn't have a fertilizer spreader for the ranch.

In 1996 or so, Thurman was visiting with Donnie Gay, the eight-time world champion bull rider, and Baxter Black, the famous cowboy poet. Thurman said he wasn't a very good bull rider and told them about a bull named Showboat that he tried to ride at a Longhorn rodeo in 1971. Baxter asked him if he could make a poem out of it, which resulted in "Two Jumps."

"TWO JUMPS" BY BAXTER BLACK

Two Jumps said he used to ride bulls. In spite of his name, he tried.
He had grit, determination, and bravado on his side.

Unfortunately, he lacked skill. He was naturally inept
And as life laid down her cowpies, that's precisely where he stepped.

But even a hard luck cowboy's entitled to one guru
Whose faith in him is undaunted, whose loyalty stays true blue.

Now, all of the young bronc stompers and bullriders knew Lecile.
A rodeo clown and hero to all who strapped on the steel.

Lecile knew the bulls and broncs and always offered advice
On rodeo, on love and life, on learnin' to sacrifice.

It was over at the chutes at Knoxville when Two Jumps heard the phrase
That would stay with him forever, long after those heady days.

Lecile was walkin' toward him. No doubt to wish him well.
Two Jumps cut eyes at his pardners to make sure they all could tell

It was <u>him</u> Lecile had chosen to pass along for this ride
The words he was meant to live by. He fairly bursted with pride.

Two Jumps was pullin' his bullrope, the rosin startin' to smoke
When Lecile looked over the chute gate, squinted his eyes, then he spoke.

"Two Jumps," Lecile confided, "to really make yourself proud,
Ain't no way you can ride this bull...so hang up and thrill the crowd!"

BOBBY AND LENORA ROWE

Bobby and Lenora Rowe were a husband-and-wife team that worked for Longhorn. Bobby was an outstanding saddle bronc rider, and in fact was the IRA world champion at one time.

He was the arena director of the Longhorn show, and he was very talented at that also. Later on he started his own rodeo company, Imperial Rodeo, which was a very successful company.

Lenora, Bobby's wife, was an outstanding horse trainer, and she was the embodiment of class in a performer. She was extremely talented, good looking, and had a great presence in the arena. Backstage, though, she was just another one of the hands. If you saw her during the day, she'd be grooming horses or doing any other cowgirl work that needed to be done. Lenora could also blow her nose the cowboy way. She'd take a finger, stop up one side of her nose, and blow. Then she'd stop up the other side and blow.

We were in Greenville, South Carolina one year, waiting around during the performance. Lenora was all dolled up and ready to go in and do her thing. When they called for her, she took a finger and stopped up one nostril and blew, and then she did the same with the other. Then she went out into the arena.

Lenora did her act, put her finger in the air to really sell the finish, and got a standing ovation. I saw that and thought to myself, this lady is so classy that she can take the same finger she blew her nose with and use it to get a standing ovation. To me, that was the ultimate.

MUSIC IN MY ACTS

I began incorporating music into my acts during this time with Longhorn. I was really into music because I played music, so many of my acts, even the spotlight ones, had music in them. I might not say a word through the whole act, but there would be a theme song all the way through it. One of my favorite songs to use was "The Pink Panther Theme," because I loved the groove and loved that character's slinky moves, which I incorporated into my physical comedy. After a few years of using that, a musician for a band that was working with the rodeo wrote a song for me called "Lecile's Blues." It had that same kind of feel, but a more relaxed tempo, and it just slowed me up and made me work a little more.

In the '50s and '60s, all you had was a record player for music, and it was just a mess to work with. Somebody had to put the records on there and, at a certain time, had to put the needle down in the right spot. Making things even worse, the record player was usually on the announcer's stand, which was usually by the bull chutes, so it was always bumping and moving and making the record scratch and skip.

I was really able to incorporate music and sound effects into my act when I finally got a cart machine. It was a tape deck that took these big cartridges, like they used to use for commercials in radio stations. I would take the cartridges to the recording studio, put whatever sound effects and music I wanted on there, and mix that with my verbal comedy live in the arena. Jerry's wife, Jeanne, would operate the cart machine for me. On my cues, she would punch the button to make it play. After it ran its course and stopped, she'd do that again at the next cue.

GOING WIRELESS

The cart machine was a huge leap in technology, but the wireless microphone is what really opened things up for me. Before the wireless mikes, the rodeo announcer had to repeat every line of a joke to the audience, because he had the microphone on the announcer's stand and that's the only way the crowd could hear the comedy. It took a long time to get through a joke, and even though the announcers had great voices, they couldn't tell the jokes as well as a clown could. So I started experimenting with the wireless mikes and, as far as I know, I was the first clown to use them.

I asked Bruce if I could try one, because he liked to keep a pretty tight rein on things, and he said I could. The first place I ever used one was in Detroit. We were in a coliseum on the fairgrounds, and right down the road from it was a beer joint. I was out there in the middle of the arena doing a bit and it was going pretty well, when all of a sudden we all started hearing a whole bunch of cussing and something about the Germans and Italians trying to kill each other. Come to find out, these two groups of drunks had gotten mixed up at the bar, and of course the police were called. The problem was that the signal from my wireless mike to the base that was hooked to the house wasn't as strong as the signals from the police radios in the cars that were responding to the fight. It caught me off guard, but I finally got the thing turned off and then recovered as best I could. When I walked out of the arena, Bruce told me to take it off and leave it off. It took a while for me to be able to talk him into trying one again. I had to wait until they became stronger and more reliable, but once they did, I think I was the first to mix all that together.

I have a pretty good repertoire of acts – about twenty that I do regularly – but I'm also known for my walking and talking. I tell little stories, make witty comments, and banter with the announcer. I do that because rodeo is made up of all kinds of cracks and crevices, which are lulls in the action when maybe somebody's having trouble getting down on a bull, or a bulldogger can't get back in the box. I watch and see about how long I think they'll be involved with all that, and then I try to do a little piece of comedy to entertain the people and take their minds off of whatever's going on. I try to glue together all those cracks and crevices without smearing glue all over the rodeo.

Whenever I'm asked about my comedy, I always say, "You do everything big." Your moves and props all have to be exaggerated. If it's a firecracker, it's as big around as a stick of firewood. If it's a shotgun, it's as long as a broom. So as the rodeo got bigger, so did my acts.

SPOTLIGHT ACT

The spotlight act was the first really elaborate one I came up with. Longhorn was doing a lot of indoor arenas and stadiums, and they used the lighting systems to great effect. I wanted to build an act around that, so I elaborated on something I had seen Emmett Kelly do with Ringling Brothers. I thought he was so great. It was a mime act, and it had to do with sweeping the spotlights up and doing things with them. We'd have a dark house with a spotlight about six feet across that I'd sweep up into a "pile" until it was about a foot across. Then I'd swat it with my broom, and it'd splatter back out to its original size. I'd sweep it up, swat it, and then they'd take four spotlights to make four little spots on the ground. Finally I'd sweep them into a pile again and into my sack. I had a flashlight in there, so when I reached down to pick up the sack, I'd switch on that light and throw the sack over my shoulder. They'd cut all the spotlights, so all the crowd saw when I walked out of the arena was that little light glowing through my sack. It was really complicated, but Longhorn carried their own lighting crew, so we all worked together really well. Jeanne Belles, the spotlight caller, would call the spots and get the operators to do what I wanted to do. They were all used to working with me, so we were tight.

MISSION IMPOSSIBLE ACT

The next act I came up with was one I called "Mission Impossible," which was obviously inspired by the TV show. This act also made extensive use of the spotlights. The announcer would say, "Mr. Harris, your assignment is to recover a stolen diamond. In ten seconds, this tape will self-destruct." The tape would blow up and I'd wander around until I found this "safe," which was a box big enough for a person to squat down in. I'd get a clown buddy to hunker down in it with this big "diamond," which was the size of a basketball. I used mirrors to create facets, so when the spotlight hit them, it would glitter like one of those disco balls. I'd be messing around with something and my buddy would get out and run off with the diamond. Then the safe would blow up in my face.

When I was at home building "Mission Impossible" with Butch Berry, a buddy of mine that fought bulls with me, I was using a dull old circular saw to cut some plywood. It kept getting stuck, and when it did, I'd have to reach down and grab the guard to pull it back. I did that all the time with no problem, but this particular time I grabbed the blade and it cut two of my fingers off. It cut clear through the bones so that there was just some skin holding them on. I flipped them back over and folded my hand so they'd stay on such as they were, and Butch and my wife and I all headed out to the doctor. We got in to see him, and when I opened up my hand and these fingers just kind of fell out, he said, "That's way too much for me." He then told us to go straight to the hospital, so we got back in the car with Ethel driving. We never should have let her drive, because she doesn't do very well in these situations, and I was feeling like I needed to get to the hospital pretty quick.

Ethel missed a turn on the way into Memphis and we ended up in this historic area with a lot of nice homes. I just leaned back in my seat and tried to be cool with it so as not to excite her, but I kept hearing her point out all the sights for Butch. "This over here is so-and-so's house, but it used to be so-and-so's." She was doing a tour guide kind of thing while my fingers were just about to fall off, so I finally said, "Stop the damn tour deal and get me to the hospital." I didn't learn until later that she was lost, but she didn't want me to know that, so the tour was her way to keep me from getting excited.

We finally got to the emergency room, and by that time my hand was really hurting. They took me back and put me up on this slab, and the doctor came in and asked me what I did for a living. I knew then what was fixing to happen: he was just going to snip that skin and cut my fingers on off if I told him I was a clown. So I told him I was a concert piano player.

When he heard that, he got on the intercom and called a nerve doctor, a bone doctor, a meat doctor, and the whole bunch. The room was just full of doctors. They didn't put me all the way out when they started on me, because the nerve guy was putting the different nerves back together and tugging on my fingers and asking me if I felt it as they did that. Then the bone and meat guys did their thing until they finally had my fingers all put back together.

When I was in recovery the next morning, a doctor who I'd known for years and had put me together many, many times came in to see me. He asked the other doctor what had happened, and they walked out of the room and visited there for a minute.

Later that afternoon the emergency doctor came in and asked me how I was doing. I told him I didn't think my hand was doing very good. He asked, "Well, do you think you'll be able to play piano when you get healed?"

"I don't really know. We'll just have to see."

"I know you won't, by God, because you sure couldn't play one before you came in here. I guess you know I know who you are and what you do for a living. You're a damn clown. You know, that's pretty damn bad to tell a lie like that."

"Look, you were standing there with a pair of scissors looking at my fingers. Do you think I was going to tell you I'm a clown?"

He finally admitted that he really was just going to snip the skin and cut my fingers all the way off. The doctor that told him what I really did for a living, until the day he died, reminded me of that story every time I saw him.

MOSQUITO ACT

I had a mosquito act in the early seventies that made good use of the cart machine. I'd go out into the arena and lie down and try to go to sleep, but this mosquito would start buzzing around and keep worrying me. I'd swat at him, he'd zip away, and then he'd slip back up on me. Finally I could see where he lit, so I'd take my hat and slam it down on him. Then I'd pull a great big firecracker out of a burlap sack. This firecracker was as big around as my leg, and I'd take it over to the hat to blow it and the mosquito up. I'd light the fuse, run and hide, and the fuse would burn until it fizzled out. I did this two or three times trying to figure out what was wrong with it, so I'd pick it up and shake it and look all bumfuzzled. Inside the firecracker was a twelve-gauge shotgun, and after I shook it a few times, I'd pull the trigger to make the shell explode.

This act was so rank that I got to where I dreaded setting the gun off. I never knew how exactly it would blow up, so I just tried to stay behind it when I blew the firecracker up and made a big commotion. Then the mosquito would laugh at me because he had escaped once again. I'd sit straight up in disbelief, they'd kill the spotlight, and that was the act.

The sound effects for this act were great. My son, Matt, and I went into the recording studio to get the mosquito sounds. He played trombone in school, and we found out how to make it buzz like a mosquito. He got the mouthpiece and put a length of rubber hose on it like the EMTs wrap around your arm. He'd blow on that and get that *bzzzzz* sound. One time we couldn't get the sound quite right, so we drained all the water out of the commode in the studio and stuck the tube down there with a microphone so we could get it just like we wanted it.

GOLF ACT

The next act I came up with was also in the seventies. They were beginning to show a lot of golf on TV and everybody was talking about it, so I figured that would be a popular one. I knew nothing whatsoever about golf, so I asked Donnie Gay, the eight-time world champion bull rider, if I could go out with him and his buddies to watch them play and learn about the game. I wanted to pick up on the terminology and rules and figure out enough to build a comedy act. I was spraying balls all over the course, but Donnie was a good golfer, so somewhere on the first few holes he made a birdie. By the end of the day, he had made three birdies and I wasn't hitting them any straighter than I had to begin with, but I was so enthralled with golf that I went up to the clubhouse and bought the set of clubs I had rented to play with that day.

The very next week I was playing with somebody else, and I made the comment that I had played with Donnie Gay recently. "By the way, he got three buzzards during our game."

"He got what?"

"Three buzzards."

"What's that?"

"I'm not sure, but evidently it's when you get one less thing than you're supposed to, or something like that."

Well, it got back to Donnie that he had made three buzzards in a game and to this day, every time I see Donnie, he'll ask, "Have you played any golf and made any buzzards lately?"

Of course I had to make the props bigger for my act because you do everything big in comedy. At that time, the Champion Golf Bag factory was in Collierville, so I told them I'd advertise their business if they made me a great big bag. Bobby Ballard, my friend from high school, was a chemist, and he helped me make the huge fiberglass clubs that I still use today. They were also experimenting with plastics to make bowling balls, so I used one of their molds to pour my great big golf ball. I still love to do this act.

I was doing a rodeo in Brawley, California with a bullfighter named Shorty Gorham. The golf act requires a "popcorn salesman," so I recruited Shorty to help me out. The popcorn salesman is up in the stands doing his thing, and every time I go to hit the ball, he yells "POPCORN!" and interrupts my backswing. I finally get tired of it and go over to him and knock all his popcorn out of the boxes.

Before we did the act that first night at Brawley, I took a bunch of popcorn boxes to the concession stand and asked them to fill those up. I told them I didn't care where the popcorn came from since nobody was going to eat it, so they just swept a bunch up off the floor and gave that to me.

We did the act, Shorty played the popcorn salesman to perfection, and everybody loved it. After the rodeo, Shorty came up to me and said, "You know, Lecile, I could've sold a lot of that popcorn. They were offering me all kinds of money for it." That was pretty common: people would try to buy it and then they'd get mad when whoever it was wouldn't sell it. I told Shorty, "You can't do that. Number one, we need it for the next act. Number two, they swept it up right off the floor, so it's nasty.

When we did the act the next night, Shorty yelled "POPCORN!" during my backswings just like he was supposed to do. I walked over to the stands after the third time to slap the tray out of his hand, but he didn't have a single box. I looked at him and asked, "Shorty, where's all the popcorn?"

"I sold it."

There was nothing I could do at that point except knock the empty tray out of his hand, so I did that and went back out and finished the act. After the rodeo, I went up to him and said, "Shorty, I can't believe you sold all the popcorn! You know we need it for the act, and I told you how nasty it was!"

Shorty said, "They gave me $10 a box for that popcorn." He had been carrying twelve boxes, so that was $120. I was pretty upset about it, though, so I kept on hollering at him. When I finally quit, he asked, "If I give you half the money, will you get off my back?" I agreed, but I never did get my half.

FLYING HAT ACT

My favorite rodeo clown was Dudley Gaudin, "The Kajun Kidd." Dudley also happened to be a buddy of mine, and he had a flying hat act that was just great. I had loaned him my golf act to finish his career with, so when he retired, he gave me his flying hat act. He drew a diagram of the act on a paper sack, signed his name, and wrote "I give this act to Lecile."

Nobody could figure out the flying hat, but it was really very simple. I had a thread tied from the top of the coliseum down to the fence that went around the arena. As I was walking and talking during the bit, I'd go over there casually and take that thread and attach it to my hat. Then I'd talk about having a trained hat, and I'd just sling it. Naturally it'd just ride that thread out there and come right back to me. The other clowns would say they could do it, but when they slung their hats, they just hit the ground, of course. Finally one of them would say something about it being all in my hat, so I'd unhook it real quick and hand it to them, and of course it hit the ground when they slung it. Then I'd bet them I could do it again, and when I slung it, they'd shoot it with a shotgun and it'd fall right to the ground because I'd unhooked it.

Nobody could figure this act out because nobody thought I'd go to the trouble of climbing to the top of the coliseum, going out on the catwalk, and running a thread down. This clown that was working the act with me one time hadn't seen me set it up like that, so he wanted to know how I did it.

I told him, "I have a hat with a magnet in it. Then I have a receiver that picks up this magnet and it's electrified so it attracts the magnet." Then I'd point to something up in the stands. It could be a little box, a panel, anything. "All these buildings are different sizes, so I have to come out the day before and adjust the power so it ends up in the right place back to me."

"OK, but what makes it go way out and come back?"

"Well, I have a guy in the stands with a little box. It has an antenna on it, and he uses that to control the power. He turns it off to make it fall or turns it on to make it come back to me." I was telling him all this during a performance, and I pointed to a guy up in the stands with a transistor radio, who was probably listening to a ballgame or something. "You see that guy? There he is."

He took all that in, and after the rodeo he came up to me and said, "I've been watching that guy. He'll pull the antenna out and push it back in. Then he'll twist the knobs on the box. Now I see how you do it." He believed that for a long time, until I finally told him years later how it worked. Then he didn't believe me because he wanted to believe the magnet story.

CRAWLING HAT ACT

I also had a crawling hat act. Every time I'd go over to the hat and try to pick it up, it would move away. I'd say, "A bug's got my hat. There's some of the biggest bugs here in Mississippi that I've ever seen!" I'd keep trying to pick it up until finally I'd get so mad at it that I'd shoot it with my shotgun and it would blow up. Then I'd go over and lift it up and there would be a giant pair of women's bloomers under there. The announcer would ask me what kind of bug it was, and I'd say, "It was a ladybug!"

Some of the cowboys would see this act week in and week out and they never could figure out what in the world made it work. One time I was down in Louisiana and they brought a busload of special-needs children to see the rodeo. I did the crawling hat act, and after it was all over, one of the little kids from the special-needs school called me over to the fence and said, "Hey, Mr. Clown, I know how you did that." I asked him how I did it, and sure enough, he told me exactly how it was done.

TOUCH OF CLASS ACT

One of the last acts I built with Longhorn is called "Touch of Class." It's a classic. Jerry, the announcer, and his wife, Jeanne, the lighting and sound coordinator, were on the road one night going somewhere. They were just talking, trying to keep each other awake, and they came up with this idea. "Wouldn't it be really funny if Lecile could somehow be involved with an opera singer?" So they wrote it out on a napkin and kind of sketched it together. The next time they saw me, they told me they had an act for me, and I just took it from there.

My wife's mother, Frances, who we called Fanny, was an opera singer, so I got her in the studio to record the vocal "O Solo Mio." She must have been close to seventy years old then, but she still had a strong voice. When it came time to tape it, I told her, "Fanny, I want you to just back up and blare it really strong." She sounded so good on that take that for the next one I grabbed her by the shoulders and shook her to make her voice waver. Then it was just what I wanted. Every time I do "Touch of Class," I think of Fanny. To me, it's my top act.

Matt and I were doing "Touch of Class" one night in front of a sold-out crowd. In this act, Matt plays the opera singer, so he dresses up in a woman's outfit. At the end of the act, I went to get a hold of his skirt and jerk it off like I always did, but this time he grabbed it by the waistband and said, "No. You can't."

"Why not?"

"I don't have any underwear on."

"Nothing?"

"Nothing."

Come to find out, we had been on the road so long that he ran out of underwear, so he took it all, including the pair he had been wearing, to a fluff-n-fold place. By the time we went around to pick it up, they had closed, and he forgot he was still going commando for the act. I started to snatch his skirt off anyway so he wouldn't ever forget his underwear again, but I decided to let him get out of there with a little dignity that time.

Matt could really look like a woman because he has good bone structure, and a little bit of skillfully applied makeup can really do wonders. He was all dressed up another time for that act, and right before we went on, he had to go to the bathroom. He naturally just went to the men's and walked up to a urinal between these two guys, which cleared them out right quick. Matt was all dressed up like the lady opera singer, so he slung his gown over his shoulder and went about his business. Out of the corner of his eye he saw a guy looking all nervous down at the urinal on the end, so he just turned to him and said, "What's the matter, haven't you ever seen a woman use one of these before?"

THE CLOWN'S TAKIN' A SHIT!

We were doing a performance for a packed house in Texas one night when all of a sudden I had to go to the bathroom pretty bad, so I went over to the Port-A-Potties they had set up behind the stands. The only one that was open didn't have a latch on it, but I couldn't worry about that since I had to go so bad. This was a big job, so I sat down and commenced to do my business. I was just about to wrap it up when this kid opened the door and hollered, "Hey y'all, the clown's takin' a shit!" I couldn't reach the door, so everybody in the stands turned around and looked at me sitting there with my pants around my ankles. I didn't know what else to do, so I just tipped my hat, gave a little wave, and finished the paperwork.

A LITTLE ABOUT BULLS

I was still fighting bulls while I was with Longhorn and developing all these acts. Since I had been fighting bulls for quite a while by then, I was much further along with that than I was with my comedy. So I would sweat my acts. What I mean by that is I would think about them and worry about them. The order of the rodeo events worked out well for me, though, because bull riding is always at the end of a rodeo. Therefore, by the time I was done with the comedy and it was time for the bull riding, I was like, "Wow, that's done!" Then I was relaxed and warmed up and ready to fight bulls.

You never know what's in a bull's mind. There are some bulls that normally won't go after you, but you can never depend on that. If they've got balls, they're liable to get you.

A friend of mine had a bull that he raised from a calf. I saw it the last time I was up at his place, and it probably weighed close to two thousand pounds. My friend would go in the pen with him, scratch his back, feed him out of his hand, and pet him just like he was a puppy.

A couple of weeks after that he called me and said, "Boy, I sure have a lot more respect now for what you bullfighters do for a living." When I asked him why, he said that this supposedly friendly bull had run him over. While this guy was in the pen working on a gate, the bull came out of nowhere, rolled him up right under a truck, and still tried to get him.

Bulls are smarter than most people give them credit for, and there's no way you can make a bull fight or buck if he doesn't want to. The flank strap is just a cue to let him know it's time to buck. It doesn't hurt them, because a bull isn't going to buck if he's hurting. Putting the flank strap on a bull is like putting gloves on a boxer and saying, "OK, the bell's about to ring."

The bulls are babied. Every rodeo association has very strict rules about their treatment. For instance, the rules say that the clown barrel has to have padding on the outside of it to keep from hurting the bull if he hits it. There's no rule saying the barrel has to have padding on the inside to keep the clown from getting hurt. Also, there are veterinarians on call 24 hours a day and present at every performance. The animals are on an athletic diet that consists of mostly protein, so they get big with muscle but not fat. They get vitamins in their water; you and I don't get that, but they do. These bulls are pampered because they're very expensive. Some of them are worth over $50,000, so they're not going to be abused in any way.

If there's such a thing as reincarnation, I want to come back as a bull – either a good bucking bull or a good breeding bull. A bucking bull bucks eight seconds a day at the most, one or two times a week; the rest of the time he's eating. And a breeding bull, well, we know what they're doing; that ain't a bad life at all.

A STORY BY RONNY SPARKS

Lecile's bull savvy is the best I've ever known. He always told me, "Put 'em in your pocket. Whatever you get done with him, you can't jump him." Lecile could also straight up tell you how to fight just about any bull in particular.

It was 1989 and we were at the Dixie Nationals. I drew 801, Nightmare on Elm Street, which belonged to Harper and Morgan. When I asked Lecile how I could fight the bull, he said, "Set the barrel about halfway down the pen. That's where you need to be, but don't try to jump him. He's gonna come out and blow right by you. When he bounces off the calf-roping boxes, he's ready to fight." And he did exactly that.

I got a bunch of good stuff done for the first thirty-five seconds or so. I did some fakes and good rounds, but then he left me. I figured that was a good time to jump him and get out, so when he spun around and headed back to me, I took off into the air. When I left the ground, he stopped and backed up, so I landed right on top of his head and stayed there long enough for Tommy Evans to take a picture. When I pivoted off the bull's horn and hit the ground, he hooked me and threw me. I got up, but he hit me a second time and spun me around pretty good. After he hit me a third time and knocked me down, I was trying to get up and he hit me in my right arm and broke it right in the elbow. The fight was over.

I walked out the side gate holding my arm, where Lecile was leaned up against the fence. All I heard him say as I went by was, "Kid, I said you couldn't jump him."

Lecile always told my brother Donny and me that watching us fight bulls was almost like watching himself, which is about as good a compliment as a bullfighter could get.

WHITE LIGHTNING

Longhorn leased most of their bulls from Sloan Williams, who had a heck of a set of bulls. Some of them that I remember were Rocket 88, Slim Jim, Short Stack, Rodeo Red, Grasshopper, Zulu, White Lightning, and Cream Puff.

Longhorn was interested in putting on a big show, and White Lightning played right into that. He was a big, pretty, white Brahma bull with great big horns. At the start of the bull riding they'd kill the lights, throw the spotlights on one chute, and introduce him. They'd start this really powerful music, swing that gate open, and White Lightning would strut right out. He'd paw the ground, snort, and really set the stage for the show.

CREAM PUFF

Cream Puff gave me a lot of trouble. He only had one horn, but he hooked me with it a lot. Most bullfighters will naturally go to the muley side to stay away from that horn. A one-horned bull figures that out after a while, so he's ready for it. For that reason I always went to the horn side, just to throw him off a little bit. That also gave me something to grab a hold of. If I needed to get away, I could push off of it. If I needed to get behind him, I could pull on it. But believe me, a one-horned bull knows he doesn't have but one horn, and he knows exactly where it is at all times.

A STORY BY DONNY SPARKS

It was my rookie year and we were at the Old Fort Days Rodeo in Fort Smith, Arkansas. Harry Vold had provided the fighting bulls and it was the last day of the Wrangler Bullfight. I was feeling sick that day, so I sent Daddy in to see who I had drawn. He came back and told me I had drawn Crooked Nose, which was a one-horned bull that hooked just about everybody who tried to get by him.

I went to Lecile's dressing room, told him I had drawn Crooked Nose, and asked him what I should do. Lecile said, "Everybody who gets hooked always goes to his muley side. You need to go to his horned side. I'd fake him real hard to his muley side, go to his horned side, and see what happens." I heard that advice and figured I'd be a dead man, but I thought I'd try it anyway.

When I called for Crooked Nose, he came roaring out and blew right by me. He didn't stop until he got to the third barrel, and then he whirled around and headed right for me. I stood there as long as I could, gave a hard fake to his muley side, and then went to his horned side. When I did that, he just sort of fell over on his side. On the strength of that move, I ended up winning the round that night. I drew him twice more that year — once at the Wrangler Bullfight in Billings and once at the National Finals — and I won those rounds with him too. Crooked Nose was a famous bull that ended up in the Hall of Fame, and I credit Lecile with helping me to figure out how to fight him.

We were at Fort Smith another time when Lecile walked up to me and asked how I was feeling before I went out to fight bulls.

I said, "I feel good, nice and relaxed."

"Relaxed?!? You need to get your motor runnin'!"

When I asked Lecile how I could do that, he took his open hands and slapped me across the face five or six times. That really got my motor runnin', and I went out and won the round that night. It became our little ritual such that every time he saw me, he'd give me a good slap or two before I went out, just to get my motor runnin'!

Lecile has been a great mentor and friend to myself and many others in the rodeo world.

PLAYBOY AND THE DETROIT WRECK

There was a muley bull called Playboy that was a bad little bull. A muley bull doesn't have any horns, and they were harder to fight than horned bulls because you didn't have anything to grab hold of. Their head was really slick, so if you tried to get your hand on it, they'd be up under your arm and into your ribs before you knew it. They'd also get you down on the ground and try to mash you paper-thin. They had no horns to stop them, so they'd just mash and mash and mash. I've even seen them drop down on their front knees and lie down on you and mash you. Playboy was a master of all these techniques.

One night in Detroit, Glen Bird, the IRA champion bull rider from Weatherford, Texas, drew Playboy. Glen rode him the full eight seconds and when I got him off, Playboy turned me around some kind of way and threw me straight up into the air. I turned halfway over on the way down, so Playboy waited on me until I got just right and popped me in the back just like a ping-pong ball. He broke five transverses in my back, although I didn't know it at the time. I couldn't get up, but I had propped myself up on my arms and I saw Playboy coming back. He was about to tear my head off, and there was nothing I could do about it.

One of the pickup men was Butch Bond. He was a hell of a cowboy, and he could some kind of rope. Just before Playboy tore my head off, I saw this loop go over his head, and Butch dallied. That means he roped him and took off the other way, which pulled the bull off center just enough that he passed right by me. Had he not done that, Playboy would have hit me head-on, and that would have been the end of Lecile.

You really don't have much time to think when something like that's going on. About all you can think is, "Damn, this is gonna hurt," because it all happens so fast. From the time Playboy picked me up and threw me in the air until I flipped and came back down seemed like forever. But when you're on the ground and something's happening, it's like the blink of an eye. Some people say if a bull gets you down, you should just lie there and play dead until he stops. That's bullcrap! You don't ever quit fighting. You don't ever quit trying to get out.

I never experienced my life flashing in front of my eyes or anything like that because I was too busy noticing everything and trying to get out. I could see little details like the hair on his leg and the dirt between his hooves. When I was a boxer, I was taught to concentrate on what I was going to hit, so when I squared off with somebody, I'd pick out something like a pimple on their nose. Then I'd focus on that and just wallop it. So I applied that training whenever I got run over. I'd focus on a knee and push, or lock onto a horn and pull, or do whatever I could to get out from under a bull. When one gets you down, the really scary part is wondering what they're going to do to you before you get up.

My traveling buddy at the time was George Taylor. The ambulance came to get me, so George hopped up front and we headed to the hospital. They had the siren screaming as we went wide open down Woodward Avenue in Detroit on a Saturday night. The EMT in the back with me told me we were almost to the hospital, when all of a sudden we pulled over on the side of the road, turned the siren off, and stopped. We didn't know what was going on, so after a minute the guy attending to me slid the little window to the cab back and asked why we were stopped. The driver turned around and said, "This guy riding up here with me wanted to stop for some donuts." My EMT couldn't believe it, but the driver said, "Yeah, he knew it was going to be a long night and he was hungry so he wasn't going to have nothing to eat." George came on out pretty directly with two dozen donuts and off we went, speeding the rest of the way to the hospital.

When we got to the ER on that Saturday night in Detroit, there was every kind of wreck imaginable in the waiting room. People in there had been whipped with chains, cut, stabbed, shot, you name it. That place was packed. They got me on in quick though because they thought my back was broken pretty bad.

George and I were the only ones in the examining room for a while, so we got into the donuts. He ate a half-dozen and I ate a half-dozen. They finally came in, did some X-rays, and left again. So we split another dozen donuts. Finally they came and told me I had five broken transverses, so they were going to have to admit me.

I shared a room with a guy who they had found in a bathtub in a motel somewhere. He had gotten it pretty bad, with a broken arm, two broken legs, and a bunch of broken ribs. He seemed to just sleep most of the time.

Later that morning a nurse came in with a little cup of orange juice. I asked her when I was going to get breakfast, and she told me that was my breakfast. I couldn't have any solid foods because they didn't yet know the extent of my internal injuries. I told her I had already eaten a dozen donuts, so obviously this wasn't going to be a problem if I had a proper breakfast, but she said she couldn't do that.

By noon, I was starving. For lunch they brought me a bowl of imitation split-pea soup. It wasn't even real – it was imitation. I told them I really had to have something more than that, but they wouldn't budge. Eventually I noticed that the guy over there next to me wasn't eating. They'd bring him full meals, but he didn't eat them because he just came to every now and then for just a minute. His meals sat on his little rolling table a few feet out of my reach, and they looked good. Since I was in traction, they had this four-foot long metal rod with a hook on the end of it that I could use to hook to the bars and pull myself up if I needed to. I took that hook, snagged his table, pulled it over to me, and ate his lunch. When I was done, I pushed his table back over so nobody was the wiser.

That went on for two days, with me getting every meal of his. His plate would always be clean, so they thought he was doing good. They'd come in and see that he wasn't awake, but I'd say, "Oh yeah, he comes to and eats and then he goes back to sleep." So I guess this guy probably almost starved to death while I was there.

Evel Knievel had tried to jump a bunch of buses somewhere in Detroit, but he missed and busted up his collarbone. He was on the same floor as I was, so the newspaper sent somebody down to interview us. The reporter told each of us what had happened to the other, and the headline in the paper the next day read: "They Each Say the Other's Crazy."

I kept telling the doctor that I needed to go because I had to get to Milwaukee for the next rodeo. He wasn't having any of it at first, but he finally told me that if I could get up and walk down to the checkout desk and back, then I could leave. George helped me up in the bed, but when I sat up, I passed out. He got me up again kind of halfway standing, but I passed right back out on the bed as soon as my feet hit the floor. Obviously this wasn't working, but I told him I felt like I could do it if I had some kind of back brace. So George went down to the nurses' station and asked for one, but they wouldn't give him one because the doctor didn't order it. He ended up being gone for about a half hour before he came back with a brace. I asked where he got it and he said, "I stole it out of a stock room."

We put it on and it helped me stand up but I still couldn't walk. George said, "Let me go get another one. That room's full of them." He brought back another that was a hard plastic one, and we tightened it up over the first. I walked to the end of the bed and had to quit. "It's just not enough," I said. George thought it might help if we had another one, so he brought back a stretchy one that he pulled over the other two. That helped a lot, but I was still kind of losing my balance. The other guy in the room had a walker, so George took that and gave it to me too.

With all that, we gingerly walked down to the nurses' station and George said, "We're checking out." The nurse told me I couldn't because there was no paperwork to that effect, and I said, "Well, the doctor told me if I could walk up here to you then I could check out, so the papers have to be up here somewhere." When she said she didn't have them, George said, "Let me go back to the room and see if they're in there."

He left and didn't come back for a while, so I asked the nurse if she would please go down there and see what his problem was so he could come back and help me to my room. When she left, I slipped out and caught a freight elevator downstairs. A few minutes later, George met me in the lobby and took me out to his truck, and then we drove on to Milwaukee.

I fought bulls that weekend with those three braces. They'd spray me with the CO_2 fire extinguishers and freeze my back. I'd fight a couple of bulls until it started hurting again real bad, and then I'd go over to the fence, get sprayed again, and fight some more bulls.

Milwaukee was the end of that spring run, so that gave me a little time off. I needed it because I was having a lot of trouble with my transverses. They're these little wing-looking things that come off your spine, and if you break them and they float around, they'll really bother you. I was having a lot of trouble with mine, so I thought I was going to have to have an operation on my back, which I really dreaded.

One day my dad called me and told me to come down to his house. "I can't even straighten up to get out of the chair," he said. I don't know what had happened, but he was in a fix, and wanted me to take him to the chiropractor. I said, "Dad, I don't know if we need to do that or not. I don't think they do much good." But he insisted, so we went. They helped me get him out of the car, into a wheelchair, up a ramp, and into the office. I had been sitting in the waiting room for about thirty minutes when he came walking out ramrod straight. When I saw that, I said, "Somebody knows something I don't know."

I thought about it for a week and finally decided I'd go give that chiropractor a try. He looked at my back and told me if I got operated on, the chances of me doing the things afterwards that I currently did would be slim. I was in my early forties by then and had just started fighting bulls the way I wanted to fight them, so that wasn't a very good prognosis. But the doctor said, "Let me just try to straighten you out." And over the course of a few months, he did. I would not have been able to do anything without him. My back was such a mess that when he got through working on me, he hung before and after pictures of my spine up in the waiting room.

GEORGE TAYLOR

George Taylor was a traveling partner of mine during the Loretta years, and we argued all the time. We were both Type A personalities, so we just couldn't get along. In his mind he was always totally right about everything, while I thought I was, so we were always getting into arguments. Once we actually got into an argument about the proper way to fold a towel. To this day, I'll be helping Ethel do laundry and she'll say, "You're not folding that towel like George told you to do it."

George was from Cleburne, Texas, which is right outside of Fort Worth. He had comedy acts and was also a trick roper and barrel man. I had comedy acts and was a bullfighter. Most rodeos couldn't afford two guys with comedy acts, so for a long time we never worked together since we both did comedy. But Longhorn was big enough to hire two guys with acts, so George worked the barrel and I fought bulls.

George had some of the most irritating habits in the world. For instance, he had a little gap between his two front teeth that he spit through all the time. It didn't make any difference where he was. He could be in your house, your car, anywhere. Habits like that one just wore me out.

George was a terrible driver, so I drove most of the time, even if we were in his rig. One night we were on the interstate headed to Detroit and were just getting into town. He had been lying in the back seat asleep, but he woke up and climbed up front, where he started spitting on the floor.

I said, "George, stop spitting on the floor."

"It's my damn truck."

"I don't care whose truck it is. Stop spitting on the floor."

He kept on until I finally said, "George, if you spit on the floor again, I'm going to stop and put your ass out."

"Not out of my own truck, you tall son of a bitch!" He hardly ever called me Lecile. He was a little short shit, so he called me that instead of calling me by my name.

Well, it wasn't two minutes later until he spit on the floor again, so I pulled over to the side of the road and said, "Get out."

"I ain't gettin' out of my own truck!"

"You need to get out or I'm going to put you out – whatever you want to do." He knew I could whip his butt. I had stuck him up on the wall so many times where his feet weren't even touching the floor. So I got out, went around and opened the door, and asked, "Are you going to get out or do you want me to get you out?"

"I'll get out, you tall son of a bitch!"

When he did, I got back in, locked all the doors, and drove off. It was pitch dark and he was on the side of the interstate in Detroit, so I felt bad about it even though I was so mad. I pulled over after about a mile and figured I'd leave him back there until daylight, so I leaned my seat back to take a nap. After about an hour, I heard somebody beating on the window. "Hey, you tall son of a bitch! Let me in my truck!"

I rolled the window down about two inches and said, "I'll let you back in if you promise you won't spit on the floor anymore."

"I ain't gonna promise you nothin'! That's my truck!"

I rolled the window up and leaned my seat back again. In a minute he knocked on the window and said, "Okay, you tall son of a bitch, I won't spit on the floor no more." So I opened the door, he got in, and we drove on to the rodeo. Sure enough, he didn't spit on the floor again after that.

Later that year we were getting ready to overnight from Madison Square Garden to Jacksonville, Florida. We were leaving the arena and there was Billy Don Haynes hitchhiking on the sidewalk with his horse on a lead rope. Imagine that – hitchhiking with a horse in downtown New York. I knew Billy Don was going to Jacksonville too, so I told George we should pick him up and take him along with us. Of course George didn't want to, and we got into a big fight over it, but I gave in since it was his rig. We drove all the way through to Florida and never spoke a word; I mean not one word. When we pulled up to the coliseum in Jacksonville, there was Billy Don with his horse. He had caught a ride and beat us down there.

We worked that rodeo just like we did all the others, and our comedy never suffered as a result of our disagreements. We'd walk into the arena and have our usual dialogue that was sharp as ever. But when we walked out, we didn't speak again, even though we were staying in the same room.

We finished the rodeo and headed home. It was Thanksgiving, so we stopped somewhere to get turkey and dressing. He sat down across from me and said, "Happy Thanksgiving, you tall son of a bitch."

"Happy Thanksgiving, you little shit."

And that was all we said from Jacksonville to Collierville.

George and I shared a hotel room on the road. I was fighting bulls pretty heavy by then, and I stayed keyed up all the time. I often dreamed about fighting bulls, so I might go over and push George out of the bed or grab him to get him out of the way of a bull, all while I was sleepwalking.

One particular night we were staying in a little motel in Ada, Oklahoma. This place had a great big red and yellow neon sign out front that flashed all night long. It was also across from the fire station. I had finally gotten to sleep at some point after midnight when the fire trucks across the street cranked up. They wound their sirens up and floored it out of there, and of course they woke me up immediately. I was so startled and tired that I didn't really know what was going on, but I saw that red and yellow sign flickering through the curtains, so I thought the hotel was on fire.

I told George to get up and get out because the place was on fire, but he said he wasn't getting out of bed. I heard that and decided I was going to save his life. I got a chokehold on him and dragged him out of bed and out the door. We made a pretty big commotion on the way, so everybody in the motel came out to see what was going on. When we got to the parking lot, I was standing there in my underwear with him in a chokehold and he didn't have a stitch on. George didn't speak to me for a while after that.

We were working a rodeo together somewhere and I was doing a very simple act, so all I had for props was a broom and a burlap sack. George was working the barrel with me and doing a comedy routine himself, and he was also doing some trick roping, so he brought a horse, two mules, a miniature bulldog, a border collie, a basset hound, and a flock of ducks.

Somehow this rodeo got our checks mixed up. My check was in his envelope and his was in mine. He opened his envelope and saw what I made, and evidently it was more than he made. I don't know how much more, because I never saw his, but it wouldn't have mattered if it was just a dollar more. He flew off the handle and said, "I can't believe that. Here I am pulling a six-horse trailer with a horse, two mules, three dogs, and a flock of ducks. You've got a broom and a towsack and you make more than I do!" That made me mad, so I looked at him and said, "George, you can run up and down the road with a great big trailer and a horse, two mules, three dogs, and a flock of ducks, OR you can just have a broom, a burlap sack, and a little bit of talent." That really pissed him off because he was loaded with talent.

George was a talker. He could talk himself into a job, but he could also talk himself right out of one just as fast. He got crossways somehow with Bruce Lehrke, who ran Longhorn, and got fired, but then turned around and talked Bruce into hiring this barrel man that he had supposedly trained. George had found this guy back home in Texas and told him he'd get him a job with Longhorn for a percentage of what the new barrel man made. This guy didn't have a barrel, so of course George rented him his and made a little extra on top of his placement fee.

The first rodeo I was to work with this guy was in Asheville, North Carolina. I was sitting around with Bill McEnaney, who was a trick rider, the night before our first performance. He said, "You know, I'd like to learn to clown. Could I be your barrel man sometime?" I said sure, we could do that one day.

I was up early the next morning because a TV station had come out to film me fighting a bull around the barrel with the new barrel man. About a half hour before the crew came out, I went by his camper, knocked on the door, and told him to get up and get ready. I was headed off toward the building when all of a sudden I heard a huge explosion – *whomp!* When I turned around and looked to see what had happened, I saw that the door had been blown off the back of the camper and my barrel man was lying on the ground blistered from one end to the other on one side. Come to find out, the guy had fallen asleep with his propane heater on that night. The flame went out at some point, but the gas stayed on. When I woke him up and he lit his stove, all that gas ignited and blew him right through the camper door. He was burned so bad that we had to call the ambulance to come get him.

After we got him taken care of, I went over and knocked on Bill McEnaney's door. When he opened it up all half asleep and asked me what I wanted, I said, "Bill, remember last night how you told me you'd like to learn to be a barrel man one day? Well, you start this morning."

George and I used to do an act together called "Big Ball's in Cowtown." It was his act, but people identified us both with it. I wanted to do a version of it in later years, so I called him to see if he cared. I also asked him if I could have a copy of the tape of the song we used so I could re-record it and update it a little bit. He said he didn't care, but he told me he'd like to have a copy of it so he could use it with his new trick horse he was training. I told him that was a deal, and he said, "OK, I've got to go put a horse out on the exercise walker." It was a very civil telephone conversation, which was unusual for us. About an hour later, his wife called me and said, "George is dead. He came in from exercising his horse and fell over dead of a massive heart attack." When I heard that, I sure was glad our last talk had been a good one. I loved working with George. He was just hard to travel with.

SKIPPER VOSS

I used to fight bulls pretty often with a guy from Texas named Skipper Voss. Hulen Missildine and I were working a rodeo in Texarkana one year when Skipper and his traveling partner happened to be on their way to Wisconsin for a show, so they stopped in to see us.

After the rodeo, Skipper and his buddy went over to a beer joint in this area called The Pines, which was a place out in the country with nothing but pulpwooders and timber people, and they were a rough bunch. Skipper and his buddy had a beer or two before they got into a fight with some of that crowd, and Skipper got hit in the eye with a pool cue.

I had a camper that I slept in on the grounds of the arena. At about 1:30 in the morning, Skipper came around banging on my door. When I opened it, he said, "Lecile, I need some help. I boogered my head up and I need you to sew it up for me so I can get on up to Wisconsin and work." I looked at his head and saw that he was cut all the way across right under one eyebrow. It was so deep that his eyelid was just hanging there flopped over his eye.

I said, "Skipper, that's bad. You need to go see a doctor."

"Naw, naw, I don't have time to go to the doctor. You can sew it up for me."

I told him I didn't have anything to sew it up with except the black thread that I used in my flying hat act. "You don't want me to use that, because the thread is bigger and all I have to go with it is a great big carpet needle."

"I'm not leaving here until you sew it up."

"All right then, get a grip on something and hold tight."

I took that great big carpet needle and that coarse thread and sewed it up the best I could, with him hollering bloody murder the whole time. I actually did a pretty good job considering what I had to work with.

Skipper left that morning and went on to Wisconsin. I didn't see him again until a couple of weeks later when we were working another rodeo together. I asked him, "How's that eye?"

"Doing good. Why don't you look at it and tell me what you think?"

When I looked and saw that the stitches were still in it, I said, "Skipper, it's all grown together with the stitches still in there. Why didn't you get them taken out?"

"Well, I didn't want to pay anybody to do it. You didn't charge me anything to put them in, so I figured you'd also take them out for free."

"All right then, hold tight to something."

He hollered getting the stitches out almost as much as he did when I was putting them in. When I finally got done, he said, "I told everybody you sewed me up, but they all said it was such a good job that they didn't believe it was really you."

"Skipper, if they had heard you hollering at Texarkana when I put them in and hollering here when I pulled them out, then they would have damn sure known it was me that sewed you up."

CLOWN GROUND RULES

By the early eighties, I'd been working for Longhorn for almost twenty years, so Bruce Lehrke and I were close. We met every year in this particular restaurant in Mukwonago, Wisconsin to have breakfast and do the deals for the next season. As usual, Bruce and I ate and talked about the coming year and the money and all that, and I was looking forward to working with him as usual. I was just about to sign the contract when he said, "There's something else we need to talk about," and slid this little booklet across the table that said "Clown Ground Rules" on the front.

I asked him what that was all about, and he told me to read it. The first thing I saw was: "Everything that's said in the arena must be first approved by Bruce." I asked him if that meant I couldn't ad lib in the arena, and he said, "Nope, everything has to be approved by me before you can say it." That was the first rule, and after reading it, I never got through the rest of them. I said, "Bruce, I can't do this. You know me well enough to know that that's not me."

He told me to take the contract home with me and think about it. Like I'd always done, I had things going on during the week to tide me over in case something happened with the rodeoing. I worked for a company called Hancock Investments and was developing an exotic animal farm in Spring Creek, Tennessee. I had a Saturday Night Opera Barn with live radio shows. I had a couple of housing developments going, a printing company, a sign company, and Collierville's first answering service. I would do all that during the week, fly out for the weekend to do the rodeos, then fly back to my other businesses. I had so much going on that I thought maybe it was time to just get out of rodeo, so I quit.

Word got out pretty quick that I had quit, so a contractor with the Dodge City, Kansas rodeo called me and asked if I'd come work it. At that time you could only be in one association or the other: the IRA or the RCA. Since Longhorn was with the IRA, I didn't have an RCA card, but he told me not to worry about that. So about a month after I quit Longhorn, I worked my first RCA rodeo, and I've been there ever since.

The RCA was the Rodeo Cowboys Association. They later changed their name to PRCA – Professional Rodeo Cowboys Association – which I thought was extremely silly. Just because you hung a "P" on there doesn't mean you're professional. You show people that you're professional; you don't put it in your name. The IRA later added it to their name, becoming the IPRA – go figure!

My sister, Mary Jo Harris Wilson, my mother, Rubye Gray Jenkins Harris, and me – 1941.

Photo: Olan Mills.

My mom and dad, Rubye Gray Jenkins and Marvin Harris, when they were courting in Alabama.

Photographer unknown.

Bobby Ballard and me painting Maybelline, my first clown car and everyday ride – 1955.

Photo: Mary Jo Harris Wilson.

My first band, The Echoes (L-R John Wayne Garrison, Lewis Baker, Donald Garrison, Charles McOwen, me) – late 1950s.

Photo: Curtis Free.

Playing with The Capris – 1958.

Photographer unknown.

The Cisco Kid *really was* a friend of mine – early 1960s.

Photographer unknown.

Fighting Frank Harris' bull "Big Chief" – Fort Worth TX, 1960s.

Photographer unknown.

Fighting one of Clyde Crenshaw's bulls – 1960s.

Photo: Cimarron Studios.

Working with Roy Rogers – Washington DC, early 1970s.

Photographer unknown.

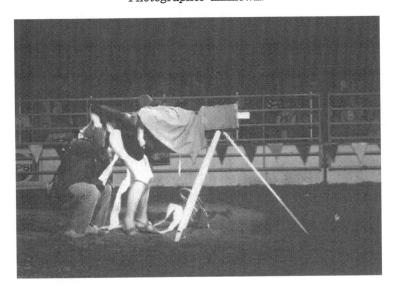

That's the darkest darkroom I ever stuck my head in.

Photographer unknown.

On the set of "Hee Haw" – 1972.

Photo: Moore Photos.

On the set of "Hee Haw" (L-R Jimmy Moore, Loretta Lynn, me, Sam Lovullo) – 1973.

Photo: Moore Photos.

Jumping one of Floyd Rumford's bulls – Kansas City MO, 1970s.

Photographer unknown.

Untying a bull rider at a Longhorn rodeo -1970s.

Photographer unknown.

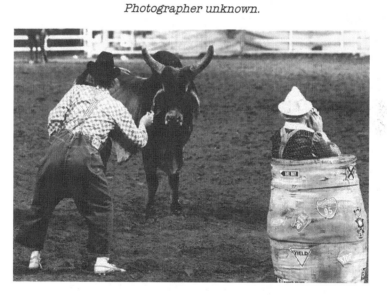

Dancing with a bull at the IPRA Finals - mid 1970s.

Photographer unknown.

Lecile Harris as "Pockmark" in W.W.
and The Dixie Dance Kings

Burt Reynolds and me on the set – 1975.

Photographer unknown.

Taking a break on the set of "Walking Tall – Final Chapter" with Bo
Svenson, the actor who played Buford Pusser – 1977.

Photographer unknown.

Loretta Lynn's twins, Patsy and Peggy.

Photographer unknown.

"Big Ball's in Cowtown" (L-R George Taylor, me, Hulen Missildine) –
Texarkana TX, late 1970s.

Photographer unknown.

Fighting a buffalo at the Ken Lance Arena – Ada OK, late 1970s.

Photo: Bush.

It's a tough job, but somebody has to do it.

Photographer unknown.

The Kajun Kidd and me.

Photographer unknown.

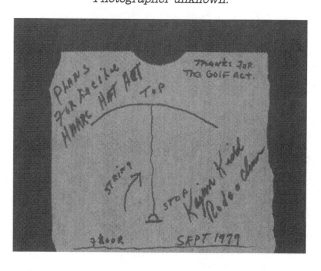

Kajun Kidd's flying hat act that he gave me in return for the golf act –
1979.

Buddy Martin and me untying a cowboy at a Longhorn Rodeo - 1980.

Photo: Tom Wodrich.

Longhorn Rodeo - early 1980s.

Photographer unknown.

Johnny Cash and me on the set of "The Last Days of Frank and Jessie
James – 1986.

Photographer unknown.

Bill McEnaney and me in the Mexican version of the shootout act.

Photo: Tom Wodrich.

Dancing with Harper & Morgan's "Red Nine" – Lake Charles LA, 1989.

Photographer unknown.

"Touch of Class" – 1990.

Photo: Tommy Evans.

The famous Wonder Brothers (L-R Benjie Barnes, me, Lamar Barnes, Bill Zeigler) – Montgomery AL.

Photographer unknown.

A great company of rodeo friends (L-R Jerry Diaz, Randy Corley, Hadley Barrett, me, Harry Vold, Matt Harris, John Payne) – Colorado State Fair.

Photo: Jeff Belden.

Matt Harris and me working the taxi act – Fort Smith AR, 1997.

Photographer unknown.

Me and my girls (L-R Christi Gray Harris Lalonde, me, Ethel).

Photo: David "Rockin' Dave" Witzer.

Me and Phil Gardenhire after a performance at the Calgary Stampede –
1998.

Photographer unknown.

Matt Harris in the barrel and me dancing with a bull at the Pikes Peak
or Bust Rodeo – Colorado Springs CO, 1998.

Photo: Susan Lambeth.

A prank pulled on me at the Kansas City Royal Rodeo - 1999.

Photo: Tommy Evans.

My real wife, Ethel, and me at the Rodeo of the Ozarks.

Photo: Bedford Camera.

"Black Bart" act – 2000.

Photo: Jeff Belden.

Dancing with a bull at the Dixie Nationals Rodeo – Jackson MS, 2001.

Photo: Jeff Belden.

Whoa, lady – you broke the butt off my car!

Photo: Robbie Freeman.

Matt Harris and me doing "Mr. Friggins" – Lafayette LA, 2002.

Photo: Jeff Belden.

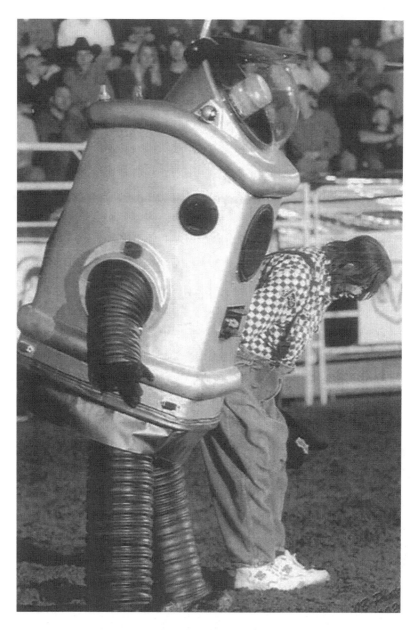

Matt Harris (in the robot) and me doing "BR549" at the Dixie
Nationals Rodeo – Jackson MS, 2003.

Photo: Jeff Belden.

I developed my "Hole in One" act in the 1960s when golf was on the
upswing, and I still perform it today.

Photo: Way Out West Rodeo Photography.

As most people call it, the "Whoop It in Here" act.

Photo: Jeff Belden

MEMORIES OF LECILE BY KEN KNOPP

The first time I saw Lecile was way back in '67 or '68, when I was about 12 years old. Lecile was probably about 30 then, but as I now remember, the dude stayed 39 years old for two decades, then 49 for what seemed like another decade, so I am not sure how old he was then or how old he really is now. My father had taken me and my brothers down to the see the Loretta Lynn Longhorn Rodeo at the Detroit Fairgrounds. I don't remember much about the rodeo, but I do remember well the tall, gangly, funny clown.

In that part of the country at that time, there wasn't much of a PRCA rodeo presence. Most rodeos were produced by the IPRA, and Bruce Lehrke's Longhorn Rodeo Company was the best. About 1979 or so I went to one of Lehrke's rodeo marketing schools in Nashville. Two years later, when I graduated from college, Bruce hired me as a publicist.

My first real association with Lecile was in the early fall of 1981 when Longhorn started its winter run of coliseum rodeos out East, which included Philadelphia PA; Hampton VA; Greenville SC; Lakeland FL; and Charleston WV. That spring we went out West to Houston and San Antonio and then produced several more shows that summer up North in Ohio, Michigan, Kentucky, and Wisconsin. It was during this full year's run that I got to know the real Lecile Harris. For whatever reason, I was drawn to him. It was certainly his humor that made an impression, but looking back I think perhaps it was also his friendly, easy-going personality. He was a solid leader in the company and always fun to be around, so I hung out with him as often as I could.

That year was Lecile's last with Longhorn and the IPRA before he moved over to the PRCA. He had worked some rodeos previously for James Harper and Ralph Morgan, so when he made the big move to the PRCA, they immediately booked him for all of their rodeos. I worked another year for Longhorn, and then in the spring of 1983 James Harper hired me as the

Marketing Director for the Harper and Morgan Rodeo Company. For the next eighteen years, Lecile and I worked together at some sixteen to twenty-four rodeos each year and grew to be very close friends. I got to know his wife, Ethel, and children very well during this time. Lecile, his son, Matt, (a barrel man and sound man) and I spent a lot of our free time together on the road and other times outside the rodeo trail as well. In many ways Lecile became a father figure to me. He was old enough to be my father (I think, though he has lied to me so much about his age that now I sometimes think I am older than he is) and was always willing to dispense advice to me about money, working, the rodeo business, family, friends, and even women (this last area was always a bit hazy with Lecile too, like his age).

Lecile's comedic abilities are legendary. There is no need for me to expand upon that here, but I would like to note that although I have seen every one of Lecile's acts dozens of times, I always found myself watching him again for every performance. Though I knew every line by heart, I always found him doing something new to make me laugh out loud once again. The rest of the crew and all of the cowboys felt the same way, because I always looked around the arena during Lecile's acts to see the roadies and cowboys all just as mesmerized as I was. That is a special testimonial to his talent. Nobody can touch him for comedic creativity, timing, and spontaneity. Lecile is a legend in the rodeo business, but to me he is like my brother or dad. Though time, space, and civil propriety will limit my contributions, I am happy to provide a few of my favorite memories of Lecile Harris to this book.

Lecile always liked to fight. Even in my era, but more so in his day, fighting was a common thing among guys. Call it rite of passage, competition, sport, or just fun; it wasn't a big deal. Fighting came pretty naturally to Lecile and, many times, pretty quickly.

One year we were in the little town of Lauderdale, Mississippi, home of the Ralph Morgan Rodeo. Twice a year, every April and August, we went to Ralph's for lots of fun, food,

Southern hospitality, and great crowds. Usually all the spectators were respectful to the acts, but one Saturday night in the middle of the rodeo a big, loudmouth, drunk redneck started heckling Lecile.

Now, Rule #1 for any spectator at any public event is to NEVER, EVER heckle the guy with the microphone. Trust me, it will not turn out well and you WILL lose. This is especially true with Lecile Harris. It didn't happen very often, but when it did, it was always a sight to behold Lecile embarrassing a heckler. It was a sport for him, and he was damn good at it.

On this particular night, the big ol' drunk hollered everything to Lecile that he could think of: foolish thoughts, cuss words, epithets, random answers to nobody's questions, and other garbled and obnoxious oaths. Now you have to understand that Lecile takes his craft very seriously. It's comedy, but it's also serious business. His friends could mess with him a bit during his act, but if you were an outsider, you would most certainly be taken down in brutal fashion.

Well, Lecile got his fill of this guy pretty durn quick and started hollering back at him over the microphone. Of course, at first the crowd didn't know if this was part of the act or not because it started off sort of casually. Lecile's initial comebacks were the usual stuff like "Yeah, I know buddy, I acted like that when I had my first beer too" or "If you have to go that bad, the bathrooms are out back." My personal favorite was: "Would somebody get a shovel and clean that up?"

Even after all that, the drunk still didn't let up. When Lecile finished his act and came out of the arena, he was hopping mad and heading into the stands to go whip that redneck's ass. We talked him out of it, though, because neither professional etiquette nor time allowed such things, and went on with the show.

The drunk kept getting drunker and more belligerent. Every time Lecile was in the arena, this guy started in on him. By now the whole thing had gotten old, so the crowd had gotten sick of the jerk too. He was big and surly, though, so nobody did anything to stop him.

By the last event, bull riding, the tension between Lecile and the drunk had built up to a boiling point. Lecile was doing his walking and talking and bantering with Phil Gardenhire in between bull rides. The drunk had been uncharacteristically quiet for a few minutes when all of a sudden a BIG FIGHT broke out in the stands. Of course the drunk redneck was right in the middle of it. Apparently somebody had finally had enough of him, and the response was immediate and violent. One bunch of people was directly involved in this fracas and the other bunch was just trying to get out of the way.

Lo and behold, out of nowhere, Lecile ran over to the fence, vaulted it like a giraffe in baggy Wranglers, and launched himself into the bleachers. He waded through the crowd to get to the drunk and wailed away on him with all he had. His microphone was still on the whole time, so everyone in the arena heard things like, "Get out of the way and let me at that sonuvabitch! You want some of me? Here – have some!" Lecile was having a helluva time flailing all over this guy, but the crowd was stunned and not sure what to make of it.

Fortunately for the drunk, the police weren't far behind Lecile, so the whole thing probably only lasted about thirty seconds. But what a spectacle! After the police broke it all up, Lecile hopped down the stands and over the fence to retrieve his hat and wig. By this time the crowd realized that all this was NOT part of the act, so they spontaneously erupted into a huge roar and standing ovation. Lecile just stood at the top of the fence, proud as he could be, doffing his hat and looking like he had just been elected Mayor of Lauderdale.

Like I said, Lecile loves to fight. Most of the time it was funny to see him get worked up, but other times, not so much. Back in the day, the Harper and Morgan Rodeo Company was known for their opening productions. They were big show-biz type events with a Western or patriotic theme, and they always included choreographed music, stunts, and lots of pyro. We got so good at them that in 1990 the NFR in Las Vegas had us come in to put together all of the opening productions. That was quite an honor and a lot of fun.

Each year, Harper and Morgan tried to top the previous year's production. We all pitched in to make it work and it was always challenging but a lot of fun and great camaraderie. It could also be very hard to be that creative every year. It took a lot of time and energy and was often stressful too. One year, James Harper assigned announcer Phil Gardenhire, Lecile, and me to put together the next year's opening. At this time, Lecile was no spring chicken, being probably 58 at the time, but still tough as nails. I was about 38, so both of us were old enough to know better but still young enough not to care.

We started working on the production that summer, getting ready to debut it on the next winter run. We had decided on a general theme and plan, so we promised to get together in late August at the Ralph Morgan Rodeo in Lauderdale that year to finalize it. Lecile and Phil told me to write the script based on our agreed-upon ideas and to have it ready at the rodeo when we could all be together to work out the details.

As it so happened, I spent a lot of time and effort completely writing it all out that summer – theme, scripts, costumes, choreography, lights, and so forth. When we got back together in August, both Lecile and Phil liked the general idea but hated the way I had developed it. In fact, both said it "sucked." Well, naturally that hurt my feelings – no, it pissed me off! We worked on it all weekend but couldn't agree on certain details because they had their ideas and I had mine. On Saturday afternoon, the three of us were out by the rodeo arena, next to the big H & M tack wagon with the painted Western-themed mural on the side. Time was getting short, as we had to soon present the plan to Harper and Morgan so they could begin procuring the materials required to implement it. But, of course, we were still arguing back and forth. It was Lecile and Phil against me, and things were getting heated.

Lecile said, "Look, your idea doesn't make sense! There's no continuity, so people won't understand!"

I looked at him and said, "Well, yours is boring."

That raised Phil's hackles, who said, "Boring? At least it's not stupid!"

We went back and forth like three school kids until Lecile finally got personal and hollered, "Look, you damned Yankee sonuvabitch! It doesn't matter what you want! We're gonna do it our way!"

Well, to this day, you can call me almost anything but a Yankee. I saw red when he called me that and grabbed him by the shirt to push him backwards. Quick as a flash, he grabbed me around the throat with both hands and stuck me up against the side of that tack trailer. As my feet dangled a foot off the ground, with Lecile's nose just about touching mine, I realized that the situation didn't look good for me. More words were spoken at high volume until thankfully Phil stepped in and defused the situation.

We went our separate ways to cool down, and after a little while I asked myself what the hell I was doing. Lecile was (and is) a tough old dude, but more importantly, he had been (and remains) a great friend of mine for many, many years. It was a silly thing, almost like brawling with your daddy. The funny thing is, that incident seemed to make us grow ever closer, and today he is like a father to me still and I love him dearly. Even funnier is that this confrontation has become a long-standing joke between us. I always say that it was a good thing Phil Gardenhire stepped in just when he did, because it was fixin' to get ugly. To this day, whenever I see someone that knows Lecile, I always tell them, "Hey, the next time you see Lecile, ask him about the time Ken Knopp had to kick his ass," which never fails to get a laugh out of him.

As long as I have known Lecile, he has always had one hard, fast, cardinal, never-to-be-broken RULE: no matter how desperate you are, or how bad it gets, or how little time you think you might have, you can NEVER, EVER do a big job in the Clown Dressing Room commode. I mean NEVER! You gotta pee? OK, fine – but take a crap? Don't try it, don't ask, don't even think about it. Go somewhere else!

You see, quite often the dressing rooms at the coliseum buildings that we worked were small, sometimes being just 15' by 15' and only including a "one-seater" bathroom. When someone went in one of those and let go one of those large, nasty, foul, paint-peeling bowel movements – hell, you couldn't get away from it. There was only so much oxygen in these confined spaces, and we sure didn't want to have to inhale anybody's concentrated fecal molecules in that little room.

Now, one has to understand what the clown dressing room represents. It is NOT just the place where the clowns dress and get ready for the rodeo. To us and the crew it is also our hangout, our refuge, and the place we gravitate to before, during and after every performance. It is and will always be a holy sanctuary for testosterone exercising and male bonding. It is a place of respite, crude humor, disgusting jokes, grandiose (but always partially true) stories, and hilarity that easily surpasses anything heard or seen by the crowd out in the rodeo arena. Like Las Vegas, everything you say and do there stays there. Only one thing can violate this harmonious boys' club and surely bring the wrath of all speedily down upon your head: go in there and sit on the pot. It was such a serious matter that at every single rodeo Lecile would tape a large handwritten sign on the door of the dressing room that read in BIG, BOLD, Sharpie-black letters: "Keep Out! Clown Dressing Room. NO TOILET." It was Rodeo Law as sure as the Ten Commandments, the Constitution, and the Bill of Rights.

One winter run we were working an indoor arena somewhere in the South. In the middle of the rodeo, Lecile had finished one of his acts, so three or four of us happily reposed back to the dressing room. As soon as we stepped inside the door, we were enveloped by the most vile, gut-wrenching, nose-scorching, eye-burning stench ever rendered by a human gastrointestinal system. To this day, the smell defies accurate description. One could not be sure if the sewer had just backed up or the wall had somehow cracked and Jimmy Hoffa's body had been found. It was horrible. Of course, Lecile launched into a spiteful rage, hollering "Who crapped in the dressing room?!?" to nobody in particular. Spinning around to the closest person to him, he got nose-to-nose with one of the bullfighter clowns and bellowed, "YOU?" Of course the clown denied it, so Lecile spun around towards me, pointed that long index finger into my face, and shouted, "Kanappy! You crapped in here didn't you?" I reminded him that I had been in the arena with him the whole time and therefore had a solid alibi. After further questioning of all parties failed to reveal the perpetrator, he puffed up and said, "That's it! The next person I catch in here taking a crap is gonna get their ass kicked! And I mean it's gonna be bad." He stomped around cussing and throwing stuff for a while, and it took a few minutes for him to calm down and for us to air out the room, but in a short while all was back to normal.

Just a couple of weeks later, we were in Montgomery at another indoor rodeo. This particular building had the usual small dressing room and single toilet. Just like before, Lecile had finished the bareback bronc riding, so several of us headed back to the dressing room to kill a few minutes while the calf roping was going on. We walked through the door with the usual handwritten sign from Lecile on it, grabbed chairs, and started shooting the bull like usual about nothing in particular.

Lecile had removed his wig and was sitting in a folding chair looking into the mirror, working on some makeup for his next act, when I first heard it. There was a shuffling sound coming from somewhere. It was fairly quiet at first, but then another one of the bullfighters also heard this scuffing, scraping sound. We all got real quiet until we heard a determined grunt, followed by a gentle sigh.

I looked at Lecile to see if he had heard all this. He was still looking into the mirror, but now he was frowning and I could see a vein in the side of his head throbbing. Right about then – *SWOOOOOOSH* – the toilet flushed. Nobody said a word, and we all turned to look at Lecile.

I was so excited because I knew what was fixin' to happen. I could hardly stand the wait because this was gonna be good! We heard a zipper zip and a buckle buckle and then the door of the toilet stall flew open with a crash. Out climbed the biggest, ugliest, most gristle-headed steer wrestler I had ever seen. This guy was a virtual Greek statue, every bit of 6'4", with a square jaw, broad shoulders, tiny waist, and arms so bulging that his shirt looked like it was going to come apart at the seams. He turned toward us and strode athletically through the room, looking more like an NFL linebacker than a rodeo cowboy. As he passed Lecile, he said in a guttural voice to no one in particular, "Hey, how y'all?" Nobody said anything, but we all watched Lecile and waited for his response. Just before that big boy went out the door, he turned around and muttered, "Uh, sorry about that." And then he was gone.

Nobody said a thing. We all just sat in stunned silence looking back and forth at each other and Lecile. Finally I couldn't stand it any longer, so I said, "Hey, Lecile! What was that you were saying about kicking the ass of the next person you caught taking a crap in the clown dressing room?" Lecile just kept working his makeup, never taking his eyes off the mirror, and after a long, unconcerned pause said, "I'm a clown, not a dummy!"

KANSAS CITY ROYAL RODEO

The Kansas City Royal was a great big rodeo that had something like thirteen performances. A group of the city's firemen would take their vacation every year and do the grip work for the rodeo, which meant they set the props out and that sort of thing. But what these guys really lived for was the prank they pulled during the last show of each year. This prank was always a classic because they put so much work into it. They would study my act for the first twelve performances to see what they could come up with and how to do it. They even filmed the act and then took that back to the firehouse to watch so they could have a greater degree of precision when executing the prank.

I did the piano act my first year there. In that act, there's a point in time when I raise the lid up on the piano and pull a guitar out of it. I performed this act twelve nights without incident. When I lifted the lid on the thirteenth night, a firecracker went off and a covey of quail exploded out and hit me right in the face. They got me good with that one, but I figured it was a one-time deal since it was my first year there, so I never gave them any thought after that.

The next year, I went back with the robot. At the beginning of that act, I'm standing in the dark off to one side, and the robot's in the spotlight singing a song that's just pitiful. I'd always interrupt it by running out and saying, "Whoa, whoa! That doesn't work. We need some rock n' roll!" After I did that, I'd walk back over to the fence to pick up what I called my Robot Tool Sack, which was a duffel bag with some jumper cables and a saxophone in it.

On the last night of the rodeo, I went over to pick up my bag, and it moved about two feet out of my reach. I reached for it again, and it moved again. The firemen placed the props, so they had hooked a line to my bag and were pulling it so I couldn't grab it. By this time I realized what was going on: I saw that it was only going one way, so I stepped around to block it. Unbeknownst to me, they had also tied a line from above, so when I went around and reached for the bag, that sucker went straight up in the air. They let it dangle about three feet over my head, and when I jumped up to grab it, they'd just snatch it up out of my reach.

I played that game for a minute before I just decided to go on with the show. I walked over to the robot, his butt caught on fire, and a great big spray of fireworks shot out of the top of his head. When that went off, they poured a 55-gallon drum of water off the catwalk directly onto me and the robot. There's a picture of it somewhere, and it shows a big ball of water right over my head. That much water coming from that high up drenched me from top to bottom and almost knocked me down.

The next year, I was doing the baseball act with Rudy, J.G. Crouch, and Leon Coffee. I was at bat when all of a sudden I felt these arms come around me and grab my hands. I couldn't see who it was, but I could look at the hands and tell it was a girl. I could also tell she was well endowed by the way she was mashing into my back. I turned around and there was this stripper, with hardly a stitch of clothes on, that these guys had hired. We went through that whole act with her right there in the middle of it.

When Leon and I went back the next year, this guy there had a petting zoo with an elephant in it. Whenever we had a little time, if somebody was having trouble getting down on a bull or something like that, I'd just go out into the middle of the arena and pat my foot until the announcer, Phil Gardenhire, would pick up on it. He'd ask me, "Lecile, what are you doing?"

"I'm patting my foot."

"Why are you patting your foot?"

"Well, the mayor of Kansas City hired me to stand here and do this."

"What exactly are they hiring you to do?"

"I'm keeping elephants away."

"Lecile, that's ridiculous. There's not an elephant loose within five thousand miles of here."

"I'm doing a good job then, ain't I?"

It was almost like a "Who's on first?" thing that we did at least once every night. I usually initiated it, but on the last night, Phil said, "Lecile, come here."

"What have you been doing since you've been in Kansas City?"

"Well, I've been here at the rodeo."

"I heard the mayor of Kansas City hired you to do a job."

"Yep, they did."

"What do you do for them?"

"You see me patting my foot? The city hired me to do that because it keeps the elephants away."

"Well, you're not doing a very good job."

I didn't know it, but Leon had dressed up like Tarzan and ridden an elephant up right behind me. When Phil said I wasn't doing a very good job, the zoo guy cued the elephant, which made this great big roaring sound right in the back of my head, and I mean it scared the living crap out of me.

Leon and I were fighting bulls in Kansas City another year. He was easily spooked, so one of the best pranks the firefighters ever pulled capitalized on that quality. Kemper Arena was a coliseum that had a very tall ceiling. The firemen kept talking to us all week about a guy who had fallen out of the ceiling and gotten killed. They'd talk about what a terrible scene it was and how bad they felt for the guy, and all that made Leon really nervous. He didn't like hearing about that at all, and he didn't like the idea of putting on a performance right there where that had happened.

On the night of the last show, one of the firemen came up to me and said, "Listen, nobody ever fell out of there. We're going to put a mark on the arena floor, and when you get a little time during the bull riding, we want you to get Leon as close to that spot as you can."

So I did. All of a sudden we heard this blood-curdling scream, and then somebody was falling out of the ceiling. The firemen had taken a mannequin and put it in overalls that said

"Kemper Arena Staff," so it looked just like a real person. Leon looked up, saw this thing coming down, and turned absolutely white. It hit the ground right in front of him, and it was just like that mannequin and Leon were on a seesaw. When it hit, Leon shot straight up in the air and ran right out of the arena. He went through the grand-entry gate, over another gate, up a loading ramp, and out into the parking lot, all without stopping. We went ahead and finished the bull riding, and nobody had seen Coffee since the prank. We finally found him hunkered down in the back of an empty horse trailer. Needless to say, he was a mad dude when he found out what had really happened. He figured I certainly must have had something to do with it, but I really hadn't. That's how much trouble the firemen of Kansas City would go to just to pull a prank.

RALPH MORGAN

James Harper and Ralph Morgan bought the Steiner Rodeo Company, which was a prestigious rodeo company with lots of color, action, acts, and excellent stock. James and Ralph had the whole package. They liked a troupe of their own announcers, clowns, acts, stock, everything. This way they had total control over the show and were better able to put together a full production with the pageantry, entertainment, comedy, rough stock, and pretty girls.

Ralph, Matt, and I were at the Kansas City rodeo one year. The hotel we were staying in happened to be having a cross-dressers convention. When we came in after a performance one night and got in the elevator, it was full of all these great big guys dressed to the nines and all dolled up for their formal that night. We kind of looked at each other, but we went ahead and squeezed in between them. When we did, one of them put his arm around Ralph and said, "You know, I have always wanted me a cowboy," and I mean Ralph turned just as red as a tomato.

We were all staying in the same room. Ralph and I each had a bed and Matt had a little foldup cot. I was sound asleep when I heard Ralph say, "Lecile, what's it feel like to have a heart attack?"

"I don't know, Ralph. I've never had one."

"I think I'm having one. I'm hurting real bad."

"I don't think so, Ralph. Just relax and turn over on your other side."

I had just got back half asleep when Ralph asked me, "Lecile, what would you do if you had a heart attack?"

"I don't know, Ralph. I've never had one. I think you might have heartburn. Let me give you a Tums."

"What's a Tums?"

"You've never had a Tums?"

He was fifty-something years old and he'd never had a Tums. I gave him one and cut the light out.

I had just gotten back to sleep when I heard something slam shut like a giant mousetrap – *whap!* I jumped up and turned on the light, and there was Matt folded up in that bed with his knees in his mouth. I pried the bed apart, got Matt out, and finally got everybody settled back down. Then I went back to bed and was almost asleep again when I heard Ralph say, "Lecile?"

"What, Ralph?"

"I'm so glad I wasn't having a heart attack."

RUDY BURNS

Rudy Burns was a Cajun from Gonzalez, Louisiana who came to Harper and Morgan full-time as a barrel man. He started out fighting bulls and then got really good at working the barrel. Rudy and I clicked right off the bat. He's a little guy, at least a foot shorter than me, so we looked a little like Mutt and Jeff. Rudy and I came up with a lot of bits that we did around the barrel during the bull riding.

Matt was the sound and lighting director at this time, so some of the comedy involved him and the sound design. Rudy and I would be standing beside the barrel, and I'd tell the announcer, "This barrel is really something else. Rudy has everything in there. He's got a couch. He's got a coffee table. He's got a fireplace. He's even got a dog in there. Rudy, is it okay if I pet your dog?"

"Yes."

"Does your dog bite?"

"No."

When I reached over in the barrel to pet the dog, Matt would turn on all this racket of a dog barking and growling and chewing, and I'd play like the dog was pulling me into the barrel. While I was in there, I'd slip on a sleeve that was just ripped all to pieces. When Rudy pulled me out, I'd look at my sleeve and say, "I thought you said your dog don't bite!"

"That ain't my dog."

We used to carry a dummy with us into the arena. We'd prop him up with a broom, and the bulls loved hooking him all over the arena. We'd name him after a politician or movie character that nobody liked, and when the bull hit that dummy, the crowd would really roar.

That was good, but I decided what we really needed was a running dummy. There was a guy named Little Bill who worked for the company, so I measured him and made a dummy the same size as he was. Then I got two identical sets of clothes so we could dress them the same, and after that you could hardly tell them apart.

Rudy brought the dummy out before the bull riding and set it up. After we let a bull work it over, I said, "I don't like that dummy. I don't want him out here." Rudy contended that it was his dummy, so he was going to keep it right where it was, but I got it and threw it over the center gate. After they bucked a bull or two, Rudy and a cowboy dragged the dummy back onto the dirt. After another bull bucked, I grabbed the dummy to throw it out of the arena again.

But instead of bringing the dummy back in the next time, they were dragging Little Bill instead. They pulled him into the arena, stuck a broom in his back, and propped him up just like the dummy. Bill knew the bulls since he worked with them all the time, so we let him pick one that we knew wasn't going to fight.

After that particular bull came out, bucked, and left, I headed over to Bill and said, "Rudy, I told you I don't want this dummy out here!" When I went to grab Bill, he reached around, took that broom, and whipped my ass all over the arena. He did that for a while and then ran right out the center gate. It really blew the crowd's mind.

The first time we did it, Ralph Morgan was standing by the gate. We hadn't told anybody about this bit except the guys who were dragging the dummy out there. When Ralph saw that dummy jump up and chase me around the arena and then turn towards him to run out the gate, it really scared the crap out of him. He lit out down the ramp as fast as he could, trying to get away from the dummy. After the show, Ralph came up to me all hot and said, "Don't you ever do that again without telling me! You like to scared me to death!" So after that, he was just waiting for the right time to get me back.

We were in Jackson at the Dixie Nationals. I was doing the shootout act there, so I had my pistol and shotgun with me. There was a particular joke I had told the night before, and Ralph just did not like it at all, so he came out in the middle of the arena during the bull riding and said, "Lecile, don't tell that nasty chili joke."

"Oh, Ralph, I got to tell it."

"Don't tell that thing. It's nasty. Don't tell it."

So when we got a break in the bull riding, just to annoy him, I started into the joke. When I did, Ralph came out with a pistol and started shooting at me, hollering "I told you!" He ran me all over the arena shooting at my feet with it, which turned out to be my .38 from the shootout bit that he had filled with blanks. At the time, though, I didn't know what it was. All I knew was that Ralph had a gun and he would use it.

We were using the dummy again one September in Memphis. Before the bull riding, Rudy would get his barrel and I would get the dummy, and then we'd head out to the arena for the main event. Most of the time we'd turn the light out to the dressing room when we left, so I'd leave the dummy propped up right next to the door so I could just reach in and get it without looking.

On this particular night, Rudy went in there and put on the dummy's clothes and propped himself up against the wall. I was running late and in a hurry, so I opened the door, reached in without looking, and grabbed under his arm. When I did that, Rudy caught me around the neck with both hands, and I mean cold chills ran all up and down my spine. It scared me so bad and made me so mad that I caught him by the throat and stuck him up against the wall. I was so stirred up I couldn't turn loose and I kept beating him against that wall while he was hollering, "Let me down! Let me down! I won't do it again!"

We were in Monroe, Louisiana when I decided to get Rudy back good. I got some rotten shrimp that a place had thrown out and put them in his barrel. I cut a little hole in it so I could put it all down in there without him knowing where it was. Then it sat outside all day getting hot and rank. When it came time to do the performance, Rudy rolled the barrel out and jumped down in it. He didn't even finish the bulls before that smell overtook him, so he came out of there throwing up all over the place. He couldn't even get back in his barrel for the rest of the rodeo.

After I was home from the rodeo for a few days, I noticed that my truck was stinking so bad I could hardly get in and out of it. I looked and looked and couldn't figure out what the deal was, but my dog finally did: Rudy had taken off all my hubcaps and filled them full of shrimp.

I was doing the piano act in Montgomery. I always have to lock the piano up somewhere so people won't fool with it during the daytime while I'm gone. At Montgomery, this location was a little boiler room with concrete walls. My piano is about six by four, and this room was about eight by six, so I only had a couple of feet around the piano on all sides to work on it and get ready.

Like most of my acts, this one involves pyro. I load my own twelve-gauge shells, and I fill them almost completely full of powder, which makes them super loud. If you don't get the shell loaded in the shotgun properly and get the breech shut tight, it might not cock and fire, which you didn't want happening in the middle of your act. I wanted to make sure it would cock and fire beforehand, so I put the shell in and closed the breech. After that, like always, I pulled the hammer back and cocked it. Everything seemed fine, so I put my thumb on the hammer to let it down easy and pulled the trigger. Well, the hammer slipped out from under my thumb, and the whole thing went off in this little concrete room.

The blast really rang my bell, so I blacked out just from the noise. When I came to, I was lying on the concrete floor. At the time, I was loading with black powder, which produces a lot of smoke, so the doors were blown open with black smoke just pouring out of that little room. Rudy was down in the dressing room, quite a ways from where I was, and he thought the boiler had blown up with me in the room. He ran down all in a panic and helped me get myself together. When I finally came stumbling out through the smoke and into the hallway, a maintenance man stuck his nose in my face and hollered, "You didn't hurt that damn boiler, did you?" I couldn't really hear what he had said, but I figured I wouldn't like it if I had, so I just reached out and got that guy by the throat until Rudy pulled me off of him. Anyway, I could barely hear anything for weeks, and I probably also had a concussion.

Another time in Montgomery, while Jerry Don Galloway and I were fighting bulls, Rudy was working the barrel. He was also doing his car act because he had started doing some of his own comedy. He got his car out to the middle of the arena and it wouldn't start. Jerry Don and I were trying to help him get it cranked, with a bunch of comedy around it, when all of a sudden a fighting bull named Ice Man broke out and made a beeline to us. We were all good bullfighters so we knew what to do, but I mean this bull would not quit. He ran us around the car, with me in front, Jerry Don behind me, and Rudy bringing up the rear right ahead of the bull. Rudy's car had no doors on it, so I cut across the car, which put me behind the bull. Rudy and Jerry Don dove under the car and I got up in the seat, so Ice Man had us all trapped. Finally he settled down enough for the pickup man to come take him out. About this time somebody's cow dog started barking back in the chutes. When I heard that, I raised up and said, "Well, I reckon y'all are gonna turn the damn dogs loose on us now." In all the excitement I had forgotten about my wireless still being on, so that went all over the arena and everybody got a real good laugh out of it.

TY MURRAY

Ty Murray was a nine-time world champion bull rider. When he was just starting out, he was a hell of a hand already. You could tell he was going to be something. He used to work on his balance by walking wooden fences for acres and acres. Then somebody told him that riding a unicycle would help his balance, so he learned to do that really well.

I'd be out there when he was bull riding, and after he got off, I'd say something on the wireless like, "Boy, that dude can really ride." On his way back to the chutes, Ty would come by me and say, "Lecile, I ain't no dude." That was just a regular thing between us, all in good fun.

We were at Lufkin, Texas one year, and the last bull of the night was one that hooked pretty bad. I had stopped fighting bulls by then so I was just doing the comedy, and we had two bullfighters. Rudy was in the barrel, and he knew this bull, so he told me, "Lecile, you better watch this one. He's a bad dude."

The bull came out, bucked the guy off, and headed straight for the barrel. I was behind the barrel waiting to see which side he was going to go around, but unfortunately he decided he would go straight through it. He hit this barrel, picked it up, and shoved it right on top of me so I was down flat on my back. The barrel probably weighed 125 pounds, and Rudy weighed about 150, so that was close to 300 pounds right there. Then the bull got on top of that, and he was probably about 1,700 pounds, so I had close to a ton weighted down on me. Well, all that broke my pelvis, but at the time I didn't know it.

I was able to get up somehow, so I started staggering out of the arena. There was a special seating area where the rodeo committee sat, and I had to pass by it. Ty Murray was sitting up next to the commissioner, whose grandson had dropped his bandana over the wall and down on the floor. When I came up on it, the guy leaned over the wall and said, "Hey, Bozo! Hand me that bandana!" Well, I just blew up all over him, but my mistake was that Ty heard it. He climbed down next to me and hollered, "Hey, Bozo! Pick the man's bandana up for him!"

I had a broken pelvis, but I was so hot that I took off after Ty trying to catch him. I ran him around and around the chutes, but of course he outran me. Rudy had been watching and listening to this whole thing, so he finally caught me by the shirt and said, "Lecile, you might as well quit. There ain't no way Bozo's ever gonna catch that little dude." Ty still calls me Bozo to this day.

PHIL GARDENHIRE

When Harper and Morgan started up, they needed an announcer to take over the reins for them. I had gotten my name out there and was working a lot of rodeos with Ralph, so when he asked me for a recommendation for a good announcer, I immediately named Phil Gardenhire.

Phil, in my opinion, was the best young announcer to come along in a long time. He was like a son to me at times and like a brother at other times. He had the total package, so he just had a presence about him. He was a good-looking guy who always dressed sharp and rode a fine horse. His hat, leather vest, and leather chaps were all cream-colored, and he usually wore a crisp white shirt.

Phil was really the one, I think, to bring back the horseback announcer. They did it in the early days of rodeo, when the announcer was on horseback and spoke through a megaphone. But then with the advent of PA systems, the announcers went up into the announcer's stand. Phil brought it back down to the floor. When they called his name at the beginning of every performance, he'd ride through the grand entry gate wide open and come to a stop in the middle of the arena to get the show started.

Phil had such great improvisational skills that he could, as my mother would say, turn a sow's ear into a silk purse. We were in Jonesville, Louisiana and it had been raining all weekend, so the arena was really muddy. There was a great big mud hole that had water standing in it right in front of the grand entry gate. When they called Phil's name and he came barreling through the gate, his horse saw that mud hole and just shut it down, so Phil went over the horse's head and landed face down in the mud. About all you could see was the top of his hat and one arm sticking up, holding the mic so it wouldn't get wet. He rolled around in there a few seconds until he was brown from head to toe and then jumped up and said to the crowd, "Well, how do you like me so far?" That's just the kind of personality he had.

Phil had a large vocabulary, so he had many catchphrases that he used in the arena. He's the one who came up with "the greatest show on dirt." Harper Morgan Rodeo Company still uses that term, and the Calgary Stampede and so many others have used it. He would use words that the average cowboy had no idea what they meant. "Plethora," for instance. Phil would learn these words just so he could use them in his announcing. Sometimes he'd even ask my wife if she had a good word he could use, because he knew she speaks such proper English and has such a vast vocabulary.

Phil's timing was rock solid because he was also a professional drummer. We had both made a living years before that playing drums. My son, Matt, had also been a drummer before he went to work with Harper and Morgan as their lighting and sound coordinator. You may not have anything else going for you if you're a drummer, but you've got to have timing. So if you put three drummers in an event to all work together – me doing the comedy, Phil doing the announcing, and Matt doing the music and lights – you had timing that was just unreal.

Matt would challenge us both with his music, which kept us sharp all the time. We worked together week in and week out with Harper and Morgan, so everybody was on the same page. It was just a neat entertainment package. People started booking all three of us together for other rodeos because they'd seen our chemistry with Harper and Morgan. The other rodeos had their lighting and sound people, so Matt would work the other end of my acts at those. For instance, if I was doing the camera act, he was the lady getting her picture taken. He played lots of different characters, but I always just played Lecile, so it was easy for me.

Phil and I witnessed so much rodeo history. We were working Central Point, Oregon in 1991 when we saw something that, in my opinion, will never be repeated. That night the judges announced what they said was a perfect bull ride. Each judge scored it 50 points, which made it 100 points – a perfect score. That's the only one in the history of rodeo. When the score was announced, Phil and I were speechless. We couldn't believe what had just happened. Whether it was perfect or not, it's down in the record books as the only perfect bull ride, and I don't think another announcer or clown will ever stand in the arena and see another 100-point bull ride.

A STORY BY RANDY CORLEY

In all my years of rodeo, I never got to work with Lecile as much as I would have loved to. If I had, I promise there would be many more stories to be told. Having said that, I can mention two things that Lecile is not fond of: drunks in Vernal messing up his robot act and country singer Michael Martin Murphey. I can say these things openly because I'm sure they won't make the book.

Let me tell you of a time when Lecile, Matt Harris, and Phil Gardenhire were all at the Calgary Stampede. They would work the first five performances and then head to Vernal. I would fly into Calgary the day after they left to announce the last five performances. This particular year, I came in a couple of days early. My room wasn't available until the next day, so Lecile invited me to stay with him and Phil and Matt. Their room was equipped with two double beds and a cot (of course Lecile and Phil each got a bed to himself – I always felt sorry for Matt on the cot).

I bunked with Phil, but had a tough time staying asleep. I couldn't figure out why until I woke up yet again and heard Phil and Lecile talking in their sleep. That's what kept waking me up. As I laid there listening, I realized they were actually mumbling clown jokes and bits back and forth in their sleep. I finally got up about 5AM and got dressed to head down for some coffee. I stopped at the door as I left and turned back and hollered as loud as I could, "No wonder you two work so good together! Shoot, you practice all night long!"

LITTLE BLUE PILLS

Back in those days I stayed pretty keyed up all the time, so I would fight at the drop of a hat. I was always on edge, but I didn't know why. One particular day Phil and I were in Pueblo, Colorado, and had just finished a round of golf with Matt and

Steve Scribner. We had been talking all morning on the course about how we needed to go get a good greasing, which meant we wanted some good ol' greasy fried chicken, so naturally we found a Kentucky Fried Chicken to satisfy our cravings. We walked in and I told the girl behind the counter that I wanted a bucket of fried chicken. She looked at me and said, "We're out of fried chicken." I looked at her and said, "What? Is this not a Kentucky Fried Chicken?" She said yes, it was, but they were out of chicken. Well, I couldn't understand how you could be out of chicken at a chicken place at eleven o'clock in the morning, so I just went off on this girl until Phil pulled me out and we went across the street to a Red Lobster. The first thing I did when we walked in was ask them if they had any lobster. They said they did, so Phil told me to just settle down and eat.

I was still a little edgy from the KFC deal by the time we got through and headed out to my van. We loaded up and were getting ready to leave when this guy on a bicycle pulled up beside us in the parking lot, grabbed a hold of my mirror, and asked, "Have you got a couple of dollars for lunch?" I said I did, but I had already eaten. He said, "I mean for me." I looked down at his bicycle and it looked brand new, so I said, "No. Why don't you have any money? Why don't you get a job? You've got a brand new bicycle. You can do things. You can deliver stuff on your bicycle. Why don't you take that bicycle and use it to make a living, or sell it and go buy yourself something to eat?" I just chewed his butt up one side and down the other until he figured he didn't need all that and tried to leave. When he let go of my mirror, I just caught his arm and yanked him back up to the window and said, "I'm not through." So I just commenced to chewing on him a while longer until Phil or Steve convinced me to turn him loose.

The next week I was at home putting a roof on a shed behind my house when I got a real dizzy spell and had to actually hang onto the trusses up there until I got over it and was able to get down safely. I was sweating and my heart was running away with me, so I thought I better go to the doctor. He ran some tests and found out that I had arrhythmia because of too much adrenaline in my system. Talk about being in the wrong line of work! Anyway, he gave me a little blue pill called a beta blocker that slowed things down a little and took a bit of the edge off.

A couple of weeks after that, Phil and I were working a rodeo in Fort Worth. We had been there all week and really needed a good meal, so we went to a Bonanza steakhouse with the Scribner brothers. When I ordered a T-bone, the waitress told me they were all out of T-bones. The guys were all on the edge of their seats waiting on me to explode, but I just calmly looked at the girl and said, "That's fine, I'll have the chicken." After she walked off with our order, Steve looked at me and said, "You know what, Lecile? You ain't near as much fun as you used to be before you started takin' them damn little blue pills."

PHIL'S DEATH

I was sitting at home one day when I got a phone call from Mike Duplissey, a buddy of mine in Poteau, Oklahoma, who said, "Lecile, Phil's dead." Well, when I heard that, I just couldn't believe it.

It was April the 14th, 1999. He had dropped off his son, Tyler, to get a haircut. After that, he took his income tax to the post office to mail it. Finally he picked up Tyler and they headed home. Heavener has one traffic light. The light was green, so Phil went through it – just as a drug addict all hopped up on speed ran the red light and barreled right into Phil's truck. That guy's lick drove Phil's truck into a light pole, which broke off, crushed the cab of the truck, and hit Phil right behind the neck. It killed him instantly. Mike was telling me all this and I asked, "Are you sure Phil's dead?" He said, "Lecile, I'm standing here lookin' at him."

Well, that just turned me wrong side out. The rodeo world lost the best announcer they had, and I lost a son, a brother, and a great friend – all because of a guy who decided to do drugs that day. Timing is what Phil was all about, and that guy's timing didn't agree with Phil's.

We were at Ralph's in Lauderdale, Mississippi that week. The rodeo had to go on there, but when it was over, we all got on a private plane in Meridian and flew to Oklahoma. The only thing that got me through that funeral was something the preacher said: "This is not Phil lying here. It's his overcoat. And this overcoat was what God gave him to wear while he was here. But Phil is already gone." Even hearing that, I couldn't go look at him. I knew he was dead, but it was months before I could accept that he was gone and he wasn't coming back.

There are many great announcers out there at the top of their game – Hadley Barrett, Randy Corley, Bob Tallman, Boyd Polhamus, Mike Mathis, and Wayne Brooks, to name a few – but even though they're all superb in their own ways, they themselves will tell you that Phil was probably the most perfect and unique package of an announcer that there ever was in rodeo.

A STORY BY ANDY STEWART

I've been watching Lecile since I was six years old. I got to see him and the great Phil Gardenhire work together for many years in my hometown of Monroe, Louisiana. When I saw those two guys for the first time, I thought every professional rodeo in the world had a stellar announcer like Phil and a great clown like Lecile.

As my career has progressed and I've worked with Lecile, he has taught me so much about showmanship and what to do to keep things moving in the arena. He told me one time, "Son, timing isn't everything; it's the only thing."

I owe a lot of my success to what Lecile has taught me. For him to be in the business of entertaining people for about sixty years is just a testament to the talent he is.

THE WONDER BROTHERS

I worked the Montgomery rodeo with Harper and Morgan for at least twenty years in a row starting in the early eighties. Montgomery was the Southeast Livestock Exhibition, and it was really big beef country around there.

The first time I ever worked the rodeo, I saw these two guys standing around the back of the building just watching the stock. They never would say anything to anybody. They'd just stand and watch. If I had to describe them, I'd say they looked like characters out of "The Beverly Hillbillies."

I kept seeing them hanging around outside looking at the stock, but I never did see them inside for any of the rodeo. Finally, after the second or third year of that, I went up to them one day and asked, "Guys, would you all like to go in and see the rodeo?" They said they would, so I got them armbands that let them go wherever they wanted to go.

These two characters were Benjie and Lamar Barnes from Pine Level South, Alabama. Benjie was the younger one, and he must have been in his mid-thirties at the time. He was the first one in his family to ever finish high school. Lamar was the other one, and he must have been about forty. They lived with their momma and daddy and cleaned chicken houses for a living. Benjie was the Head Chicken Crap Cleaner and Lamar was the Assistant Chicken Crap Cleaner. If you ever wanted to make their day, you just took them to Waffle House. Benjie and Lamar were so enamored with the rodeo and had such a sense of wonder about it that I started calling them the Wonder Brothers, so pretty soon everybody was calling them that.

The Wonder Brothers and I got to be pretty close. They were always there at Montgomery to help me unload. It didn't make any difference what time I got there, because they would be there. They'd help me take my props, makeup, and things into the dressing room, and then they'd just hang out there. When I left to go work in the arena, they escorted me to the floor. After that, they'd go up into the stands somewhere and watch the act. Then they'd meet me back at the dressing room.

One year I was doing the baseball act with Rudy Burns and Matt. There's a part at the end of that act where they start to pull the base away from me to keep me from making a home run, so I stop and yell "Time!" Then I turn and point somewhere up in the stands and say, "Lady, it's against the law to pull your clothes off at the rodeo!" Rudy and Matt would turn around to see her, and then I'd step on the base for a home run.

The Wonder Brothers had seen this act four times, because it was the last night and there were four performances every year. When we all got back to the dressing room, Benjie went over to Rudy and said, "I can't believe you fall for that every time. We've watched it four times in a row and we still can't find her." Well, that's just the kind of people they were.

Rudy had gotten me pretty good at the Memphis rodeo with the dummy deal, so he wanted to do something similar with the Wonder Brothers. One night we were all sitting around the dressing room and he said, "Fellas, they got a big bad dog here that escaped from the pound. He's got rabies and he'll attack anybody anytime. They say he's in the building here somewhere." Of course Benjie or Lamar one said, "You know, I think I saw that dog."

The dressing room had a shower, and Rudy told me to get Benjie over there next to it a while after he told that story; then he'd come out growling and raising hell. When I got Benjie in place, Rudy came through that shower curtain snarling and barking – I mean like you never heard. But as soon as he got close, Benjie got him in a headlock. Benjie was scared so bad that he couldn't turn loose, so he was just clamping down with those huge arms and hands like hams. He had Rudy by the head and was spinning around in a circle with Rudy's feet off the floor and face turning purple. He got all the way across the room until he got to a corner where he couldn't sling Rudy around, so I got over there and got a hold of him, but I couldn't get Rudy loose. It was like trying to pull a vise off of something. Benjie was so scared he was crying, and Rudy was all out of air and about to pass out by the time Benjie turned him loose. So Rudy got his little payback for pulling a similar stunt on me with the dummy.

I went to the lobby after every Montgomery performance to sign autographs. The Wonder Brothers would each buy a program every night. Then they'd go stand at the end of the line, with their arms crossed and their feet touching at the heels and making a little "T," and wait for me to autograph their programs. We had four performances a year for twenty years, and they bought a program and got it signed after every single one.

I noticed that Benjie and Lamar had a preference of not letting anybody stand behind them, so one afternoon I conducted an experiment to see just how adamant they were about that. Matt, Bill "Zig" Zeigler, the Wonder Brothers, and I were standing around the parking lot talking one day. I started telling a story to Zig, who was an outstanding trainer for Justin Boots. As I told it, I'd take a couple of steps to get behind the Wonder Brothers, who would immediately move back behind me. I'd hold a minute, move a step behind them, and they'd move right back behind me. I wanted to see how far they would go, so before it was over with, I was hollering at Zig from all the way across the parking lot. He knew what I was doing, so he went with it. Over a period of time, I started working my way back up close to Zig, and they followed right behind me without ever realizing we had gone all the way across the parking lot with me shouting at the top of my voice.

The Wonder Brothers never shaved from one rodeo to the next. They'd let their beards grow out all year, but then they felt like they needed to shave for the rodeo. One year Benjie walked in and it looked like somebody had gotten after him with an axe. He had skinned marks on his face where he had shaved real close, and then there were a few hunks of hair about the size of your thumb that he had just missed completely. Of course the Wonder Brothers were brown as a biscuit because they worked out in the sun all summer, but where they'd shaved, they were white as a sheet. I had never seen anybody cut themselves all to pieces this bad shaving, so I asked Benjie what he used.

"Daddy's straight razor."

"Did you use shaving cream?"

"Nope. I didn't even use a mirror."

Donnie Gay was in Montgomery one particular year to do the color commentating for the bull riding. He'd sign autographs in the lobby until it was time for the bulls, and then he'd head out to the announcer's stand. It was kind of like a little balcony, with a three-foot outcropping that sort of hung out over the chutes. They'd throw the spotlight on the bull and introduce him, and then they'd shine the spotlight on Donnie in his location.

On this particular night, the Wonder Brothers had been wandering around looking for a place to sit. When they saw this little outcropping, they hunkered down in there to watch the rodeo. It came time for the bull riding, so Donnie headed up to the stand, saw these two big ol' burly guys crowded into his space, and said, "Fellas, y'all got to get out of the way. I've got to get in there."

Benjie looked at him and said, "I don't think so. We got here first."

"No, you don't understand. I've got to announce from that point right there."

"No. We got here first and we're gonna stay here."

By the time the spotlight came up on him, Donnie had wedged himself between the Wonder Brothers, who were just sitting there with their arms crossed telling Donnie the whole time that they were there first.

Every time the Wonder Brothers came from Pine Level South to Montgomery for the rodeo, they'd stop at a truck stop that had day-old donuts for sale. They'd get a dozen donuts each for the road, and these guys could some kind of eat. They'd easily finish them before they got to Montgomery, which was about twenty-five miles.

One particular day when they walked into the rodeo, Benjie was covered in grease from head to toe and Lamar had a black eye and a busted lip. I asked them, "What in the hell happened to you all on the way up here?" Benjie looked at me and said, "I whopped him." Mind now, whopping to them wasn't the same as hitting. Their whopping would probably kill an average person. They had huge hands, like hams, and they didn't know their own strength. When they whopped each other it made a thumping sound, like a truck had run into a cow or something.

Anyway, come to find out, Benjie's truck had busted a throwout bearing when they got back on the highway after stopping for donuts. He walked up and down the road picking up the parts to the bearing and then put it all back together right there on the shoulder. By the time he got all that done and got back in the truck, Lamar had eaten all of their donuts – all two dozen. Benjie told us that story and said, "That's the reason I whopped him."

Benjie had two trucks; Lamar didn't have one at all, but he did have two girlfriends. I asked Benjie why he didn't trade him one of the trucks for one of the girlfriends so they'd each have one apiece, and Benjie said, "Well, we tried that, but he wanted to give me the old fat one."

Lamar said, "Yeah, and you was trying to give me that old truck you run through the bobwire fence."

"But I painted it."

"Yeah, with a gallon of yellow latex and a roller."

I had to see that, so I asked Benjie if he'd bring it to the rodeo one day. He did, and I grant you this was the brightest yellow truck you've ever seen in your life. He had rolled the whole thing with yellow latex paint and then taken a razor blade and scraped out around the windows so he could see to drive.

The Wonder Brothers didn't travel much, but they eventually started coming to the Lauderdale, Mississippi rodeo. Of course they always came in Benjie's truck because Lamar didn't have one. His truck had a cab-high camper on it, so that's where he slept and kept his food. He stuffed his sardines, Vienna sausages, mustard, and bread under the mattress. Lamar wasn't allowed to sleep back there because it wasn't his truck.

At that time, Lauderdale had a parking lot that was on a hill with a pretty good grade, and it had a cyclone fence around it. One night Benjie parked somewhere on top of the hill, got in the camper, and went to sleep on his mattress. Lamar stayed up front and stretched out on the seat where he slept. Some time during the night he rolled over and kicked the truck out of gear, so it went flying down the hill backwards until it hit the cyclone fence. Benjie couldn't get the door to the camper open, and he had the keys to his truck in his pocket, so he had to stay there in the back all night until the next morning. That's when Lamar was able to get somebody to help him push the truck up a little so they could get Benjie out of the back, who was pretty steamed at this point.

We were standing around that night listening to this story and I said, "Benjie, I heard Lamar wasn't up there by himself. He had one of his girlfriends with him and they rolled over and knocked the truck out of gear." When I said that, Benjie came up from the ground with that big ham of a fist, hit Lamar in the chest, and knocked him flat on his ass – *whop!* Lamar got up and they were about to sure enough get into it, but by then I realized what I had done and said, "Whoa, Benjie. I was just kidding with you. He didn't have a girl up there with him. At least I don't think he did."

After that episode, Lamar decided he didn't want to sleep in the truck anymore, so he went to the Army surplus store and bought a little six-foot pup tent. It had a pole at each end holding it up in the middle, like a triangle, and it was open at both ends.

There came a big rain on the first night Lamar slept in his tent, and all the water drained off that parking lot right through it.

The next morning I asked Lamar how he had slept. He said, "I was sleeping real good until the water got up to right about here," and he traced a line from the top of his head, between his nose and ear, and down the side of his body. That's how high the water got when he was lying down on his back in his tent, so after that he got back in the truck.

Doug Ollie, a Justin trainer, had heard Bill Zeigler, Matt, and me tell stories about the Wonder Brothers for years, and he always thought we were exaggerating. He just didn't believe all that until he came to Montgomery for the first time.

Lamar had seen a Justin sticker on my hat and he really loved it, so I told him to go see Doug. When Doug gave Lamar that sticker, you would have thought he had just given him a brand new truck or something. Shortly thereafter Benjie came in, backed Doug into a corner with a menacing look, and asked, "Where'd my brother get that sticker?" I came in right about that time and said, "Doug, you really ought to find him a sticker."

After that Doug said, "I never believed there was really anybody like that, but they were everything that everybody had ever said they were and more. And they were just as genuine as they could possibly be."

One year Benjie and Lamar were going to Florida to work cattle at a rodeo, so they bought a camera since they'd never seen the ocean. They couldn't wait for us to get back to the rodeo next March to see the pictures they had taken.

Benjie showed me a stack of six or eight pictures that all looked the same. All they showed was the sand, the ocean, and the sky. He asked me what I saw, and I said, "The sand, the ocean, and the sky." Then he pointed out a little dot in the corner of the first picture that you could barely see even if you were looking for it and said, "No, that's a fellow riding a kite." It was somebody parasailing, and Benjie had taken pictures of this thing until it went plum out of sight. He flipped through the pictures and showed me that the dot got smaller and smaller until it finally just disappeared from view. They weren't able to take any pictures up close, but they just really wanted me to see that guy riding that kite.

We couldn't imagine the Wonder Brothers at the beach, so Matt asked them, "Guys, what did y'all have on?"

Benjie said, "Lamar cut the legs off his Wranglers and made him a swimsuit. I cut the legs off a pair of overalls and made me one."

"Did your heads get blistered?"

"No, we had our hats on."

"What about your feet? Did you blister your feet?"

"No, we had our boots on."

So they were on the beach with cutoff britches, cowboy hats, and cowboy boots.

The Wonder Brothers always took the funniest pictures. One time they brought a picture that we just could not figure out. Doug Ollie and I turned it up and down and around and every which way to try to make sense of it. Later that night, in the middle of the rodeo, Doug called me over to the fence and said, "I finally figured it out." They had taken a picture of the louvers on the bottom of a door somewhere. They had never seen one like that, so they took a picture of it.

Another time they brought a picture of a dirt road that split around a clump of woods and then met up on the other side. I asked Benjie what it was, and he said, "That's a picture of the road to our house. You can go either way."

We had always wondered where the Wonder Brothers lived, so they brought us some more pictures of their place. The first picture Benjie showed us was of their house, which sat on rocks about three feet off the ground. For the next one, he had crawled up under the house and taken a picture of a hound dog laying up under there asleep. The next picture was of some chickens under the other side of the house, and the next one was of the actual chicken coop. Doug looked at that last picture and asked Lamar, "What's that growing up there against the chicken coop?"

"I don't know, just some kind of weed."

"You know what, I think that's marijuana."

"I don't think so. We don't grow marijuana. We don't have nothing to do with that stuff."

"You know that's illegal, right?"

"Yeah, but we didn't plant that."

"Well, maybe it just came up wild. Y'all didn't have to grow it."

The next day they came back and Benjie said to Doug, "Lamar's in trouble with Daddy. You know that marijuana you said you saw in that picture? Lamar tried to set it on fire and he burnt the chicken coop down."

Benjie came to the rodeo one spring and said, "Well, I got my own place now. I'm not living with Momma and Daddy no more." Come to find out, he had bought a trailer for $300. I couldn't imagine what kind of place he had gotten for that little bit of money, so I asked him about it.

"It's great. I've got lights and a TV in there and everything, but it ain't got no floor so I have to watch where I walk."

Lamar said, "You ain't got no lights. You've just got a stenshon cord runnin' across the road from Momma and Daddy's house."

"Yeah, but it's my place and I stay there. And I can watch whatever TV I want to."

Lamar was still living with his mother and daddy, so I asked him what he thought about Benjie's new place. He said, "I like it where he's at because when he plays that TV too loud, I just unplug the stenshon cord."

When the Wonder Brothers weren't cleaning the crap out of chicken houses, their side job was building fences. Without a doubt, they could build the prettiest fence you ever saw. Their fences were ramrod straight and tight as a banjo string.

One time Benjie brought a picture of a fence he wanted me to see. The way they had braced the corner post was absolutely perfect, just a work of art. I looked at it and said, "Benjie, how did you get this picture?"

"I just took it."

"How did you keep him from moving?"

"Keep what from moving?"

"That fawn."

There was a little baby deer laying in between the corner post and the brace, but they never even saw it. They were taking a picture of the fence, not the deer.

When the Wonder Brothers built a fence, it was going to be on a straight line. If you didn't want a fence built right through your barn, you better not point that way and tell them to go from here to there with that barn in the middle.

One spring they had the wire for a new fence all laid out. There were a lot of big rattlesnakes over toward Pine Level South, and they were mating at this time of the year. When rattlesnakes mate, dozens of them will get wrapped up in a pile all hot as a firecracker.

It just so happened that their fence line ran right through a wad of mating rattlesnakes, so Benjie asked Lamar, "What are we going to do? This post is supposed to go right there in that bed of rattlesnakes."

"I don't know, but that's where it has to go."

Benjie decided to go get some gasoline to pour on them. By the time he got back, Lamar had cranked up a chainsaw and gotten right in the middle of that bed of rattlesnakes and was just whacking it like you'd use a machete, except it was a chainsaw. Benjie said that when he got through, Lamar was standing right there where that post went and there were little pieces of snakes, each no more than two or three inches long, laying all over the place. When I asked Lamar if Benjie's story was true, he said, "Yeah, that's where the post had to go." If there had been a gorilla there, Lamar would have cut the gorilla all to pieces and put the post right through what was left.

Benjie and Lamar Barnes had no earthly idea how well known they were. People all over the rodeo world, many of whom never even met them, know all about them because of all the stories that have been told. All you have to do is mention "The Wonder Brothers" to somebody and they know exactly who they were, what they were all about, and what they meant to me.

MEMORIES OF LECILE BY DR. LYNN PHILLIPS

I knew Lecile, and I knew Lecile well, long before I ever met him. What I'm trying to say is that Lecile Harris is bigger than life, and his reputation precedes him. You see, I grew up around rodeo. I had contested and announced amateur rodeos for several years before I ever got my PRCA announcer's card. So obviously I'd studied my lessons. Lecile was already a legend by the time I started working those amateur rodeos, so that long-legged, goose-necked, hillbilly bullfighter – a master of hijinks and tomfoolery – is one of the men I studied from afar. I watched him dance with bulls to Three Dog Night's "Joy to the World" and saw his acts and antics at rodeos all across the South.

When I finally got my pro announcer's card back in 1979, I showed up to announce one of my first ever rodeos in Grand Prairie, Texas. I hadn't met Lecile by then, so when Neal Gay told me that Lecile was the clown, my pulse quickened, my throat went dry, and my mind began to race. "Welcome to the big time," I thought to myself. I also began to wonder if I was up to the task, because I knew Lecile's acts were intricate. I'd seen them, and they required perfect timing on the part of everyone involved – especially the announcer. I knew if I screwed up his act that day at that performance, then I was through as a rodeo announcer.

But I soon learned that I had absolutely nothing to fear. You see, Lecile took me under his wing and gave me a little coaching, so we sailed through his acts that day without a hitch. That began a friendship and working relationship that has now spanned about thirty-five years and hundreds of rodeo performances across the continental United States and Canada. He is a friend, a mentor, a buddy, and one more fine guy.

How best to describe Lecile? Well, if you were to take the legs of a track star, the timing of a fine Swiss watch, the comedic genius of Red Skelton and put that in a gangly package with the grease-painted face of Emmett Kelly, then you'd have Lecile Harris.

I've had the pleasure of working Lecile's acts hundreds of times. Sometimes his acts go really well and sometimes they go to pieces, but it really doesn't matter. Either way, the crowd's always laughing, and you leave with a smile on your face. You know, it's my heartfelt belief that on those rare occasions that Lecile's acts do go totally awry, that's when they're the funniest. I'd like to tell you about one time I saw it happen myself. You could see that train wreck coming down the tracks a long way off, and there was absolutely nothing Lecile could do to get off the tracks before it arrived at the station.

We were in Harrison, Arkansas back in the mid-nineties. The sound man for this rodeo was "old school," or what you might call "technically challenged." His idea of playing music during the rodeo was to pop in an eight-track tape of Johnny Cash and let it roll through the whole performance. Lecile was planning to do his famous baseball act that night, so before we even got started, Lecile had spent an hour with this sound man explaining to him that he would play the music from "Chariots of Fire" at this particular time and place in the act when it had to be played. On and on the instructions went, but the sound man assured Lecile that he had it covered.

It came time to do the act that night. There were two other baseball players on the field, with balls and strikes being called, when Lecile finally hit the ball and headed to first base. Now what's supposed to happen after Lecile rounds second and heads to third is this: the theme to "Chariots of Fire" starts playing and the whole baseball field, including Lecile running, goes into extremely slow motion. So what did we hear as Lecile rounded second and headed to third? Silence, and the sounds of crickets. Yep, you guessed it: the sound man had gone to sleep at the wheel. Lecile went into slow motion for what seemed like an eternity, but was only seconds, and nothing happened. Finally he stopped, slowly swiveled his head on that long, crane-like neck of his, and looked right at that sound man. Lecile, with that long-legged, loping gait of his, came charging across the arena. In four or five strides, he reached the bucking chutes, and in stride, with cat-like quickness and agility, hit the third slat of that bucking chute, and vaulted into the air. His momentum carried him right onto the announcer's stand. Then, to the shock and chagrin of that sound man, he commandeered the entire soundboard. Moments later, we heard the melodic notes of "Chariots of Fire" as they came blazing out of the loudspeakers. Just as quickly, Lecile vaulted back over the fence, bolted across the arena to second base, and went into his slow-motion run just like nothing had ever happened. Now, for a moment, that huge crowd sat in stunned silence, but when they realized what had happened, they all just fell out laughing.

TRAVIS ADAMS

Travis Adams, an outstanding bullfighter, was working his first Wrangler Bullfight for Harper and Morgan. I was out on the floor talking to Rudy, who was in the barrel, when I looked over and saw Travis. I could tell he was nervous, so I called him over and asked, "Are you scared?"

Travis said, "I'm scared to death."

"Well, come on over here and take a look in this barrel."

When he leaned over to see what was in there, all he saw was a bare behind, because Rudy had taken off his long handles and turned his butt up to flash him. Travis took one look at that and then just looked at me and shook his head. When I asked him if he was still nervous, he said, "No sir," and went out and won the bullfight.

REMEMBRANCES OF LECILE BY CLAY COLLINS

It's pretty hard to know where to start when talking about the impact that Lecile has had on my life. To me, he's Pappy, and one of the great men in my life. For some reason, he took me in and taught me how to fight bulls and how to be great at it.

I only fought bulls for a year as an amateur before I got my pro card, so I didn't have a lengthy background in rodeo. I can say that I got my pro card that quickly because of Lecile.

My association with Lecile started in about 1996, when James Harper let me fight bulls at my first pro rodeo. I got to the venue early and was sitting outside the dressing room when I heard Lecile talking to somebody as he came down the hall my way. I was so nervous, because I knew he was a legend and I was still very new to the rodeo world. He walked up to me and asked, "Kid, what are you doing here? Can I help you?"

"Yes sir, I'm here to fight bulls."

"Really? Who told you that?"

"James Harper."

When Lecile heard that, he told me to just sit there a minute, and then he walked off. I guess he got the story from James, so he came back and said, "Kid, get your stuff and come on in."

I remember trying to get dressed myself while I was watching Lecile get ready. I just stood there with my mouth open in disbelief that I was in the locker room of a legend.

I fought bulls that night and I guess I did something that got Lecile's attention. When it was all over, he said, "Kid, you did all right." Then he went to James Harper and said, "James, you need to hire this kid for the run and let him work all your rodeos. He's gonna be good." So I was hired on the strength of Lecile's endorsement, and almost twenty years later we're still working together. Lecile taught me everything I know in the arena: bull savvy, reading animals, knowing what to do, knowing when and where to go, how to get in and get out, how to get into the pocket and stay there. He taught me all that.

I was at the Wrangler Bullfights one year with Lecile and the Kajun Kidd. I drew J16, Ice Pick, a bull that was really tough. When it came time to fight him, I could get in the pocket with him, but he'd throw me right out as soon as I got there. After it was over, Lecile came up to me and said, "Son, come over here and let me introduce you to the Kajun Kidd." This was another legend I'd heard about and I couldn't believe I was meeting him. We walked up to him and Lecile said, "Kajun, tell him what you told me."

He looked at me and said, "Son, why do you work so hard to get to the pocket and then give it up so easy?"

Kajun was probably in his seventies and not in the best of shape at the time, but he got up off his bench and started showing me how to get in the pocket and stay in there. It's one of the greatest moments of my career: standing there with Lecile Harris and the Kajun Kidd while they taught me how to fight bulls.

The next night I had E1 Electric, the fighting bull of the year. This bull was mean and fast, so he came out like a missile when I called for him. I threw a huge fake, dove into the pocket, and for the first time ever I was able to get to that pocket and stay there. As mean and fast as he was, that bull couldn't get me.

I remember it being the very first time I was able to just walk around a bull. I was in that pocket and it was a feeling like no other. I remember thinking while I was doing it, "This is what it feels like. This is what they're talking about."

Lecile taught me how to fight bulls both in freestyle and cowboy protection. He had his own way of doing it, and he taught Travis Adams and me that method. Lecile taught us how to be smooth: get in, get control, and get out. Protect the cowboy and protect yourself so nobody gets touched.

A lot of people in the rodeo world think it's "cool" for a bullfighter to go flying through the air, but Lecile taught us to always stay on our feet. He said we were no good to anybody if we went flying through the air, whether we had jumped or gotten hooked. Every time that happened to me, I could see Lecile in my mind's eye saying, "Don't leave your feet!"

When a bull is fought correctly, it's a work of art. I remember Ty Murray telling me one time that he could always tell when he was in the presence of great bullfighters. He'd finish the round and come off and ask, "Who was fighting bulls?" He meant that the bullfighters were so good that he didn't even notice them.

In 2007 I was leaving the golf course in Seguin, Texas when I got a phone call from the PRCA. The man on the other end said, "Son, you've been selected to fight bulls in the National Finals Rodeo in Las Vegas. Are you available?"

This was the greatest rodeo in the world asking me that question, so I said, "Hell yeah I'm available!"

After I hung up the phone, the very first person I called was Pappy. I told him the news and we both got so excited that I think we both started crying. Lecile said, "Son, I want you to do me one favor. When you step into that arena, I want you to remember Pappy." Well, when I walked through the gate on that first night, I thought, "This is for Pappy."

I'd call Lecile after every performance so he could tell me what I'd done right and what I'd done wrong. I had been fighting bulls about ten years and was working the biggest rodeo in the world, but I was still asking Pappy what I could do better. And I was still doing that after fighting bulls at the NFR in 2008 and 2009.

I owe my career to Pappy. I owe everything to Pappy. He not only taught me how to be a great bullfighter, but how to be a great man. Out of all the people in the rodeo world, he and I both would tell you that he was like my dad. To put into words how much I love and respect him and how much he meant to me, I would have to sit down and write my own book.

MULE DUNN

I was working a rodeo in Lafayette, Louisiana with a buddy named Mule Dunn. He was tougher than a nickel steak, but I never heard him say a single cuss word. The closest thing he got to that was "Mammy whammy!" Everything was a mammy whammy. It was always funny to see this great big ol' rough-looking guy from Alabama talking about a mammy whammy. Mule and I were fighting the bulls, and our barrel man was Bill McEnaney.

This particular night Mule came over to me and said, "Pappy, I want to do something spectacular tonight!"

"What did you have in mind?"

"I got on a brand new pair of cleats, and I'm going to jump a bull!"

"Mule, you can't even jump three inches off the ground, much less jump a bull."

"Yes I can! I'm going to jump Wide Track!"

Wide Track had horns that came straight out like a forklift, and he was a bad fighting bull. I didn't feel good about

Mule's chances at all because Wide Track was what we called a "mushog," which is a bull that just wants to kill you. He would come out and blow by you the first time, then go all the way to the other end, turn around, and line you out. He'd stand there for a minute until you started walking to him, and then you'd get to a certain point of no return. That was the distance at which he'd twitch his ears, move his head, and take off at you. When that happened, you had to take off running towards him while he ran at you, and when he dropped his head to hook you, that's when you'd jump right over him.

I could do this because I'd done it many times before, but I didn't think Mule could. I said, "I'll tell you what let's do. You run towards him and when he drops his head to hook you, instead of jumping over him, you just fall flat on the ground. That'll spook him and he'll jump right over you."

"You think that'll work?"

"Better than you trying to jump him."

So they let Wide Track out, he lined Mule up, and as soon as they headed towards each other and the bull was about to hook him, Mule dropped flat to the ground. The bull was scared half to death and jumped over him clean as a whistle and the crowd just roared. Mule came over to me just as proud as a peacock and said, "I really thrilled 'em, didn't I, Pappy?"

Mule felt so good about that first night that he wanted to try it again the next, but I told him, "You can't do that. He saw what you did last night, so the chance of him allowing you to do it again is slim."

"Oh yeah, Pappy, he'll do it again."

So they paired off again that next night and headed towards each other at full speed. Right before Mule got to Wide Track, he dropped down sideways to roll under the bull as it jumped over him. When he did, Wide Track picked that sucker up just like a forklift and slung him straight up into the air. The arena had these little flags flying on nylon string, like they have at car lots, and he pitched him high enough that Mule got hung up in the flags and pulled them all down as he hit the ground like a sack of hammers. I got Wide Track's attention and got him on out of the arena, but Mule was still out cold as a codfish.

The EMTs were just standing there looking at him wondering what to do, so Bill and I walked over to see what was going on. Bill took one look at Mule laid out cold in his new cleats and said, "Lecile, if he don't make it, can I have them new shoes?"

TRUCKER CUSS FIGHT

Bill McEnaney has a distinctive speech pattern that he used to his benefit in his clowning, kind of like Mel Tillis did with his singing. We were traveling down the interstate through Kentucky one night talking on the CB when this trucker came on who had the same speech trait that Bill does and asked, "Has anybody seen any bears out there?" I understood the guy perfectly since I was around Bill all the time. Bill, on the other hand, had never been around anybody else who talked in this particular way, and therefore couldn't understand him, so he went on the CB and asked him what the hell he was saying. The trucker repeated his question a couple more times, and each time Bill came back on and said he couldn't understand him because he talked so damn funny. The trucker finally became irate and started cussing Bill, so I figured I'd jack with him a little bit. I got on the CB and started cussing him right back, using this same speech characteristic. He started cussing me because he was tired of us making fun of the way he talked, so we just got into a big ol' cuss fight going down the highway. Finally he asked me where we were, and I told him we were in the semi right behind him, but of course we really weren't.

Bill and I went on down the highway laughing about that, and after a while we pulled into a truck stop to get a bite. We were looking at the menus when this great big fellow walked in and sat down right next to Bill. The waitress knew him, so she tended to him first. Well, when he opened his mouth to order his food, it was obvious that this was the guy we had been cussing all that time. Bill looked at me kind of nervous like and nodded back at the guy, and I said in a low voice, "Yeah, I know. That's him."

After the waitress took the trucker's order, she moved down to Bill and asked, "What'll you have?"

Bill shook his head No.

I said, "He'll have a cup of coffee."

Bill nodded his head Yes.

The waitress asked, "Do you want anything to eat?"

Bill shook his head No.

She looked at me and I said, "He'll have a hamburger."

Bill nodded his head Yes.

I ordered, we got our food and ate it, and Bill still hadn't said a word. We were just about to pay the tab when the trucker turned to Bill and asked in his particular way, "Where you headed?"

Bill got wide-eyed, shook his head No, shrugged his shoulders, and looked at me. I threw a twenty on the counter and said, "I don't know where, but we're gonna leave and start out right now." Bill cussed me all the way to Tennessee, and we left the CB alone after that.

HOWARD JOHNSON'S FIGHT

Bill and I were on our way back from a rodeo in Biloxi, Mississippi. We were in his truck and pulling his trailer with my mule and his trick horse in it. I was driving but I was getting tired, so about halfway home I decided to stop to get a cup of coffee. Most all of the places to eat had closed except the late-night ones, and this was about 2AM, so I pulled into a Waffle House. It so happened that all the bars around there had just closed, so all the drunks were getting breakfast. Right off the bat some dude hollered, "Hey cowboy, where's your horse?" I turned to Bill and said, "We need to go somewhere else, because I'll be in a fight before we even get inside and sit down."

We saw a Howard Johnson's across the highway with a lounge on one side and a diner on the other. It looked a little quieter over there, so we went in and ordered a cup of coffee and something to eat. There was a truck driver on the other end of the counter talking to somebody about trucking, and I was looking for the quickest way home, so I asked him, "Is there a shortcut between here and Memphis that a fellow might be able to take that's pretty good?"

Before he could answer me, somebody standing behind me said, "What damn difference does it make to you if there's a shortcut?" I turned around and there stood this great big ugly guy wearing a black leather jacket, black leather pants, and chains and stuff around his neck. He was standing there smiling at me and right in the middle of his front teeth was an extra tooth that stuck out and ended in a little point.

When I fought, I always picked out something on the guy's face to aim at, like a mole on their nose, or a wrinkle on their lip, or a spot on their eyebrow. But I was looking at this guy's extra tooth and thinking I didn't want to hit that because it was going to cut my fist, and the human mouth is one of the nastiest things on earth as far as causing infections. I said, "Look, I don't want to fight." I had a badge in my billfold that was a prop in the "Walking Tall" movie I had played a sheriff in, so I showed him that and said, "How would you like to spend the night in jail?"

"How would you like to have that badge shoved up your ass?"

Well, when I heard that, it was on. I turned around to Bill, gave him my glasses, billfold, and watch, and said, "I'll be right back." When I turned back around to square off with the dude, he wasn't there. I looked out the front window and saw him running past it. By then I was mad, so I took off after him. Right outside the front window was a pickup truck with a big box tied down on top of a couple of two-by-fours. This dude stopped and tried to pull out one of those, but it wouldn't budge. While he was standing there pulling on it, I came down the sidewalk wide open and knocked him fifteen or twenty feet before he ever fell down. Every time he got up, I'd clobber him again, but I couldn't knock him out. He was high on drugs, and those people are really hard to knock out. I even popped him on that little pointy tooth, which I shouldn't have. Finally he got up enough for me to get a hold of his head, so I dropkicked him, and that kind of wiped him out.

By then a crowd had gathered, and somebody said the cops were coming. That was fine with me because everybody there had seen what happened, so I had lots of witnesses in my favor. The cops got there and started questioning everybody, but by the time they got around to looking for the dude, he was gone. After they couldn't find him, they told me to just go on home. I knew that hitting him on that tooth was going to be a bad deal, and it was. My hand was swollen up so bad that I couldn't even make a fist by the time we got home.

The next week I got a call from the police down there. This officer knew me from the rodeo, and he said, "Lecile, this guy has filed assault and battery charges on you, so we have a warrant out for your arrest and a court date. He's also going to need some facial reconstruction work, and he wants you to pay for it."

"Well, you know how it all happened, and besides, his mouth was really messed up to begin with. I probably helped it."

"The best thing to do is to just not come back down here for the hearing or anything. Just stay away and let it blow over."

That all happened in October. The following spring I got a call from the guy who ran the rodeo down there. He wanted me to come work it, but I told him I couldn't. He asked me why not, so I explained the situation and said, "They told me it would be a good idea if I just didn't come back down there for a while."

The guy heard that and said, "Let me see if I can do anything about that."

I got a call from him a couple of weeks later and he said, "You know that little problem you had down here? It's all taken care of."

"Really? How'd you do that?"

"I sent a couple of pulpwooders over to his house to talk to him, and for some reason he never did show up for the court date."

VINCE GILL / MATT HARRIS

I met Vince Gill at the Dixie Nationals in Jackson, Mississippi. It was one of his first gigs. After the show, he got in the back of a pickup truck just to ride around and say hello to everybody, and he hollered at me to jump up there with him. While we were riding around the arena, I told him there was no doubt in my mind that he was going to make it. Not only did he have a great voice, but he was also an outstanding guitar picker.

After the rodeo was over, Matt and I went to Denny's to get something to eat. He was at the salad bar when a girl who had been at the rodeo came up and asked him for his autograph. Matt couldn't understand why somebody would want the sound engineer's autograph, but he signed her paper anyway. After that, another came up, and another, and another. Finally one of them came up and said, "Vince Gill, can I have your autograph?" Matt didn't want to disappoint them, so he just signed Vince's name instead of his from then on.

My mother always thought Matt looked a lot like Vince Gill, who was one of her favorite singers. Two things she really loved were Alabama football and Vince Gill. When Mother was eighty-five years old, she said that if she were sixty years younger, she'd give his wife a run for her money.

LEANN RIMES

I was working the Dixie Nationals another year. I always ran around the fairgrounds there every morning, but this particular morning it was raining, so I went to the coliseum. The building is round, and there's a corridor that goes all the way around it, so I started running on it. I had made it about halfway around when I met this little girl skating, who must have been about twelve or thirteen. I met her another time or two, since we were both going opposite directions, and we'd laugh and nod each time. Finally the concession workers were bringing in some food for the night, and they had the way blocked off, so we had to stop for a minute. She asked me what I did with the rodeo, and I told her. We visited there a little bit before the guys got done and then went our separate ways.

Later that night in the middle of the rodeo, I was standing in makeup next to the entertainment stage when this little girl came by me and said, "Hi, I was skating while you were running this morning."

"I remember. What are you doing here?"

"Oh, I'm singing."

"Singing? Who are you singing with?"

She said, "I'm singing by myself," and walked right up onstage. The announcer introduced her as Leann Rimes, and she really rocked the house.

DEEP THOUGHTS WITH LECILE HARRIS BY MARK W. DUNCAN

"Comedic genius is best defined by its simplicity." Those were the words that raced to my mind that frigid February night as I stood there in utter amazement and disbelief next to Boyd and Rolex, surrounded by a sell-out crowd of 5,214 rodeo fans in San Angelo, Texas.

Over the previous nine years, we had seen many things happen in that arena. I can honestly say that 99.9% of them – good, bad, or indifferent – were the result of careful thought, meticulous planning, diligent rehearsal, and precise execution by some of the most passionate, professional, and selfless people that have ever been assembled with the task of producing a PRCA rodeo. During that time, we had revived a rodeo that had become stagnant and disconnected for the fans, the community, the contestants, and the sport of rodeo alike. It was no longer withering on the vine as we molded it into a production that was the model that many in our industry were trying to emulate.

At the heart of that transformation sat four-time PRCA Announcer of the Year Boyd Polhamus and Pro Rodeo Hall of Famer Lecile Harris. As this display of comedic genius was playing out in a completely dark house, Boyd sat poised atop his horse, Rolex, and Lecile sat all alone in all of his glory smack-dab in the center of the arena on an old commode. Yes, those suspenders and signature oversized Wrangler jeans were down around his ankles; the iconic red-checkered shirt covered him from torso to knees; and his hat was positioned perfectly so that the spotlight didn't shadow his facial expressions.

If you think you've seen what I'm talking about, you were either present that night in San Angelo or you saw the picture on the back cover of this book you're reading. Either way, if you know anything about Lecile Harris, you know that you may be able to envision him in many different circumstances, but vulnerable is not a situation that comes to mind. Yet on this night, there he sat on that porcelain throne – exposed to the world in a comedic sense. For those of us who knew the details of the story leading up to that defining moment, we knew that Lecile was exposing an element of his comedic genius that even he didn't know existed. When Boyd introduced for the very first time "Deep Thoughts with Lecile Harris," we learned that if you're willing to take a chance, you can grow in ways you never imagined – even at seventy-something years old. This story is a microcosm of Lecile's life, one that he has lived as an open book for all of us to experience and enjoy.

If you know anything about rodeos, you know that most of them have a carnival and midway somewhere in close proximity; San Angelo is no exception. It is also common knowledge that if there is a large number of people confined to a certain area for any significant length of time, there will be plumbing catastrophes; once again, San Angelo is no exception.

For the past few years leading up to our story, San Angelo had gone to a two-weekend format. In doing so, we had created two "dark days" on which the carnival and midway continued full speed ahead but the rodeo was able to take a couple of nights off. These "dark days" were originally designed to allow those of us who were directly involved in putting the rodeo on a time to catch our breath and recover; they really served more as a time for those who saw themselves as the self-appointed experts, who were also too privileged to labor, to bitch and moan about anything that they thought important to themselves. The problem was that they really thought they themselves were important. They really could not grasp the concept that Boyd, Lecile, and I didn't really care about anything they had to say about the product we had been turning out over the past six years.

Things were financially tough in West Texas, so those sell-out crowds we were playing to night after night deserved the best that we could provide. Since we were really the only building rodeo that didn't have a concert to follow our performances, it was imperative that we bring the best entertainment that our sport had to offer. Believe you me, when I say that we brought them all over the years, we brought all of them. We had developed the philosophy that we couldn't produce a first-class rodeo without a first-class production, but unfortunately we had a real production dilemma we were needing to solve.

In the spirit of full disclosure, this dilemma was really a self-inflicted one. World-renowned *charro* Tomás Garcilazo was going to be performing the last four nights and dammit, come hell or high water, Tomás was going to finish his act under a spotlight in a dark house. We had always talked about it, but this time it was going to happen.

It is also important to know that the San Angelo Coliseum is an excellent facility for flea markets, church revivals, motocross, tractor pulls, and even midget wrestling, but it absolutely is the worst facility in the country in which to try and produce a first-class rodeo. Among many of the issues we faced was the one facing us now: it was simply that the lighting system in the coliseum was older than Lecile. Getting a dark house was no problem at all; the real challenge was covering the twelve minutes it took for the lights to cool off before they could be turned back on.

We were about to kick off our second weekend of the year. At around 2AM on Wednesday morning when the meeting between Boyd, Lecile, and I ended, everyone wearily headed back to their trailers for a few hours of sleep before the 10AM production meeting for the performance that was to take place later that night. I took a short detour by the coliseum to confirm to myself once again for the umpteenth time that twelve minutes was still 720 seconds and it still took a minimum of 720 seconds to skirt the lighting dilemma. After leaving the coliseum, I decided to cut across the midway since it had been closed for several hours. As the rodeo chairman, I usually avoided the midway like the plague since everyone there felt as if I should give them free rodeo tickets, which didn't even exist since we had been sold out for weeks (but that is in fact a chapter reserved for my book someday). But there I was, all alone, walking along this deserted midway in the wee hours of the morning, just hoping for some sort of sign or idea or maybe even a vendor who happened to sell modern-day coliseum lighting fixtures. That's when I saw it. By "it" I do not mean the Colisieum-Light-o-Matic machine I so desired. I mean sitting there under the glow of a midway security light, I saw an old white commode that had recently become the focal point of the afternoon's midway plumbing disaster. Now, I would be lying through my teeth if I told you that when I saw the "Turd Tosser 2000" I thought immediately of "Deep Thoughts with Lecile Harris," but I am telling you the absolute truth when I say that I thought immediately of Boyd Polhamus.

Now I don't want to get into any chapter of Boyd's book, but I can say this without giving too much away. For as long as I have been Boyd's favorite rodeo chairman and whenever he is in San Angelo, there has been what you might call a pattern of random things showing up at Mr. Rodeo Announcer's trailer. It started with an old wooden eagle and over the years has included trash dumpsters, Mike Cervi's blue roan, a missing police cruiser, countless adoring fans of both sexes, some annoying realtors, and countless other inanimate objects. This particular night, however, all I could focus on was getting this fecal collection unit pressed up against his trailer door before it was time for him to go feed Rolex.

Toilets were designed for one thing and one thing only, so they were not meant to be portable. Besides being extremely heavy, the damn things are kinda awkward to carry. It became apparent very quickly that I was not going to be able to move this throne by myself, so I instinctively did what I always do when I encounter something that requires assistance: I phoned George Cooper. The only reason that Boyd, Lecile, and I and all the others could even remotely focus on production issues is because George Cooper was the driving force that put together the entire physical infrastructure that a rodeo of our magnitude demanded. I will leave those specifics for George's book, but I can sum up George Cooper and what he meant to me personally and to our rodeo by simply saying this: by 2:45AM, that toilet was wedged tightly against Boyd's trailer door, perfectly leveled, clean as a whistle, and in perfect working condition.

When the phone rang at 6AM sharp, I didn't need caller ID to know who it was so I just rolled over and went straight back to sleep. After I finally awoke, everything had quietened down surrounding the events of the previous hours. But as we headed off to the 8AM production meeting, little did we know that my find was going to become an icon instead of a worthless piece of junk overturned next to Boyd's trailer.

The production meeting went just as we had expected. We went in with the lighting dilemma and we walked out with it as well. Not even George Cooper could fix it. We were screwed and it was almost lunch time. This meant only one thing: Justin Sports Medicine Athletic Trainer Bill "Zig" Zeigler, Lecile, Boyd, Matt Harris, George Cooper, and I were headed to lunch together at Franco's. Pull up to this little place any day of the year and there is a line out the door; pull up during rodeo week and you'd better have a couple of hours to kill. It was actually during the time that we were waiting on a table when the concept of "Deep Thoughts with Lecile Harris" was conceived. Listening to Lecile talk about his life and seeing that toilet in front of Boyd's trailer had me thinking. You see, besides being an authority on hamburger steaks and chicken-fried steaks, Zig has probably seen almost as many of Lecile's acts as poor Matt (his son who works the other end of his acts) has, yet every time he sees one again, he still laughs his ass off. Boyd, of course, as the announcer, knew every aspect of Lecile's routines, and the detail to which the two of them planned things down to the last detail is awe-inspiring. So as talk turned to which act Lecile was going to use on this second weekend, the discussion intensified between everyone as I began to have this crazy idea – and I do mean it was crazy.

I would like to think that I was smart enough to find a more professional time to suggest it to Lecile, but the truth is that I was a little scared to mention it in front of the crew. Any act that Lecile has ever performed has only been performed publicly after literally every minute detail has been addressed and it has been rehearsed to the point of perfection. Somehow I thought that asking him to just do an improv sit-down comedy routine in front of a packed house for the next four nights might not be received well. With that in mind, I waited for the right moment, which came as the three of us crawled into Boyd's truck and headed back to the fairgrounds. I said, "What if Lecile followed Tomás and did his act under a dark house?" I might as well have farted the question from the way it was received. Lecile's answer to my question was pretty simple: "I don't have an act that will work under a dark house." For the sake of time and space I will forego the conversation that followed as we drove back to our trailers, but I can tell you that I learned more about Lecile's craft than I had ever known as I listened to him talk about all of the elements that must go into an act in order for it to be successful. It was summed up by his parting statement as we dropped him off at his trailer: "Comedy is *deeeeeep*, Duncan. It appears to be very superficial, but in order for it to be effective, you have to put some *deeeeeep* thought into it. Later, dudes!"

So when Boyd and I got back to the trailer, we put some *deeeeeep* thought into things. Tomás needed three minutes of dark house to finish his routine, then another thirty seconds to accept his applause and exit the arena. Surely Boyd could sell a sponsor or something for another minute or two. That led to the idea of running the sponsors' flags under a dark house, and the next thing we knew, we were at seven minutes of dark house. All we needed was five more minutes, but in production, that can be an eternity. So it was with the thought of eternity in mind that I suggested my crazy idea to Boyd. It was really pretty simple: ask Lecile to come sit on a toilet in the middle of the dark arena; have him entertain folks for five minutes with an act he had never performed; and then turn the lights back on. You can imagine Boyd's response and, believe you me, Boyd can respond when prompted. What he responded with was actually not what I expected, but it was golden.

You see, when I hired Lecile in my second year as rodeo chairman, having never met him nor seen his act, I did it strictly on Boyd's recommendation. Lecile introduced San Angelo to his "walking and talking" style of comedy, the banter between him and Boyd, and his robot and baseball acts. The crowd loved him.

A few weeks later, I fired Lecile – not because I wanted to, but because I was told to. You see, some of those experts I mentioned earlier got their feelings hurt when they discovered that Lecile was going to play to the crowd and not to them individually. He was trying to connect with that family on row twenty-two who had saved their money all year to come to the rodeo; he was not just there to humor those chosen few who sat in the box seats that surrounded the arena floor.

The problem was confounded by the fact that there was no family on row twenty-two or even row eleven for that matter. We were trying our best but we couldn't give tickets away and get to row eleven. I briefly mentioned earlier that there had been a disconnect between the rodeo and its fans. This phenomenon was not just unique to San Angelo, but it was very apparent every time we finished the national anthem and started bucking out a few broncs: we had a disconnect between us and our fans.

A couple of years later, I called Lecile to hire him back, fully expecting to be told "Hell no!" but instead hearing "Hell yes, those folks were just starting to get me when you fired me!" Thus began the reconnection between Lecile and his fans in San Angelo.

This is all very important because although I am writing this I am actually just telling you what Boyd was telling me. He was going back over the previous six years and all of the things that had taken us from trying to give tickets away to now producing an event that was the hottest ticket in town. Lecile was one of the major reasons for the amazing turnaround. The fans came expecting to hear some of Lecile's classic lines; they came expecting the bantering and badgering between Boyd and Lecile; they came for the baseball act and the golf act; but even more importantly they came because Lecile had created a connection between himself and the entire crowd, from row one all the way to row thirty-four of the coliseum. They had grown to love Lecile Harris but the question was, did they really know Lecile Harris? It was with that premise in mind that Boyd invited Lecile over to his trailer to discuss what would forever be known as "Deep Thoughts with Lecile Harris."

The specific details of the discussion that ensued in Boyd's trailer will forever be kept between the three of us because it really was a defining moment of our friendship, but also because it would not be good reading for most of you. Fast-forward to the 5PM production meeting and that is when the whole idea really came together.

"Hambone, we need twenty seconds of bed music to set it up."

"Lisa, we need a ground-level camera on Lecile the entire time so they can pick him up on the big screen."

"Spotlight operators, here's the order you'll hit him with and here's the pass-off sequence."

"George, we need to get that toilet in the middle of the arena without anyone seeing it being put there."

"Randy, we need cool graphics that say "Deep Thoughts with Lecile Harris" and they have to fade in on his intro and fade out when he exits."

There was lots of talking but the guy that it was centering around just sat there in silence. He just sat there in that production meeting as quiet as a mouse, and that is not what you usually get when you invite Lecile to a production meeting. He was just looking around the coliseum, staring at all of those seats, and you could tell the wheels were turning in the mind of that comedic genius.

Hambone asked, "Lecile, how will I know when you are finished so I can start your exit music?" His reply was very simple, and it was actually the last sentence Lecile uttered to any of us until show time some two-and-a-half hours later: "Don't worry, dude. You'll know."

And know we did. We got our twelve minutes of dark house that night and the nights that followed, but more importantly we got five minutes of some of the rawest, most genuine, selfless emotion you could ever imagine. That all happened in those few brief seconds that transpired with Lecile just sitting there on that commode. Imagine if you will, sitting on your commode, as if you were all alone in deep thought, contemplating the meaning of life; then you suddenly realize that you have literally been caught with your pants down in front of an arena full of people. Lecile did just that and he did it to perfection. He also did it under a spotlight in a dark house that was totally silent as well.

You could have heard a mouse break wind as Lecile sat there on that throne with 10,428 eyes looking directly at him. You could FEEL a connection between Lecile and everyone in the coliseum that few entertainers will ever experience and few audiences will ever know. The silence was deafening, yet it spoke volumes to everyone present. When the lead-out music started and the graphics ran, Lecile didn't even acknowledge that anyone else was present until Boyd said, "San Angelo, I give to you Deep Thoughts with Lecile Harris!" Surprisingly he didn't appear startled, embarrassed, or even uncomfortable that more than 5,000 folks had just unexpectedly walked in on him in his bathroom back home in Tennessee. No, in that brief moment, he was actually welcoming to everyone who was there. He didn't just welcome us into his bathroom; rather, he welcomed us into a side of Lecile Harris that none of us knew existed and in some ways even he didn't know existed. He simply stood, pulled up his pants and suspenders, flushed the toilet, put down the lid (as if out of respect for all of the women present), straightened his hat, and then with the most perfect pitch and timing one could ever imagine said, "I was just thinkin'."

And the rest, as they say, is history. I really can't remember what he was thinking because it really didn't matter by that time to me or to Boyd either, but it was hilarious. What mattered was that he thought more about those folks up there in those stands than he thought about his own personal self. He held over 5,000 people in the palm of his hand, and in those few minutes, he allowed them to experience every emotion that is necessary in order to get to know who Lecile Harris really is.

Hambone did in fact know when Lecile was finished. He simply doffed his hat and, with perfect posture and timing, followed his lead-out music into a chasm of darkness. When the lights came back on after twelve minutes exactly, they came back on at full strength to a full house of fans who were giving Lecile Harris a full standing ovation for what was a breathtaking display of comedic genius.

As Lecile exited the arena, he looked Boyd and me straight in the eyes and, with that effervescent smile and that gentlemanly Southern charm, simply said, "Later, dudes."

A STORY BY BOYD POLHAMUS

I have so many great memories of working with Lecile. His comedy is just so natural. You never have to work to fit in a joke because the joke always seems to fit no matter what we're doing or when we're doing it.

One of the funniest memories I have of Lecile happened at the Rodeo of the Ozarks on one Fourth of July. He was telling a story about how he won a door prize at Wal-Mart. Lecile wanted to say he won one of those oscillating fans but really said, "I won one of them ovulatin' fans."

I said, "Excuse me, sir?"

"You know, one of them ovulatin' fans that swings from side to side." When he said that, I just started cracking up. Then he asked, "Well, what's the real word then? What is it?"

"I'd tell you what it is, but ovulatin' is a lot funnier than the real word."

Lecile has done a lot of that over the years. He's always had a knack for taking a normal word and making it funny. I love the man and I'm just proud that I was working rodeos at the same time he was.

RENO WRECK AND BOB TALLMAN

I was still fighting bulls at 52 years old. The average bullfighter now may make it to 30 or maybe 35. I was beginning to lose agility, but I was compiling knowledge. When you start learning to fight bulls, you study the bull riders and watch them get down. You watch how they wrap their hands and which one they put in the rope. You learn whether a particular bull has a habit of coming out and spinning to the right or spinning to the left, or whether he's a straightaway, or whether he's bad about jerking the riders down on his head. You learn all of these things and just kind of keep a mental record of all their habits without relying on them to do any of it. If you start to depend on them to do this or that, and they don't, then you find yourself in a bind.

So with that knowledge I was compiling, I started to move into the positions I wanted to be in a little better than when I was faster and quicker. I never was real fast, but I was always quick. That's one reason my bullfighting was so different. I didn't do all the fast passes because I didn't have the necessary speed. I had to go to the bull, stay real close to him, keep my hands on him, and work around him. I knew I couldn't outrun one, but with my quickness I could move from point A to point B in a hurry. So all this knowledge I had compiled, plus my particular style, enabled me to fight bulls longer than most people did.

But in Reno, a bull caught me and gave me a brain concussion; broke my pelvis and ankle; tore up my left knee; separated my left shoulder; broke four ribs; and bruised my liver, heart, and lungs. I was in bad shape, and at 52, you don't bounce back like you do when you're 19 or 20.

Fifteen minutes before I got hurt, Bob Tallman, one of the most celebrated rodeo announcers in the business, also got busted up when the horse he was riding bucked him off and broke his hip.

We were in the hospital together for ten days, and since we were sharing a room, we also shared the same nurse. She was a great big Swedish woman, and she walked in about two or three days after we got there and asked me in this great big booming voice, "Mr. Harris, have you had a BM?"

"No ma'am."

"Well, you'd better have one by morning. If you don't, I'll be back with what it takes to get it done."

Then she said the same thing to Bob and left. His wife and daddy were there, and they asked if we needed anything from the store. I said yes, that I needed three sacks of prunes and a can of prune juice. I also told them to get some for Bob, but he said, "I ain't eating none of that crap."

His wife left and brought me back my groceries, and I stayed up all night eating prunes and drinking prune juice. I told Bob that he better have some too, but he refused. Well, about daylight, the urge hit me. I was bedridden so I called the nurse's station, and a great big orderly came down to tend to me. I told him, "I'm fixing to have a BM."

"I'll get you a pan."

"A pan ain't gonna work."

I knew I had to get up. The problem was that my pelvis was broken and they hadn't pinned it, so it was moving back and forth if I even tried to roll over or sit up, much less stand. But I said, "Just help me back up to that shower." When I got there, I held my gown up and almost blew the back out of that shower, with Bob laughing the whole time.

At 7AM sharp our great big Swedish nurse came back in and asked, "Mr. Harris, have you had a BM?"

"Yes ma'am, I sure have."

"Yes, I see it on your chart here. Good, good. Mr. Tallman, have you had a BM?"

Bob said, "Yes ma'am, I have."

"I don't see it on your chart."

"Well, they must have forgotten to write it down."

The nurse looked at me and asked, "Mr. Harris, do you think he's had a BM?"

I said, "No ma'am. I know he hasn't. I tried all night to get him to eat some prunes but he wouldn't do it."

When the nurse heard that, she turned back to Bob and said, "Mr. Tallman, you should have eaten the prunes."

They dragged Bob back to the shower and the nurse gave him an enema that you would've thought was killing him. I never heard so much screaming in my life. When it was over, he came back white as a sheet and sweating bullets, so I asked him, "Tallman, you think you might want some prunes now?"

A STORY BY BOB TALLMAN

I came to Jackson, Mississippi in the eighties to work the Dixie Nationals Rodeo for the first time. This being my indoctrination to Southern culture, I was eager to fit in, so I probably tried a little too hard. Having that mindset when I first met Lecile at this event, I decided I was going to teach him a thing or two.

Lecile considered Mississippi his home country since he was born there and lived right across the border in Tennessee. He knew exactly where he was going with the act, and I was just supposed to fit my part into it. Phil Gardenhire, who I consider to be the greatest rodeo announcer that ever lived, had worked hundreds of performances with Lecile, so he had his timing down impeccably.

I decided I was going to learn that right then and there, but I had very little training with Lecile. When I met him, he said,

"Listen, kid. I'll start, you follow, everything's gonna be fine and they'll love it." Right…

When it came time to do the performance that night, Lecile strolled out, like the gangly ape he is, to do the piano act. Lecile is the only person I know who can go to the thrift store, pick up the clothes that nobody else would even think about buying, wad them up, never wash them, yet put them on and look like a prince.

You have to remember that technology has changed a lot since then, so the sound effects didn't always hit exactly when you wanted them to. That wasn't a problem for Lecile. He had been in movies and on TV and was also a professional drummer, so his timing was beyond belief. 99% of all rodeo clowns and acts never figure this out, but timing is the key to all success.

My job was to follow him: he'd lead with the comedy and I'd follow as the straight guy. But I wanted to be funny, and every time I tried to be funny, Lecile would give me this look that seemed to say: "Just shut the hell up." I asked him once during the act if he was going to sit down and play the piano. When I did, he just looked at me and said, "That's my line." That sort of thing went on throughout the performance, and the people absolutely loved it. I thought I was a real part of the act, but I later found out that I was actually just in the way.

I understand that this is a book with stories designed to last for one bowel movement, so you're probably waiting for the story to end so you can get the paperwork over with and finish the job. With that in mind, let me just say that nobody in the world can do an act like Lecile. His timing is above and beyond anybody else's.

EYE-OPENER

The Reno wreck was an eye-opener that told me at 52 years old it was time for me to stop fighting bulls. I realized that I didn't want to get out of the rodeo business altogether, so I had my comedy to fall back on. Fortunately, not like it is now, I was forced to do comedy when I was young, because back then you had to do comedy or you didn't work as a bullfighter. So I learned my comedy as I was going along, and it turned out that was a good thing.

Back in the old days, we didn't have nearly the pressure we do now. A lot of that is due to all this politically correct stuff. People used to come to the rodeo and kick back and say, "Entertain me." Now they dare you to make a mistake or say something they can put in the paper or make something out of. Instead of just laughing and enjoying it, they're picking it apart. My goal is to never have to quit, so I develop my acts or change them up a little every year to stay current. But I don't do political stuff and I don't do religious stuff, because it's just going to offend somebody.

A lot of people look at things now just to find fault. You can be in an arena with 8,000 people and have a bit that you think 7,999 of them would enjoy, but if you think that one person is going to take it and use it against you, then you have to watch it. Society in general is like that, whether you're at the rodeo or in church. And if you turn on your TV, you can hear stuff that's just damned embarrassing to you. I wish TV was family entertainment, but it isn't, and these people that complain at the rodeo have no problem putting their kids in front of the TV to watch something rank. Rodeo is family entertainment, and that's the way we want it. We take care of the kids at the rodeo.

I'm able to get away with more things than a lot of clowns because of my age. But there's a difference in being nasty and colorful. You don't ever hear me say anything nasty. Colorful maybe, but not nasty. I do a bit where I ask the announcer if he knows what a "badonkadonk" is, and when he says he doesn't, I'll ask a lady in the audience to stand up and turn around to show everybody. In all the years I've been doing that, I've never had a single one not to stand up, because it's their few seconds in the spotlight. And you wouldn't believe the number of people who come up before the rodeo and tell me that they're going to be sitting in section so and so, and would I do the badonkadonk thing with their wife or girlfriend or whatever. They just want that little bit of attention.

There are some words you can say because they're funny, even though they're a little bit naughty. I talk about having a thong on backwards in one of my bits. I can say "thong" and get away with it because it's a funny word, but I couldn't say "panties" because it's not. I learned that by watching W.C. Fields. One of his favorite words was "kumquat." That's just a funny word.

I'll mispronounce words to be funny. Believe it or not, I minored in English in college. People hear me today and think "No way!" But I had a really good English professor in college who knew I was doing some standup comedy, and I never will forget what he told me one day: "If you want to use the English language in a comedic way, you are going to first have to learn to use the English language in the proper way."

You have to be able to talk on people's level. If I go do a speech at a pilots' convention, I don't use the same vocabulary that I use at a children's home. When I go to Canada, I can't say, "That feller's no kin to you," because they'll have no idea what I'm talking about. I have to say, "He's not related to you."

I'm good at painting pictures with verbiage. A good example of that is the story about me taking my Uncle Vick to get a shave at the barber shop. I talk about the barber putting that wooden ball in his cheek to poke it out and make it smooth so he could shave right over it. An orthopedic surgeon heard that story one time and told me, "You're the damnedest storyteller. When you were telling the story about Uncle Vick and the barber, that was so visible to me. I could see the ball and then I could see his face when he got through shaving with all the wrinkles in it. And I'm soaking all that up and then – *wham!* – you bust me with that punch line."

MEMORIES OF LECILE BY LES MCINTYRE

I first met Lecile at the Calgary Stampede some twenty or twenty-five years ago. The late Bill Kehler, the ultimate Canadian rodeo announcer and my mentor, introduced me to Lecile one day after I had watched him work the afternoon rodeo performance. The minute I saw him walk into the arena, I saw that this was a man in control of everything – the crowd, announcers, contestants, everyone! He got everybody's attention just by walking into the arena with an old corn broom. His look, motions, and demeanor were all one of a kind. You just had to watch him, and the cool part was that he hadn't even spoken yet! He had the ultimate rodeo clown look. His makeup made you want to feel sorry for this poor hobo-looking dude, yet at the same time, laugh your head off at him. When Lecile finally spoke, it was with calculated purpose. It was slow, with that undeniably funny and appealing Tennessean accent that made you laugh and, at the same time, respect and be attentive to every word he said. You just felt drawn to the man even though you didn't know a thing about him. His humor, timing, and delivery were impeccable, which is something I've grown to appreciate even more now after thirty years of announcing chuckwagon races and twenty-five years of pro rodeos.

I never will forget that day in Calgary when I first met him in his full costume and makeup. An hour or so later, Billy and I were on our way back to the main grandstand to do my radio show for the chuckwagons, when this car pulled up in front of us. Bob Tallman and his passenger, a tall, good-looking black-haired fellow, had stopped to talk to Billy and me before they headed out to dinner. The passenger didn't say much, so Tallman did all the talking – surprising? When they pulled away, I asked Billy who the guy with Bob was, thinking he was a calf roper from Texas or something. When Billy told me that was Lecile Harris, I couldn't believe it!

Fast-forward some twenty years. My traveling partner and dear friend, Bill Kehler, passed away suddenly right in the middle of the Canadian rodeo season. It was a life-changing experience for me and many others who knew him. As a result of his passing, I inherited most of the bigger rodeos that Bill had been doing for years. The first one I did was the Ponoka Stampede, the largest seven-day rodeo in Canada, and the entertainer that year was Lecile Harris. I was scared to death and felt like I was in over my head as far as working with a rodeo clown of such great stature! I will never forget our first production meeting. I was nervous as heck when we entered the meeting room, and was preparing to introduce myself to Lecile, but he beat me to the draw. He stuck out his hand and, with that unmistakably unique Tennessean accent, said, "Hi, Les. It's real good to see you. It's been a long time and I'm really looking forward to working with you, dude!" For me, that was the best thing I could have ever heard, and it was the start of a special friendship that I will cherish forever.

Lecile and I have worked Ponoka and Strathmore together a few times. In Strathmore, I get to work alongside Bob Tallman. What more could an announcer ask for than to share the arena and microphones with those two legendary icons? But it's the storytelling after the show that fascinates me the most – the lifetime of incredible experiences these two have created and enjoyed together! What an honor for me to have experienced it.

One time in Strathmore, Bob was, I think, somewhat overloaded with all the things going on in his crazy, busy world. As a result, Lecile had been challenged during the performances by Bob's meandering away from the purposes and punch lines of some of Lecile's stories and jokes. Before the rodeo one day, Lecile said to me, "Les, here's what I want to do today. I want you to pick up with my comedy and not let Tallman cut in there with all his bullshit and mess it up for me!" Well, I laughed so darn hard when he said that, but it was true. I'd listened to them all week and it was fun to watch! What a pair they are. But I was so impressed by the fact that someone as great as Lecile Harris would even let me play his game, especially alongside Bob Tallman. I will be forever grateful to that man, who is so sincere, down to earth, humble, and real.

We were in Strathmore another year, and Lecile had just arrived from somewhere in the United States where it was 110 degrees. It was 65 in Strathmore, so he was freezing. After the production meeting that morning, Lecile came up to me and said, "Man, do you have a jacket or something I could borrow? I'm freezing my Tennessee ass off in this Canadian weather!" It just so happened that earlier that week I had purchased a fancy jacket of some kind that I had never worn, so I lent it to him for the week. When he brought it back, I hung it in my closet and have never worn it to this day. It's still there, in case he needs it again!

I was interviewed once and asked to say something about Bob Tallman's career, so I said, "Tallman did for rodeo what George Strait did for country music!" And I will say this about Lecile Harris: "Lecile has done for rodeo what George Jones did for country music!" Lecile is the KING of rodeo entertainers!

CAR ACT

I had a long convalescent period at home after I got out of the hospital from the Reno wreck. I was watching a lot of old comedy just to stay tuned up, and I saw a Laurel and Hardy episode that really tickled me. They were riding along a street in San Francisco in an old Model A. When they pulled up behind a streetcar and stopped, another one behind them didn't stop, so they were sandwiched between them with their car folded up in half and the wheels just a little ways apart. When the streetcar in front took off, Laurel and Hardy drove off with that car folded up into a big point.

I had seen people do car acts before, but I had never wanted one because they were such a pain. You were always having to work on them because they'd always quit or break, plus you had to haul them around. I knew all that, but I just couldn't get over that bit I had seen Laurel and Hardy do, so I decided to build one myself. I asked Ethel to go to the hobby shop and get me a model kit of an old Model A. I sat there in bed and put it together, painted it, and then got a hacksaw and cut it in two so I could fold it up and see if it would work. Once I saw that it would, I drew up plans that were to scale for a real car.

The main problem I had was how to make the car fold up and down. I was talking to a friend of mine about it over coffee one morning when he said, "Why don't you use a winch?" That was good because I didn't know squat about hydraulics, so he designed a system for me. Jackie Robertson, a good friend of mine from Weatherford, Texas who had been a rodeo clown and barrel man himself, built the frame and put the motor in it. I got the body down in Florida, painted it how I wanted it, and took it to Jackie. He called me after a couple of months and told me to come try it, and I was just thrilled. That's how the car act was born and it's become a real hit.

MR. FRIGGINS ACT

Then came "Mr. Friggins," which was a takeoff on "Big Ball's in Cowtown." I was looking for a musical act that could match me, an untalented musician, with a talented one. I play the standup bass with this classically trained violinist, which was Matt, and we just cannot get it together. I named the guy Roland Wiggins, but I'll mistakenly call him Mr. Friggins, which is kind of like me calling Black Bart by the name of Black Butt. My main inspiration for this act was Charlie Daniels, who has been a friend of mine for a long time.

HARRY VOLD

Harry Vold is probably the best-known rodeo stock contractor and producer in the business. They call him "The Duke of the Chutes," and that's referring to the John Wayne character. When he speaks, everybody listens, because he's just loaded with wisdom and witticisms. One of my favorite sayings of his is one that I must've repeated dozens of times. I'd be upset about a rodeo going poorly because maybe the weather was bad or the crowds were thin, and Harry's famous line about that was "Lecile, the check's the same."

One time we were in Colorado Springs doing the robot act. There was a huge storm coming over the mountain right as we were about to go on. The rain started peppering down and lightning was popping all around. Matt was inside the robot, which was about eight feet tall, plastic, and painted silver. Harry thought this robot was made out of metal, so he looked up at the sky and then turned to me and said, "Lecile, don't send that kid out there in that tin can with all this lightning going on. Let him stay here with me while you go out there and tell a joke."

"Harry, you don't want him to go out there, but you want me to go out there and tell a joke?"

"Lecile, you're a lot older and he's got a lot longer to live. Go ahead."

We were at a rodeo one year taking part in the introduction. They usually like to honor dignitaries, such as a mayor or governor, at the beginning of a rodeo. They introduced the honoree, Harry, and finally me. They were on horseback and I was on my little mule out in the middle of the arena. When it came time for the national anthem, this little girl came out and sang it absolutely horribly. It was so bad that it was just embarrassing. After she finished, Harry turned to the fellow beside him and asked, "My God, who was that?"

"That was my granddaughter."

"Oh, what a fine job she did."

KENNY BERGERON

James Harper used to make a lot of money selling wheezers, which most people just called cowboy boomerangs, at his rodeos. He'd have the bullfighters go out and throw them all around to get the people excited.

Kenny Bergeron had never thrown a wheezer, so the first time he did throw one, it went straight into the dirt. The next one flopped around like a wounded duck. The next one hit the wall. He never did really throw one right. Of course James was watching all that.

When Kenny finished, James met him at the gate and asked, "Son, do you like fighting bulls for me?"

"Yes sir, I sure do."

"Well, I don't give a damn how good a bullfighter you are. You better learn to throw a wheezer by tomorrow night or you'll be looking for another job. I recommend you go buy one to practice with."

ROBOT INCIDENT AT VERNAL

I first had a robot act back in the '70s, but robots had evolved so much since then that it was time to update it, with the help of a friend, Miles Muller, working on the body. Robots had changed from boxy, square things to transformer-looking deals, and they also got bigger. I made my new robot eight feet tall, put lights on it, and filled it with lots of pyro. It's so big that when Matt stands inside, he looks out a one-way curtain about halfway up. Matt's arms are way out in the robot's arms, so he has to use his chin to click the switches on a panel that control the lights and pyro. There are two switches on each side that turn on the lights and one in the middle of those that sets off the pyro, which shoots out the top of the robot's head. In honor of my friend Junior Samples from "Hee Haw," I named it BR549, The Singing Robot.

An interesting story about this robot happened a few years ago in Vernal, Utah when I must have been about 69 years old. It was a Sunday matinee and there was a huge crowd. We got to the point in the act where I pick up a saxophone and start playing along to "Bad to the Bone." I had my back to Matt, so I didn't really see this happening – I just kind of felt it – but a guy ran out of the stands, jumped on top of the robot, and knocked it down.

The miracle of it all was that the guy didn't get his face burned off. We hadn't set off the big pyro with the middle switch yet, so evidently Matt's chin must have been just a little off to one side or the other so that he missed that switch. Had he not, the pyro would've blown up right in the guy's face, because he jumped up right on top where it all went off. That would've been really bad, and it's a good thing it didn't. I would've hated that, but he had no business being out there in the first place.

Matt didn't know what had happened because he could hardly see out the front curtain. He thought maybe a bull or pickup horse had hit him, but he knew it wasn't me. By the time I realized what had happened, the dude was running off, so I flung my saxophone at him like a boomerang. I just barely missed him, which was his good luck: that big tenor sax would've laid him out colder than a pawnbroker's heart. But I just barely clipped his hair a little bit, so he kept on going.

I saw the bullfighter, a friend of mine named Clifford Maxwell, not too far away, so I hollered out, "Clifford, catch him!" Well, that was just like siccing a dog on the guy. Clifford ran across the arena and caught ahold of his leg as he was trying to climb over the pipe-rail fence around the arena, which was about six feet tall. The guy got one leg over the top rail, but Clifford had him by the other leg and wasn't about to let go. I hollered out, "Hold on, I'm coming!" When I reached them, I grabbed the dude in a wrestler's headlock and then, just like the wrestlers do when they jump off the top ropes of the wrestling ring, I piledrived him headfirst straight into the dirt.

I kept him in that headlock when we landed and rained down right hooks on him until the security and cops came to arrest him. He was a big boy, and you could tell he thought he was a hotshot because he wore a t-shirt with the sleeves cut out to show off his muscles. The cops were trying to get the handcuffs on him but they couldn't because his arms were huge and he was just outmuscling them. I finally had enough of that, so I stood up and dropkicked him in the face. He quit resisting then, so I said, "Y'all can go ahead and put the cuffs on him now." When they stood him up, his face was a bloody mess. The head cop came up and asked, "What happened to his face?" One of the security guards said he thought the guy hit it on the fence when he fell off. The head cop just nodded and said, "That's good enough for me."

I saw the police chief the next day at the rodeo, who told me a little bit about the guy. The chief was a real good friend of mine, so I asked him if I could go see the guy down at the jail. The chief said he couldn't let me do that because it was against all the rules, and he asked me why I wanted to see him. I said, "I just wanted to ask that guy how it felt for a 69-year-old clown to whip his 29-year-old ass in front of a full house."

BLACK BART

The next act I came up with was "Black Bart," which I sometimes call "Black Butt." I got this idea from the big shootout in "The Good, The Bad, and The Ugly," and I even use that music on the front end of it. It's basically a remake of my Mexican shootout act, but in order to be politically correct, I can't call the characters Mexicans. However, I can call the act "Black Butt." It amazes me that you can say "butt" in the arena and "pissed off" on TV, but I can't say that a guy is a Mexican. What is that all about?

One night in Lauderdale, Mississippi at Ralph Morgan's rodeo, I decided I wanted to try to make this act work in an open arena. When I performed it in the coliseums where we usually worked, I'd run a string from the catwalk above all the way across and down behind the chutes. Then I'd tie a rubber duck to it with a parachute on it about the size of a bandana. When it came time to do the act, I'd go out there with my shotgun, which the announcer said I couldn't use because this was a pistol shootout and that wouldn't be fair. We'd go back and forth until I'd finally get so mad that I'd jam the butt of the shotgun down on the ground, making it go off. That was the signal for the sound engineer to punch the button to make a bunch of quacking sounds, which would get weaker and weaker until the rubber duck floated down to land at my feet. I'd pick the duck up, say a little prayer, and then put it back down and kick dirt over it in order to bury it with a little dignity.

That's how it was supposed to work. I'll let Mike tell what really happened that night in Lauderdale.

THE REST OF THE STORY BY MIKE MATHIS

Jerry Don Galloway was fighting bulls at Lauderdale that night, so Lecile enlisted his help to make this act work outside. Ralph Morgan's arena is open-air, with covered stands on the east and west sides. Lecile told Jerry Don to stand outside the arena behind the east side stands and, when he heard the quacking sounds after the gun went off, to throw the duck over the grandstands and out into the arena. It didn't matter how close it came to Lecile, because he'd just walk over to wherever it landed.

When Lecile did the act and his gun went off, James Harper, who was doing sound that night for some reason, punched the button for the quacking sounds. But there was no duck. We all looked around for it a few seconds until James hit the quacking button again. Still no duck. We did that a couple more times until Lecile hollered, "Throw the damn duck!"

Jerry Don had felt like the duck was too light to make it over the seats, so he had packed it full of rocks to weigh it down and make it go farther. When he heard Lecile hollering to throw it, he reared back and threw it as hard as he could. I looked up and saw the duck sail over the east side bleachers, across the arena, and land with a huge *thud* on the cover of the west side bleachers. The crowd didn't even see the duck; they just heard it when it hit that tin top.

The act was over so Lecile walked out of the arena, where he met Jerry Don, who looked at Lecile and said, "Why didn't you bring the duck out?"

"Jerry Don, you threw the damn duck over the east side bleachers, clear across the arena, and onto the top of the west side bleachers!"

Jerry Don thought about it a second and said, "Well, I guess I put too many rocks in it."

TRIXIE

After that came "Trixie," which is the new version of the toilet act. It got pretty old digging so many holes big enough to accommodate a barrel. Besides, most of the coliseum floors are concrete. So what I did was build an outhouse that collapses on all four sides. It was about the size of a refrigerator box, with the old-timey moon and stars on the door. In this act, I'm a magician and Trixie is my assistant. I put Trixie in the outhouse and try to make her disappear, but she never goes away. After several unsuccessful tries, I get in there to see what's going on. Then she shuts the door and throws a firecracker over the top in there with me. When it blows up, I hit the outhouse on all four sides and it collapses around me, where I'm squatted there with a toilet seat around my neck.

THE WHUPPIST ACT

My latest act is actually from about fifty-five years ago. Bud and Dub Grant were both great trick riders and ropers, and Bud had a whip act that I would help him with. I would hold his targets and he would pop them out of my hand with some comedy in between.

Fifty-five years later I decided to put my own version together and call it "The World Champion Whuppist." I was working a rodeo in Waco, Texas about 2007 or so. I was in the dressing room with a bullfighter there named Rick Chatman, and on the first night of the rodeo, I asked him if he knew of anybody who could plait me a big colorful whip ten or twelve feet long and about as big around as your wrist. We were down there for nine nights, and on the last night he brought me a whip just like I wanted. I took it home and it sat in the prop room for almost a year before I looked at it one day, remembered Bud's bit, and thought I needed to put that together.

BISHOP ARNOLD

Bishop Arnold, from Scottsboro, Alabama, is the guy who travels with me now. He and his family used to travel to the rodeos in Alabama, Georgia, and Tennessee about fifty years ago. He was just a kid then, but his daddy worked for the stock contractor so Bishop would always help him with the animals. Bishop would also come help me with my mule, my acts, and things like that. By the time he turned about 15, he'd come to my house and help me around the place for the summer when school got out. He'd work around the farm and our restaurant during the week, and then we'd head out to a rodeo on the weekend. I'd pay him by the week, but I didn't give him his money right then. When it was time for him to go home and go back to school at the end of the summer, I'd give him all his pay and he'd put it in the bank. He did that for three or four years until he graduated from high school, so by that time he had made enough money from rodeo to go to college. After he graduated from college, he worked for the fire department for thirty-five or so years, and he's about 60 now. When Matt retired from the road, I needed somebody to help me out on my acts, so I called Bishop and asked him what he was doing. He said he wasn't doing anything, so now he travels with me again.

VIRGINIA WRECK

The Virginia wreck was the last major wreck I had. I think I was 71 years old, so I had quit fighting bulls about twenty years before that. We were doing the Sunday afternoon matinee, and I was working the crowd on the right side of the chutes while they were penning a fighting bull on the left side. I told the sound man, Randy "Stretch" Mayer, to turn up "Sweet Home Alabama," and I turned my back to the chutes for just a few seconds, which I normally don't do. This bull passed by one of the bullfighters, went around the barrel, and then I guess he saw me. People were hollering to warn me, but I never heard them because of the music. This bull hit me from behind and threw me ten or fifteen feet up in the air. I came down on what must have been the only rock in the arena, which put a hole in the top of my head and knocked me out.

Stretch was the first off the music stage to me. They loaded me up and took me to the hospital, where they found out I had two fractured vertebrae, a broken shoulder blade, and a bruised liver, spleen, and lung. Once they patched my head up, they wanted to keep me overnight, but I saw no reason to stay there. Matt and Ethel got me in the truck and we drove all night long to get back home. The next day I went to an orthopedic clinic, where they put me in a swimming pool for rehab. I had to cancel a rodeo that next weekend, and I had the next weekend off. After three weeks, I went back to work – real slow.

I've had more than a hundred broken bones. I had to have my left knee replaced. My right ankle has plates and pins in it. My left ankle has pins in it. I have a metal bar in my chest to hold it together where a bull broke my sternum. I've had so many injuries over the course of my career, and when you get to be my age, you're going to have some aches and pains anyway. But I stay active and try to keep in shape. Ironically, when I was fighting bulls, I did less training and exercise back then than I do now. I ran a lot just to keep my legs in shape, and I also played racquetball to be able to keep my quickness, but that was about it. Now I have a gym in my house, and I work out every other day with weights. I also still box, because I always did like to fight.

Ethel and me at the Lehi Roundup in Lehi, Utah.

Photo: Donna and Mel Anderson.

EPILOGUE

I think what got me where I am today is my comedy and my ability to fight bulls. My ability to fight bulls wasn't better than anybody else's, but it was different. I wasn't raised in a part of the country where I could watch someone fight bulls and learn any good habits or bad habits. All of my bad habits are ones I got on my own. My style of comedy was really different and my style of bullfighting was really different. Loretta Lynn once told me, "To be a success in the entertainment business, you have to either be first or really different." I think I was the first to be really different.

I've been in the business for about sixty years now. One of the big honors I had was to still be chosen to work the circuit finals as a bullfighter when I was 52 years old. I worked the IFR finals for several years, doing the bullfighting and comedy part too. I've been voted "Clown of the Year" four times in the PRCA, which is quite an honor. In 2007 I was inducted into the Pro Rodeo Hall of Fame, which is pretty much the ultimate.

I think I received a lot of the honors because I had a great partner in Matt and outlasted a lot of people. They don't usually get to be my age and still do what I do. I remember my daddy telling me, "You know, you're going to meet the same people coming down the ladder that you met going up it, so watch who you step on." I can truthfully say that I paid attention to that.

I'm only working the rodeos now that I really enjoy. I used to work about a hundred and fifty performances a year, but now I'm down to less than a hundred. If I don't like the announcer or this or that, then I don't go. So I'm happy at the ones I do, and I think people can see that, so maybe they think, "Well, he's been around so long, why not give him an award?"

My accolades and buckles and trophies mean so much to me, especially at my age, but not nearly as much as when a kid comes up to me and says, "My granddaddy told me that you saved his life in the bull riding in 1962. I want to thank you for that." Nothing comes up to those kinds of things.

At my age now, I'm still going back to places I went fifty or sixty years ago. The people who were 8 or 10 years old when they first saw me are now 60 or 70. The first thing they ask is how old I am, but the next question is, "How much longer are you going to do this?"

I don't have a clue. I have never set a time to quit. I think that the day I walk into the arena and I don't feel comfortable; or I don't have fun; or I don't think I'm getting the job done that needs to be done; then I'll just walk out. There's not going to be any big hoopla about it. The next year somebody will just say, "I wonder where Lecile is?"